Roads Publishing
19–22 Dame Street
Dublin 2
Ireland

www.roads.co

First published 2014

1

Weekly World News

Image copyright
© Bat Boy LLC
Design by Conor & David
Text copyright
© Roads Publishing
Design and layout copyright
© Roads Publishing

Printed in Ireland

All rights reserved. No part of
this production may be reprinted
or reproduced or utilised in
any form, or by any electronic,
mechanical or other means, now
known or hereafter invented,
including photocopying and
recording, or in any information
storage or retrieval system,
without the written consent
of the Publisher.

This book is sold subject to
the condition that it shall not,
by way of trade or otherwise,
be circulated in any form of
binding or cover other than that
in which it is published.

978-1-909399-40-2

WEEKLY WORLD NEWS

NEIL MᶜGINNESS

ROADS

'The most creative newspaper in American history'— *THE WASHINGTON POST*

TO INCREDULITY
... AND BEYOND!

A bubble-headed space ranger named Buzz Lightyear once famously rallied the troops with the call, 'To infinity… and beyond!'

Here, at *Weekly World News*, we rally the troops with our own variation on the call, 'To incredulity… and beyond!' In pursuit of incredulity, our reporters have zip-lined down nearly every blind alley on this planet. The journey has yielded remarkable results:

We've toppled governments in seasons other than spring.
We've found the one-and-only King (Elvis, that is!).
We've decoded the riddle of the Sphinx.
We've excavated sixteen Missing Links.
We've found Santa frozen in a block of ice.
We've dined with Condoleezza Rice.
How did this all happen, you ask?

STAND UP FOR BASTARDS

Weekly World News came saucily into the world. In late 1979, our parent publication, the *National Enquirer*, found itself atop the publishing world with a weekly circulation soaring past the millions.

Enquirer management seized the opportunity by purchasing the latest technology of the times: a color printer. What came next no one could have predicted: in a world-altering application of generally accepted accounting principles, the executives decided against scrapping the old black-and-white printer in favor of printing a brand new publication on the old printer and amortizing its use!

Weekly World News was born. There we were: the black-and-white whoreson of *National Enquirer*; a happy, if somewhat accidental, monochromatic byproduct of corporate fiscal prudence in the face of the relentless march of technology.

American economic ingenuity had found a way to create this bastard publication. Surely, then, American economic ingenuity could find a way to sell it. Positioned on the bottom racks of supermarket checkout lines, with bold headlines that embraced the flippant, our beloved rag found an audience. Within eighteen months, the publication saw weekly sales spike into the millions.

TELL CURIOUS TALES BLUNTLY
Deadlines rode easy during those early days. Good sport we had in our own making. Our band of maverick journalists surveyed the world with a uniquely solicitous eye, bound by a unified mission: tell curious tales bluntly.

We covered the world from A to Z: aliens to zombies, and everything in between. For many readers, we became an indispensable guide to the politics, culture, celebrities, alien abductions and mutant freaks that shape our world.

We found talking toasters, transgendered US Presidents, lost African tribes, alien senators, Republicans like Ginzo the Dolphin, and Democrats like Clem the Wild Ostrich.

Our stories fell somewhere between the bounds of sense and bounds of nonsense. Our popularity knew no bounds. Only a wealthy Western industrial power could have found the time to create *Weekly World News*, yet the world adored us too. We were big in Japan.

By the early 1990s, though, something felt missing. If you ask me, we suffered the anxiety of influence; the bouquet of our wine surpassed its taste. Too young too soon. A classic sophomore jinx.

Our detractors emerged:
'*Weekly World News,* are you serious?'
'No, we're not serious.' We had always viewed seriousness as a form of stupidity in an uncertain incongruous world.

'Okay, then *Weekly World News* is a joke?'

'No, we're not a joke. We believe, like Wittgenstein, that the most serious and profound problems can only be discussed through humor. So you may find us funny but we're not joking.'

'Okay then, will *Weekly World News* ever grow up?'

'Guess who just turned thirty-five?'

'Okay, happy birthday, *Weekly World News*. One last question: are your stories true?'

RAISIN BRAINS

Ah, truth. That's where we would find our purpose. Francis Bacon wrote that truth must be adorned. If we lived in a world of unadorned truth, it would leave our minds barren and shrunken like raisins. To know truth you must enjoy it. We decided that we exist to put the enjoyment into truth.

If Hemingway spent his whole life trying to write that one true sentence, then we will spend the remainder of our days trying to write that one true story that will make your stomach squeeze your heart.

These times of meteors, missing planes, Mayan apocalypse and shaved celebrity heads portend great opportunity. We know that one day something will appear to shock the world. It might wash up on a faraway Moroccan beach, be discovered hiding in a Pacific Northwest forest, fall from the skies above Siberia, or be discovered in Bono's pocket during an invasive airport frisking.

Like Bono, we still haven't found what we're looking for, but when we find it the world will shudder. Until we find it, this book will have to do.

Neil McGinness
Editor-in-Chief
Weekly World News

1992

During the race for the US Presidency, George H.W. Bush and Bill Clinton are both depicted meeting with P'Lod, an alien who is to become a *WWN* regular. The candidates enjoy the unexpected publicity – Clinton jokes that it shows he has 'universal' appeal – and the next issue has exclusive, untouched photos of them reading *Weekly World News*

1979
Launched by Generoso Pope Jr

1992
Trial over the origins and ownership of the character of Ed Anger

Ed Anger

1996
Weekly World News television show launches

1980s
Circulation peaks at 1.2 million per week

1993
Features in *So I Married an Axe Murderer* – 'I'm on a *Weekly World News* Garth Brooks Juice Diet'

1997
Features in *Men in Black* – 'The best damn investigative reporting on the planet'

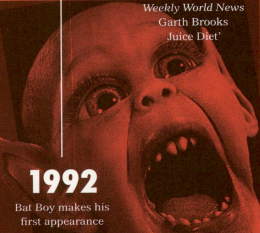

1992
Bat Boy makes his first appearance

1999

American Media, parent company of *Weekly World News*, is purchased by David Pecker. Changes are made and many of the old guard leave – Eddie Clontz, Ivone, Berger, Lind, Kulpa – to be replaced by young comedy writers

1997

Bat Boy: The Musical debuts off Broadway

2000

Bat Boy endorses Al Gore for President of the United States

2004

Begins running a disclaimer, 'The reader should suspend disbelief for the sake of enjoyment'

2000

Declared the 'Official Newspaper of the Windows 2000 Team' at Microsoft

2001

American Media is targeted in a US mail terror attack. Eight employees test positive for anthrax exposure. Seven survive, but photo editor Bob Stevens sadly perishes

1999

Weekly World News exclusive '12 US SENATORS ARE SPACE ALIENS!' is taped to the wall of the Senate press gallery, Washington DC

2007

Print publication ceases and *Weekly World News* goes online

2008
Purchased by Bat Boy LLC, led by *Weekly World News*

WORLD EXCLUSIVE!

2010
Fox announces it is developing a new comedy based on *Weekly World News*

2010
Scribner publishes the definitive Bat Boy story – *Going Mutant: Bat Boy Exposed*

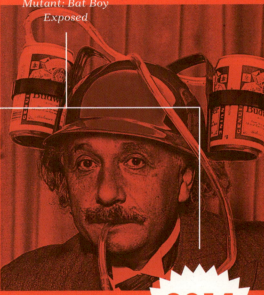

2008
Features in *Tropic Thunder*

2010
Fox News erroneously reports a *Weekly World News* story that Los Angeles will spend $1 billion on jetpacks that can fly a person up to 63 miles per hour and soar to heights of 8,000 feet

2014
Celebrates its thirty-fifth anniversary

Eerie faces control the fate of 114 shrieking passengers

JET FROZEN IN MIDAIR!

Aviation authorities are reeling over reports that a ghostly fleet of faces held a Boeing 727 jetliner and 114 passengers hostage for four hours — in midair.

And that's only the beginning. The eerie creatures not only released the plane and passengers unharmed, they actually cured 31 burned and crippled children on the mercy flight.

Aviation authorities in Bombay, India, are withholding the name of the airline pending the outcome of a government investigation of the incident.

But the pilot's report and eyewitness accounts have been released to clear up rumor and speculation that spread like wildfire after the fated plane landed in Bombay.

"We have yet to determine what happened up there — perhaps we never will," said Madhu Sarkar, a spokesman for the Indian Aviation Authority.

"But something did happen. Of that, there can be no doubt because we have proof — and lots of it."

Sarkar said the pilot told officials the Boeing 727 was cruising at an altitude of 27,000 feet on the flight from Delhi when a blinding white light ripped through the plane.

"He said he didn't even have time to react before he could feel the plane was rising at incredible speed straight up, as if in a vacuum," said the official.

"The altimeter needle almost spun off the control board before it hesitated at 53,000 feet and then dropped to zero. The passengers and flight attendants were screaming and crying — grabbing for oxygen masks and seat belts before the 727 came to a complete halt in midair."

The pilot reported that the stationary plane was suddenly bathed in a brilliant blue light, which changed to green, to red, to yellow — and back to blue.

"He said he fought the urge to cover his eyes and looked through the windshield," said the official.

"Looking back at him were human-like faces, floating like balloons a few feet from the plane."

The pilot glanced at his watch, which reportedly read 3:15, then grabbed the steering tiller because the plane was free-falling — straight down!

"It settled in softly at 27,000 feet," said Sarkar. "It was as if nothing had happened except for one thing: It was 7:15 and ground control was radioing to find out where the flight had come from!"

Just then, a shrieking stewardess burst into the cabin and begged the pilot to come to the rear of the plane.

"He went, fearing the worst," said Sarkar.

"But what he found was a miracle."

The children who were seriously injured in an industrial accident in northern India were amazingly cured, the official said.

"The pilot said he could hardly bear to look at the children when they boarded the flight for the trip to a medical center here in Bombay. They were pitiful sights.

"But now he was staring because there wasn't a scar, laceration, burn or broken limb to be seen.

"The attending physician was speechless.

"Those young people were really cured."

Medical officials confirmed that the children showed no signs of injury or trauma after the flight.

In a prepared statement, the pilot said:

"I can't tell you what happened up there.

"For several hours we were part of another time, another place. There's nothing in my experience to compare with this. The faces were human, but no bodies were attached.

"Was it a UFO? A time warp? Did we pass through an invisible door into another dimension? You, my friends, tell me."

A spokesman for the Bombay-based UFO Research Federation admitted that the group is investigating the astonishing encounter, but refused to speculate on the origin or intent of the mysterious faces.

— CHESTER QUINN

'... the plane was rising at incredible speed straight up as if in a vacuum'

Teacher wins $120,000 in cat-astrophe

A teacher who lost her job for goofing and passing out copies of a pornographic comic book to her class has won a $120,000 judgment against the school that fired her.

Teresa DeVito of Fairmont, W. Va., said she thought she was giving her eighth grade art students copies of Felix the Cat comic books, but they turned out to be Fritz the Cat comic books — an entirely different kitty.

After she was fired she sued and won a ruling from the state Supreme Court that her dismissal was wrong. The $120,000 award is for back pay and pension contributions. The Marion County School Board will also hire her as a substitute teacher and make her eligible to apply for a full-time job.

Ex-beau sues to halt abortion

Outraged Charles Buel has gone to court to keep his former fiancee from harming him — by aborting her baby.

A temporary court order prohibits his ex-sweetheart, "Sally Doe," from having an abortion. Buel, 21, claims loss of the child would cause him irreparable harm.

The suit is not an anti-abortion crusade, said Booneville, Iowa, lawyer Eric Borseth, but an attempt to define paternity rights.

10 ways to tell if your neighbor is an EXTRATERRESTRIAL!

By MARIE BOUVIER
Weekly World News

BOCA RATON — Many top scientists believe that aliens live secretly among us. The sneaky intergalactic travelers often pose as our friends, neighbors and co-workers while they learn the ways of Earth. But how can you tell invading aliens from real humans?

Weekly World News has interviewed dozens of experts and conducted exhaustive research to bring you this list of the top ten ways to recognize aliens in our midst.

1 Aliens often wear huge sunglasses to hide their eyes. Most aliens have large, staring eyes that are hard to conceal. Sunglasses help them appear more normal.

2 Aliens have cold and clammy skin. Many aliens wear synthetic skin in order to pass themselves off as human. It's never as warm as real skin, and it often feels "slimy" to the touch.

3 They smell. Aliens use all manner of deodorants, perfumes, or lotions to disguise their natural scent, which is offensive to humans.

4 Aliens are obsessed with technology. They spend hours chatting on cell phones and sending e-mails. But they're not conversing with people — they are actually transmitting data they've accumulated back to their home worlds.

5 Aliens have strange bodily proportions. The newest breeds of aliens attempt to imitate human appearance — but they never quite get it right. They are like exaggerated ideas of human perfection. Their stomachs are too flat, their chests too big, their faces wrinkle-free.

6 Aliens have strange diets. Aliens may not be able to digest most human foods. Because of this, they are limited in the types of foods they can eat, and they may become vegetarians. Watch out for people who eat a lot of melons — that's an alien favorite.

7 Aliens dance in inhuman ways. Most alien species have a completely different physiology than ours. They have the ability to move their bodies to music in a way no ordinary human can, and this results in a Dancing style that is quite breathtaking.

8 Aliens do not understand Earth's sense of humor. Forget what you saw on *Mork and Mindy*. Aliens find it difficult to understand laughter — even a simple knock-knock joke can throw them completely off. They might laugh at inappropriate times — like during a funeral — or stare blankly at the funniest jokes.

9 Aliens dress in oddly revealing clothes. Aliens find clothing irritates their flesh, so the less of it they wear, the more comfortable they are. They also like to keep their fake human skin exposed to air, to allow it to breathe.

10 Aliens ask hundreds of questions. Aliens are on Earth for research, and they want to learn as much as possible about Earthlings. They're like alien anthropologists, fascinated by human behavior and eager to study our culture. So keep your eyes open for any people asking a lot of nosy questions.

"ALIENS DO NOT UNDERSTAND EARTH'S SENSE OF HUMOR. FORGET WHAT YOU SAW ON *MORK AND MINDY*."

COPS used this startling photograph taken by a bank security camera to identify Ernie Coveley as the cucumber bandit.

'This is a —BURP— stickup!'

BANDIT USES A CUCUMBER TO ROB 16 BANKS

By JOE BERGER

Oddball bandit Ernie Coveley has been busted for sticking up 16 banks — with a cucumber!

In each case, the veggie varmint pointed a colossal cuke at a lady teller and shouted, "Give me the money or I'll blow your head off!"

And each time, the terrified teller — thinking evil Ernie was brandishing a sawed-off shotgun — meekly handed over the loot.

Veggie-packin' varmint ate the evidence after each holdup, say cops

"This may have been the strangest series of robberies in this city's history," a detective told reporters in London, England.

"To get away with a stunt like that so many times is really remarkable. But he usually had the cucumber wrapped in a trash bag, so his victims could never be sure he didn't have a gun."

After each successful stickup, elated Ernie would rush home, count his haul — then chop up his cucumber for salads or sandwiches.

"He was making enough money he could afford a new cucumber each time he pulled a job," said Detective Owen Blank.

The cuke-wielding crook normally walked up to a teller, set a shopping bag down on the counter and hauled his long green "gun" out of the bag.

The ladies he confronted were so scared of his voluminous veggie they forked over more than $20,000 during his kooky crime spree.

But the Cucumber Kid's salad days came to an end when investigators identified him from security camera photos and surrounded the home in East London he shared with a girlfriend.

When they arrested him, cops said, 36-year-old Ernie was as cool as . . . well, you know.

"He said the money was all gone, that he'd spent it all on drugs," Detective Blank said.

The wacky bandit pleaded guilty to eight counts of robbery and is awaiting sentence. Judge Edwin Jowitt warned him he's in a real pickle and should bank on a long prison term.

FISHY FIND

A fisherman in Helford, England, hauled in a human skull with his catch of scallops, authorities report. A government pathologist is investigating the grisly find.

Official traded passports for sex

A former Irish Embassy official was sentenced to 21 months in jail for providing falsified passports to foreigners in exchange for sex and money.

Kevin McDonald, 35, charged up to $24,000 for a passport that should cost $100 and piled up $400,000 in six months. He demanded sex from a number of women in London and was photographed in bed with them.

How to tell if YOU are descended from a space alien

WEEKLY WORLD NEWS

November 1, 1988 — 30587 — 65¢

GUN-TOTING MOM RESCUES NIECE FROM KIDNAPPER

Terminal patients were weighed before and after they died!

HUMAN SOUL WEIGHS 1/3,000TH OF AN OUNCE

'This proves there IS life after death,' say top scientists

Painting of Elvis weeps real tears!

Psychic makes river run backwards

Gutsy girl swims herself to death!

Oops! Cheatin' hubby tries to date his own wife at a singles bar!

MAN WAKES UP AT OWN FUNERAL – AND DIES OF SHOCK!

A FRENCHMAN declared dead by doctors woke up in his coffin at his wake — and promptly died of fright.

Now the grieving gal pal of 88-year-old Pierre Dessault says she plans to sue a hospital for 10 million euros, citing wrongful death.

Dessault was declared DOA at a Paris hospital after he suffered an apparent heart attack while frolicking in bed with his 20-year-old girlfriend.

WOMAN, 93, HASN'T AGED IN 70 YEARS!

WEEKLY WORLD NEWS

Nov. 14, 1989   70¢/75¢ CANADA   30587

He's 25 months old and weighs 103 pounds!

World's biggest baby

Guess what he eats for dinner?

Ears reveal your risk of heart attack

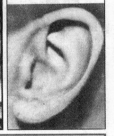

1950s AIRLINER LANDS WITH 92 SKELETONS ON BOARD!

Crook robs 16 banks — with a cucumber

Dead ventriloquist speaks from beyond the grave — through a wooden dummy!

By NICOLAS BUNCHE

The widow of a dead ventriloquist says her husband's dummy is driving her insane with its incessant sobs and chatter!

In fact, Andrea Crivelli has sought psychiatric treatment to help her cope with the belief that her husband is trying to communicate with her from beyond the grave through Franco, a replica of ventriloquist Edgar Bergen's dummy, Mortimer Snerd.

DEAD man's dummy looked like Mortimer Snerd.

Chattering puppet is driving me crazy, says widow

"My husband is trying to reach me, he wants to tell me something through Franco," said Mrs. Crivelli, 56, of Cremora, Italy.

"He talks to me late at night when I'm alone at home. But he can't say what he wants to say.

"Franco's wooden lips tremble and quake but then he tells jokes like my husband made him do when they performed on stage.

"Then he breaks down and cries in frustration. It's as if he wants to tell me something about the hereafter but can't get it out.

"It's torturing him and it is definitely torturing me," she added. "Sometimes I think I'm going absolutely insane."

Psychiatrist Joseph Accorsi is counseling Mrs. Crivelli but he refuses to discuss her case with reporters. Paranormal expert Fabio Barberi of Rome has also taken an interest in the woman's plight. And he believes that Vittorio Crivelli, who had a stroke and died on July 10, is desperately trying to tell his widow something from beyond the grave.

"Nobody has heard the dummy speak but Mrs. Crivelli. However, I am convinced she is telling the truth," said Barberi.

"I have discussed the matter with her extensively and her story and descriptions of the dummy's speech have not wavered. Besides, there are several precedents that give her story credence.

"There are at least 12 other instances of dummies speaking after the ventriloquists who owned them died.

"We have no real explanation for this phenomenon. But I would suggest to you that certain ventriloquists are able to speak through their dummies after their deaths because they were so close to them while they were alive.

"In addition, experts on the paranormal believe that because ventriloquists learn to project their voices beyond their bodies they are ideally suited to speaking to us from beyond the grave," said Barberi.

Researcher Barberi is currently writing a report on the Crivelli dummy and intends to publish it in major scientific journals on both sides of the Atlantic by early fall.

Meanwhile, Mrs. Crivelli is relying on friends and her psychiatrist to help her come to terms with the dummy's apparent attempts at communication.

"Sometimes I feel like I should get rid of Franco — it's frightening to think that he could speak on his own," she said.

"On the other hand he is my only link to Vittorio.

"I have to believe that one day he will break through whatever barrier is holding him back and say something meaningful. Right now I'm living for that day."

WIDOW Andrea Crivelli says her dead husband, who'd been a ventriloquist, is trying to communicate with her through his dummy.

Gushers of raw sewage flood couple's house!

A husband and wife watched in helpless horror as fountains of raw sewage shot out of their toilets, drains and sinks — and flooded their house!

"It was like something out of a horror movie," said Marinela Christel of Boulder, Colo. "The sewage was shooting up in fountains a foot high and all kinds of gross things were coming out.

"There was excrement and tampons and even things like toy soldiers and coins. The smell was overpowering. We couldn't believe what was happening."

Mrs. Christel and husband Gary called the fire department and city maintenance workers for help.

The men finally determined that the eruption of sewage

By DANIEL GILLELAND

was caused by a clogged sewer main near the couple's house.

But the sewage was seven inches deep before they unclogged the line and left the Christels to clean up the mess.

"We thought our troubles were over," said Mrs. Christel. "And the next day we called in a cleaning service.

"The men were just getting to work when one of them yelled: 'Oh no! Here we go again!' The sewage was flooding back into the house. I was petrified.

"For the rest of the day it would go up and down in the toilets and drains until we finally got it stopped."

Mrs. Christel and her husband spent the next five days scouring their house. They both became ill from working in the sewage — and had to get hepatitis and tetanus shots.

They estimate that damages to their floors, walls and carpets at $14,000 — an expense they hope the city of Boulder or the local water district will pay.

"I'm still afraid to leave the house," Mrs. Christel said.

CAR LEAPS DRAWBRIDGE

A woman was arrested for drunken driving after her car leaped a six-foot gap in an opening drawbridge!

Police in St. Augustine, Fla., said the 23-year-old woman was doing about 50 miles an hour when her car jumped the Bridge of Lions as it opened for a barge.

Authorities said the driver suffered only minor injuries.

Bride weds dead groom in open casket ceremony ... then goes on honeymoon with the corpse!

WEEKLY WORLD NEWS

September 26, 1989 · 30587 · 75¢

ZODIAC GUIDE FOR LOVERS!
Amazing new horoscope tells how sexy you are

THIS MAN GAVE BIRTH TO A 7-LB. BABY GIRL!

WORLD EXCLUSIVE INTERVIEW!

"I was beautiful ... when I had my baby"

12 surefire ways to beat the pain of arthritis

Real-life vampire attacks 26 women!

Man spends night in an outhouse pit!

Cops bust 540-pound wrestler Andre the Giant

Ghost ship terrifies workers on North Sea oil rig!

22

WOMAN WHO SEDUCED BOY, 13, GETS 3 MONTHS — IN CHURCH!

WEEKLY WORLD NEWS

July 25, 1989 — 30587 — 70¢

ED ANGER'S BACK! The nation's most outrageous columnist!

MY AMERICA By ED ANGER

Tests show she was born in 1819, say medical experts

SATAN WORSHIPPER IS 170 YEARS OLD!

'The Devil said to spread his word and I'd live 200 years'

TRAGIC BRIDE! Her three husbands have all died — on her wedding day!

Marilyn Monroe look-alike kills herself just like her idol!

Coed in secret sex video wins $1 million from her boyfriend!

OUT WITH A BANG! Dead man's ashes are launched in a skyrocket

CYNDI LAUPER: I was a slave girl in a past life

The world will end on Sept. 1, says holy man

'The only gossip I'm interested in is things from the *Weekly World News*. "Woman's bra bursts, 11 injured" – that kind of thing.' —JOHNNY DEPP

Female trainers make stunning accusation:
This dolphin molested us!

By SCOTTY PAUL
Correspondent

Two curvaceous young cuties hired to train a dolphin that grew human hands have quit in a huff, saying the sexy creature has learned to communicate only too well — molesting them every chance he gets.

"That dirty old dolphin is certainly no gentleman. He grabs our bikini tops, makes those disgusting dolphin noises and swims around the tank like a drunken sailor," said Sally Ray.

"He seemed so sweet and gentle at first, nuzzling up against us in the tank. Now we know what was going through his filthy little mind."

The extraordinary dolphin, nicknamed Pete, was netted off the coast of California a month ago. Instead of flippers, Pete has long arms and tiny hands.

"This is the scientific discovery of this decade," marine biologist Dr. Oto Masuda said at the time.

Masuda is one of 14 experts studying the unique dolphin at a marine laboratory in Japan.

"We had hoped the dolphin would help bridge the communication gap between animals and mankind for the first time ever," Masuda said. "But Pete apparently found his own way to communicate."

Sally and Jeannie Marshall, experienced dolphin trainers from Florida, were hired to help with the training process.

"Everything went well the first week," Jeannie said. "But the past few days have been a total nightmare. We've both been grabbed, goosed, squeezed and caressed in every place possible.

"I thought at first that dolphin didn't understand what he was doing, but that was before I saw that gleam in his eyes. He knows," she said.

The sex-crazed dolphin is now being trained by men only. "I presume THEY'LL be safe from his advances," Masuda joked.

The marine scientists had hoped to train the creature to use his hands for everyday chores. "He's learned some sign language to tell us when he is hungry, tired or not feeling well," Masuda said.

"Now we need to train him not to touch everything he sees, especially if the 'things' belong to pretty young women."

ARMED... AND DANGEROUS! This incredible dolphin first appeared in the March 17 issue of The Weekly World News. Now he's out of control!

ANIMAL trainers Sally Ray and Jeannie Marshall say they have been molested by the dolphin with arms.

TOWER OF PISA CLOSE TO TIPPING OVER!

Italy's leaning Tower of Pisa is tilting more and more with each passing year and may have to be propped up soon to keep it from falling down.

The tower's 13-foot tilt off perpendicular increased by nearly five-hundredths of an inch last year, said Michele Jamiolkowski, head of an international restoration team that examined the tower.

The team suggested placing a counterweight at the base of the bell tower on the opposite side of the lean. This should prevent further leaning, which is very dangerous to the stability of the tower, Jamiolkowski said.

HAIRBALL HORROR

Hairy-tongued kids cough up SIX fur balls a day!

By JOE BERGER / Staff writer

Heartsick schoolboy Stew Bachmann and his big sister Becky can't kick up their heels like normal kids because their tongues are covered with thick hair — and they're constantly coughing up fur balls!

"You've seen cats gagging and choking on fur balls. Well, my poor kids do the same thing six times a day — each," said their rattled dad Stewart, 41.

"It tears me up to see them so miserable when they should be having the time of their lives.

"But the doctors say they'll be stuck with fur balls as long as they have hair on their tongues — and nobody seems to have the slightest idea how to get the hair off their tongues."

Neither befuddled Becky, 11, nor her bashful brother Stew, 9, was born with the bizarre affliction. But by the time they were old enough to start school, the pitiful kids both sported tongues full of fur.

"It started with Becky when she was barely a year old," mortified mom Joanne Bachmann told reporters in Dortmund, Germany. "One day she seemed perfectly normal and the next morning she had little tufts sprouting on her tongue.

"Within a couple of days, her tongue was so furry she looked like something out of a horror movie."

The frantic parents prayed that son Stew wouldn't suffer the same indignity, but by the time he hit 12 months, the bewildered kid's tongue was as hairy as a hound dog's back.

"It's a real mess and the so-called experts are just as stumped by it as we are," said jolted Joanne, 38.

"We've taken those kids to specialists on both sides of the Atlantic, but they don't have a clue to what's causing it or how to cure it.

"So poor Becky and Stew go through life feeling like freaks in a circus. They hate to even leave the house because other kids make fun of them and adults stare and ask stupid questions.

"They have trouble talking, they have trouble breathing and they don't eat enough because with all that hair on their tongues, they can't taste the difference between broccoli and an ice-cream cone."

To make matters worse, the public schools sent the shaggy-tongued scamps packing, forcing them to attend a special school for handicapped kids 30 miles from home.

"The teachers at their old school said they couldn't conduct classes with our kids sitting there coughing up fur balls all day," said their devastated dad.

Hair first appeared on their tongues when they were both a year old!

INCREDIBLE story of the Bachmann kids' hairy tongues first appeared in the February 26, 1991, edition of the *Weekly World News*.

The bizarre affliction has docs baffled, and both Stew and Becky have since been booted out of the public school system.

The danger is real — and GROWING, warn experts

HOW TO TELL IF YOUR DOG WORSHIPS SATAN!

WEEKLY WORLD NEWS SPECIAL REPORT

By MIKE FOSTER
Weekly World News

Does your dog growl at the sight of a clerical collar? Or gleefully "do its business" on hallowed ground? If so, watch out — your beloved pet may be possessed!

That is the chilling warning of Father Brett Noughton, a leading expert in demonic possession.

"Innocent beasts are an easy target for Lucifer's minions," explains Fr. Noughton, of Raleigh, N.C. "Unlike humans, they lack the willpower to fight off an invading spirit."

Possessed dogs first exhibit behavior that is merely puzzling, then go on to become a danger to people and property, according to the expert. "In the end they always turn on their owners — when you read a newspaper account of a dog killing its own master, this is almost always a case of demonic possession."

Certain breeds are more susceptible to possession than others, including German shepherds, Doberman pinschers and pit bulls.

"These dogs have been bred over the centuries for aggression, and are more easily led to the dark side," says Fr. Noughton.

The Catholic priest, who often assists worried pet-owners, says the following are signs you have a "Devil Dog" on your hands:

- Your dog barks or growls at religious ministers.
- When the two of you walk by a cemetery, the animal tries to desecrate the dead — by urinating against a headstone.
- If you hold a crucifix or Bible in front of your pooch, it snarls, lunges or recoils in fear.
- Your dog often appears to be listening to secret voices or sounds that you can't hear. "He may be receiving his marching orders from his true master, Satan," notes Fr. Noughton.
- The canine reacts excitedly to images of death, evil and Satan.
- The dog attempts to bite or attack innocent children.

If your dog shows these warning signs, don't despair — but DO consult a trusted minister at once, advises Fr. Noughton.

"A simple exorcism can easily rid your pet of all Satanic influence."

FATHER Noughton tests a dog's reaction to a demonic image to see if the animal is possessed.

BEAUTY'S BARED BOOBS BLIND BASEBALL PLAYER

A Japanese baseball player was knocked unconscious and spent three days in the hospital after he got nailed right in the face by a line drive — a split-second after he was distracted by lady baring her breasts in the stands!

Aiko Ohruhu, 23, was playing third base when he spotted the attractive exhibitionist lifting her shirt.

Did plane missing for 35 years fly through time warp?

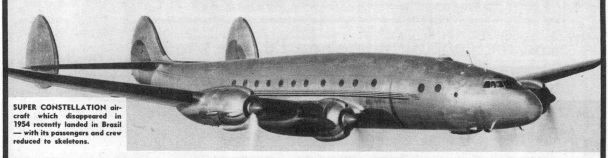

SUPER CONSTELLATION aircraft which disappeared in 1954 recently landed in Brazil — with its passengers and crew reduced to skeletons.

1950s AIRLINER LANDS WITH 92 SKELETONS ON BOARD

By IRWIN FISHER

Aviation authorities say a commercial airliner that flew out of Germany in 1954 has landed in Brazil with 92 skeletons aboard!

And while the officials refuse to speculate on the whereabouts of the plane for the past 35 years, several respected scientists, including paranormal researcher Dr. Celso Atello, say Santiago Airlines Flight 513 almost certainly entered a time warp and just flew out.

"There is no other explanation," Dr. Atello told newsmen in Porto Alegre, Brazil.

"Flight records show that the aircraft left Aachen, West Germany, on the morning of Sept. 4, 1954, and then vanished over the Atlantic Ocean on its way to Porto Alegre later that day.

"At the time aviation authorities assumed that it had crashed. But the plane landed in Porto Alegre a few weeks ago on October 12.

"It was piloted by the skeleton of its captain and all the crew and passengers were dead, too. Officials don't want to discuss explanations. But they cannot deny that this airplane had defied the laws of space and time. And God only knows how a skeleton managed to land it."

Santiago Airlines went out of business in 1956 and executives who are still alive didn't know enough about the flight to comment.

Brazilian aviation officials themselves confirmed that the vintage Lockheed Super Constellation aircraft "appeared out of nowhere" and landed at an airstrip west of Porto Alegre on October 12.

They also said that its powerful turboprop engines were still idling when support personnel found the skeletal re-

Remains of 88 passengers & 4-man crew found on aircraft — with dead pilot still at the controls

mains of 88 passengers and a four-man crew, including Captain Miguel Victor Cury — who was still clutching the controls.

Government agents are known to be investigating the mysterious flight. But they refuse to discuss anything about the airplane or the course their investigation is taking.

The official shroud of secrecy has outraged Dr. Atello and other experts who are now calling on the Brazilian government to let civilians assist in the investigative effort.

Roderigo de Manha, a re-

DR. Celso Atello

tired physics professor in Porto Alegre, said: "The public has a right to know everything about this plane and the government has a duty to tell them.

"If this plane did enter a time warp and there is evidence to prove it, the entire world should be told. Something like this could change the way we view our world and alter science as we know it.

"It is a crime to keep information like this secret — especially from the relatives of the people who perished on Santiago Airlines Flight 513."

VIRGIN MARY STATUE MOUNTAIN & SPEAKS

8:45 A.M.
FAITHFUL CROWD watches Virgin Mary statue, shown in hollowed-out area in hill above them, for signs of movement. At this point, the figure is stone-cold still.

By MARGARET STONE / *Weekly Wold News*

BALLINSPITTLE, Ireland — True believers are flocking to the local Grotto of the Virgin Mary where hundreds of eyewitnesses claim to have seen a marble statue of the Holy Mother move and speak like a living woman.

What's more, the statue has warned on at least four occasions that Christ is returning to Earth soon — and the end of the world is near.

Proof of the miraculous incidents has been provided by a photographer who snapped pictures of the 800-pound stone figure gliding along a pathway near the grotto.

"Hundreds and hundreds of people have seen the floating Virgin and heard her message that the End Times are here," said Father Bill Hannon, priest at a nearby parish.

"When she chooses to speak her voice is clear and strong. She says, 'Let there be peace among all men who have ear to hear and eyes to see. The Kingdom of Heaven is fast upon you. Christ will retunr soon, the end of the world is near.'

"When the reports first came that she had moved, people thought there had been an earth tremor or something that was causing the statue to slide. But after so many people watched the Virgin move out of the grotto and then move back again, we realized they were witnessing a miracle."

Father Hannon says the first sighting was reported last October 26, when a young woman visited the grotto early in the morning and found it empty.

Moments later, she saw a robed figure emerge from bushes and move slowly a path adjacent to the gro

The woman looked closely and was stunned alize that she was watchin statue come to life.

"The woman said the spoke to her and then retu to the cave," said Father non.

"The figure then rest the pose of a statue an came perfectly still. Whe lady told people what sh seen, nobody believed h first. But the Holy Mother repeated the early mo miracles at least once a r ever since.

"Recently a photogra took pictures of the V

‑LOATS DOWN

300-lb. figure comes to life & delivers message from God to true believers!

8:50 A.M.
VIRGIN MARY statue has floated over rope in front of opening and comes to a temporary stop several feet away.

9:00 A.M. TALKING statue has floated down to the waiting crowd, addressing them with messages of hope and love from God.

she was out on the hillside
at was proof enough for
olks.
ndreds of faithful pilgrims
visited the holy shrine
the virgin was moving
the hillside and have re‑
being miraculously cured
rious and in some cases,
erminal illnesses.
hers say their prayers for
nd happiness have been
red after a visit to the

are convinced that God is
this statue of the Holy
r to demonstrate
ondrous powers —
w us that in this
f turmoil and sacri‑
nything is possible
uly believe in Him."

Michael Jackson's nose is falling apart!

ARTIST'S conception shows how Michael's nose may soon look.

Moonwalker Michael Jackson's nose has been streamlined and realigned so often it's literally falling apart.

Frantic Mike issued a worldwide SOS after top docs in this country warned him he may have to be fitted with a plastic schnozz because his has been broken once too often during cosmetic surgery.

But even Dr. Andrew Posma, the Dutchman recognized as the best bone surgeon in the world, has refused to tinker with Michael's beak.

Dr. Posma looked at X rays and concluded that one more operation might blow Michael's nose for good. Docs say you can't go on having nose jobs forever — and after four, oft-remodeled Michael has just about reached his limit. — *Cleveland Plain Dealer.*

Frightened family hears FDR broadcast — live!

OLD RADIO PLAYS 1930s PROGRAMS!

By DEBORAH WALDROP

Telecommunications experts are said to be reeling over the discovery of an old-timey tube radio that receives and plays broadcasts from the 1930s — live!

Private electronic engineers hired by the family who owns the old Philco table set have yet to make a report.

But several sources independently confirmed that the 55-year-old receiver is in fact the focus of an "unusually intensive study" by engineers.

According to one highly placed insider, the experts have tuned in and analyzed some 12 hours of programming that was broadcast nationwide in 1934, including *Amos 'n' Andy*, the *Rudy Vallee Show* and *Walter Winchell's Jergen's Journal*.

That doesn't include the *Jack Benny Show* and one of President Franklin D. Roosevelt's Fireside Chats heard by the family who found the radio in the attic of their north Georgia home — and fled the house until engineers arrived to take it away. "I heard a Walter Winchell newscast and it wasn't the re-broadcast of a tape," said one engineer who requested anonymity.

"This was the real McCoy, either that, or the finest electronic sensing equipment in America isn't worth a damn. "We must have had half a million dollars worth of equipment stacked around that old radio. But our stuff didn't pick up a thing, no sound, no static, no nothing.

"And yet, here was this broken down Philco blaring away — I should say Walter Winchell blaring away, about movie stars and conditions in pre-war Europe and the Great Depression."

The set was discovered by two boys playing in the family attic. Their mother agreed to talk about the find only if their names and home town be kept secret. She said it had be- longed to her father and hadn't been plugged in since 1934.

EXPERTS are baffled by this vintage Philco radio that plays 1930s programs — live!

PRESIDENT Franklin D. Roosevelt prepares to broadcast one of his Fireside Chats in 1933.

BROADCAST of *Amos 'n' Andy*, featured Freeman Gosden, left, and Charles Correll.

WEEKLY WORLD NEWS
October 3, 1989

IS JOHNNY

TRIBE WORSHIPS TRUMP'S HAIR
By BECKY TODD

AN AFRICAN tribe worships Donald Trump's hair as their Supreme Being.

British anthropologist Jonathan Trevor-Tristan discovered the Womama people while on an expedition in Zimbabwe.

"Upon entering the village, I noticed that every man, woman and child was sporting blond hair that was as hard as a rock," says Trevor-Tristan. "We endured a typhoon with winds reaching upwards of 180 miles per hour and not one strand on their heads moved during the vicious storm."

THE DONALD is an inspiration.

The explorer says he was mildly curious about the Womama's hairstyle and instructed his interpreter to ask about it.

"A native explained that one of their teenagers had ventured into Kenya during his Cha Chi Ceremony, the treacherous journey boys take to become a man," says Trevor-Tristan. "In his hotel room in Nairobi he was watching Entertainment Tonight. The hostess was interviewing New York real estate mogul Donald Trump, whose hairdo sent the boy into an uncontrollable religious seizure."

The youth went to a stylist and had his own tresses done to match. When he arrived back in his village with boxes of Ash Blonde No. 109 dye and cans of Aquanet spray, the Womamas went wild with joy.

"They renounced Jesus, threw away their Bibles and erected an altar to the Hair God," says Trevor-Tristan. "The style is actually quite becoming to them. I might try it myself."

BLOODSUCKER? Artist's conception shows eternally youthful Johnny Depp with razor-sharp fangs.

THERE may be a chilling reason why Hollywood heartthrob Johnny Depp still looks just as boyish as ever at age 41: "He's a vampire," charges a top expert in the occult.

"Johnny Depp has not aged visibly since he appeared in the TV series *21 Jump Street* in 1987," says researcher Albert Linkway, author of the upcoming book, *Nosferatu: The Untold Sto-*ry *of Vampires in Hollywood.*

"We cannot discount the possibility that Mr. Depp was simply blessed with 'good genes.' Nor can we discount the possibility that he has joined the ranks of the undead."

Vampires have permeated Hollywood since the silent era, according to the expert.

"It's believed the curse dates back to Rudolph Valentino, who brought the infection over from Europe," he reveals.

That Johnny's chiseled good looks have not faded with time isn't the only fact that raise picion. The expert points to er telltale signs:

● Johnny's mysterious career resurrection. After y languishing in obscure flop *Benny and Joon* and *The A naut's Wife*, the star is now ter than ever, winning rave his performance in his late flick, *Finding Neverland*.

"This is typical of actors wh been vampirized," notes the expert. "A performer who's written off as a has-been is denly considered 'magnetic

DEPP A VAMPIRE?
'He hasn't aged a day in 17 years,' claims expert

n everyone's A-list."
● He frequently wears glasses — a common t of bloodsuckers, who st use heavy sunblock d shades to ward off dly solar rays.
● He resides in nce. "As anyone who's d an Anne Rice novel ws, France is a bed of vampiric activi- the researcher points

● Has hypnotic eyes. e starlet who encoun- ed Depp told Linkway, he had asked to drink ome one of the real blood I would have let a on the spot."
● In *Finding Never- d*, he plays the author *Peter Pan*. Notes kway: "This may be a tle message to those he know that he's ome one of the real st Boys.' "

ust because Johnny y be fond of human d doesn't mean you ld whip out a stake

instead of asking for an autograph, the expert cautions.

"Most Hollywood vam- pires do not attack strangers in dark alley- ways," explains Linkway. "If Mr. Depp truly is one of the Undead, he proba- bly has blood shipped to his mansion — or it's will- ingly donated by his ador- ing female fans."

Johnny won't be able to remain in the public eye without aging forever.

"At some point, he may go into seclusion, as the reputed vampire Greta Garbo did," says Linkway. "Or he may fake his own death.

"But most likely, he will do as Cary Grant did: he'll begin to 'age grace- fully' with the help of Hol- lywood makeup artists who add dignified gray to his hair with each pass- ing year."

THESE AMAZING PHOTOS show, Johnny Depp has not visibly ed in nearly two decades.

MORE HAIR!! STYLE IT FAST!
with WILD GROWTH® HAIR OIL

MORE HAIR! Magical increases in hair length, thickness & appearance of new hair (in bald areas) progressing to first time fullness & shoulder or below shoulder lengths. STYLE IT FAST! From coarse to fine, tangled, unmanageable, dry, dull, damaged, breaking, split ended, fly-away, weak & falling hair to strong, healthy, relaxed, body & curl holding, soft, shiny, non-greasy, bouncy, fast & easy to comb, brush, braid, blow dry, press or sit under the drier...saving money, time & comb through pain. Adds vitality, shine & natural feel to perms/relaxers. Extends perm/relaxer life for most. Replaces perms/relaxers for many. THOUSANDS OF TESTIMONIALS "Longer & thicker within one month • It grows overnight! Really, literally, magically overnight! • has made my hair grow 5&1/2 inches long • My bra length grew to my waist all in just three weeks • It is way past my shoulders & is steadily growing • very silky & easy to manage • an amazing sheen • great when you have to straighten • did make my hair softer & shinier...didn't weigh it down like hair grease...didn't take away its bounce • breakage has almost stopped...didn't need nothing else...will be saving me lots of money...a God sent for black african american hair • healthier and thicker for the first time in my whole life • white women with dry frizzy damaged curly hair need to know about this stuff too • My man is 51 & his hair was thinning. I started using it on his hair & it is growing! He's thrilled!" THE SECRET of the Black/African hair care world and proven for Spanish, Caucasian and all other hair types for over 20 years all natural Wild Growth Hair Oil is effective & safe for men & women of all ages (0-99+ years). 1 bottle lasts 1 month +. Money back guarantee. ORDER NOW! At select Sally Beauty Stores (1 800 ASK-SALLY) for $7.99. For other stores or home delivery (prices include delivery: 1 bottle-$11.39, 2-19.98, 3-28.57, 4-37.16, 5-45.75, 6-54.34, 12-79.56) by credit card (5-10 days), call toll-free 1 888 945-3476 or fax to 1 928 337-2305. Fax copy of check with shipping address for 10-15 day delivery. Mail money order (10-15 days) or check (15-20) to Wild Growth Co., P.O. Box 2940 WN, Saint Johns, AZ 85936.
Visit: www.wildgrowth.com Email: wildgro@wildgrowth.com

WEEKLY WORLD NEWS

May 5, 1992 · 60p. · 18259

First photo of pilot missing since 1937!

AMELIA EARHART FOUND ALIVE!

She's 95 years old and living on tiny island in South Pacific!

SEX MUFFINS... they energize your love life, say docs!

FREE RECIPE INSIDE!

Space aliens kidnapped my wife — and ate my dog!

Four evil-eyed creatures came in bullet-shaped starship, farmer claims

FARMER Enrique Cedillo said the creatures paralyzed him.

ARTIST'S conception of the tiny evil-eyed space creatures described by Mexican farmer Enrique Cedillo.

By JIMMY SNEAD

A Mexican farmer says space aliens kidnapped his wife and ate his hunting dog in one of the wildest close encounters ever.

Authorities will neither confirm nor deny that they are investigating the incident. But 53-year-old Enrique Cedillo says one of the aliens left behind a strange metal glove that proves his incredible story.

"They took my wife and they ate my dog. I spit on those creatures from space," said Cedillo. "Why did they do this to me when I did nothing to them?

"They are evil to the bone."

The farmer says the strange encounter took place on his farm west of Fresnillo, Mexico, on May 21. A bullet-shaped spacecraft appeared overhead as he was working in a field, he claims, and landed less than 50 feet from his house.

"Four evil-eyed creatures no bigger than children came out of the craft and marched into my house like they owned it," said Cedillo. "I started to run after them but I couldn't move my legs. I was paralyzed. I couldn't even scream."

While the farmer stood motionless in his field, the extraterrestrials emerged from the house with Cedillo's wife Carmen, 61, following like a zombie.

She allegedly boarded the UFO with one of the aliens while the other three shot and killed Cedillo's bird dog with a laser device — and proceeded to eat it raw, bones included.

"Tears were streaming down my face but I still couldn't move and had to watch those monsters eat my dog Pepe," said Cedillo.

"When they finished they went back to their ship. It made a loud whistling noise and lifted straight up in the air. It wobbled for a few seconds and then it vanished.

"When it was gone I could move again. That's when I found what they left behind, a tiny metal glove."

A spokesman for the Fresnillo Police Department confirmed that Cedillo reported his wife was kidnapped and his dog was killed but refused to say whether the incidents are under investigation.

Military officials examined Cedillo's glove but they won't comment either.

"People think I'm crazy but I'm sane," said the farmer. "If my wife was here she would tell you.

"But she isn't here. She is gone."

Children kill drunk dad for beating mom

Three schoolkids were so horrified when they saw their drunken dad beating their mom that they swung into action — and battered and stabbed him to death.

Kang Kyu-Son, 40, was knocked down by a baseball bat wielded by his 10-year-old son, then was attacked by his daughters, ages 12 and 13.

The older daughter stabbed her dad seven times with a kitchen knife while the younger girl hit him with a chopping board and a pan, said police in Seoul, South Korea.

Man's appendix cut out 20 times — it keeps growing back!

By SCOTTY PAUL

Retired barber Sergio Scali is a medical freak who has had his appendix removed every year for the past 20 years — but it keeps growing back.

"I've gotten used to the fact that I'm going in the hospital every year to have my appendix out. It's as simple as that," said Sergio, 46.

Doctors in Germany, England, Switzerland, Bermuda, as well as Italy share the mutual distinction of performing appendectomies on the scarred Sergio.

Sergio's bizarre dilemma began soon after he opened his first barbershop near Rome, Italy, in 1969. "Medics rushed me to the hospital for an emergency appendectomy," said Sergio.

The young barber was a perfect specimen of health until 10 months later when he had sharp pains in his side. X rays revealed his appendix had grown back.

"Doctors didn't have the slightest idea why I had grown more appendixes," he said. "All they knew is that they had to come out or they would burst."

And Sergio has repeated his once-a-year trip to the hospital ever since — even when he lived briefly in Germany and England, and was vacationing in the Swiss Alps and in Bermuda. Sergio has to be X-rayed every three months. "I guess the docs want to watch them grow," said the retired barber.

Sergio, who lives in Rome, is planning a trip to Naples, but it will have to wait until after July. He's due to have his appendix removed for the 21st time in mid-June.

TEN NEW COMMANDMENTS FOUND BY BIBLE EXPERTS

BIBLICAL scholar Dr. Marc Thompson believes God is still guiding mankind.

Archaeologists claim to have found 10 more commandments that were handed down to Moses on Mt. Sinai and they specifically address moral and ethical issues faced by modern man!

Drs. Jon Walters and Marc Thompson cannot yet prove that the ancient commandments came directly from God but their gut feeling is that they were divinely inspired.

The laws were written in Hebrew on stone tablets. But in plain English, they urge mankind to protect the environment, avoid birth control, preserve the family, attend church, ban pornography, enforce the death penalty, fight Satan, pursue greater spiritual understanding and knowledge, heal the sick by faith alone and feed the hungry at all costs.

"This is unquestionably the most important religious discovery since the Dead Sea Scrolls," Dr. Thompson told a news conference in Jerusalem. "The new commandments were apparently handed down to Moses along with the first 10 but were somehow lost and didn't make it into the Bible."

"We certainly don't want to make outrageous claims or insult anyone's religion. But these commandments seem to address modern moral and ethical issues. Everybody should look at them.

"There is a very real possibility that they were divinely inspired. In my mind they prove that God is still trying to guide mankind."

Biblical scholars were reluctant to speculate on the origins or authenticity of the commandments. But they were intrigued by the fact that the tablets were discovered less than two miles from the cave where the Dead Sea Scrolls were found in 1947.

Even more compelling, tests indicate that the new commandments were etched into stone about the same time as the originals, Dr. Walters said.

"It will be years and possibly even decades before we know enough about their origins to speak with authority. But until that time comes I think we can consider them to be a major discovery."

For the purpose of comparison here are the original commandments in plain English:
1. Worship the one true God only.
2. Don't make graven images.
3. Don't take God's name in vain.
4. Remember the Sabbath.
5. Honor your parents.
6. Don't kill.
7. Don't commit adultery.
8. Don't steal.
9. Don't lie about people.
10. Don't covet anyone or anything.
— NELSON MANN

GOD'S GUIDANCE: The story of the Ten Commandments was told in a Hollywood movie with Charlton Heston playing Moses.

'The most important discovery since the Dead Sea Scrolls'

1. Protect the environment
2. Avoid birth control
3. Preserve the family
4. Attend church
5. Ban pornography
6. Enforce the death penalty
7. Fight Satan
8. Pursue greater spiritual understanding and knowledge
9. Heal the sick by faith alone
10. Feed the hungry at all costs

IN PLAIN ENGLISH: The new commandments deliver God's message of encouragement. Biblical experts now believe they were etched in stone at the same time as the originals.

Japanese boozin' to beat the band

The Japanese drank more booze than ever last year — downing a whopping 2.3 billion gallons!

The government said each adult consumed an average of 18 gallons of beer and four gallons of sake.

Attack of the killer tumbleweeds

By GILBERT SALAZAR

Susan Schwinning called for help from emergency crews after being trapped in her home by tumbleweeds! Winds up to 50 m.p.h. whipped across California's Mojave Desert, kicking up dark clouds of red dust and tumbling tumbleweeds.

"There were tumbleweeds in the entry, tumbleweeds in the yard, tumbleweeds in the garage — tumbleweeds everywhere," Miss Schwinning explained.

"It's the first time I've had a call for help from someone trapped by tumbleweeds," Los Angeles County fire fighter Ruben Sandoval said.

HOUSEWIFE GETS PRIZE-WINNING RECIPES FROM OUIJA BOARD!

KIND SPIRITS are giving Michigan housewife Mary Van Maastricht nutritious recipes that delight the whole family.

By BEATRICE DEXTER

Mary Van Maastricht's recipes are out of this world, and there's a good reason why: She gets them from her Ouija board!

The Detroit homemaker says her prize-winning pies, homemade bread and crusty casseroles come from great cooks who have passed away — and then passed along their secrets by spelling them out on the ESP gameboard.

"They're tasty and easy to fix," said Mrs. Van Maastricht, 47. "If I'm stuck for a dinner idea I just pull out the board. My kids and my husband go wild over my cooking now. I don't know what I'd do without my Ouija board."

The happy housewife says she first discovered her treasure trove of recipes in 1986 while relatives were visiting her for a week. Her guests had brought along a Ouija board and urged Mrs. Van Maastricht to try it.

She sat at a table with her friends, put her hands on a small, wheeled pointer called a planchette and asked the board questions. The board answers the questions by pointing to the words "yes" and "no" written at each corner, or spells out its menus using letters printed on the board's surface.

Lucky toss

A frantic mother saved her two kids from possible death by throwing them out a third-floor window of a burning building — and neighbors caught them in a sheet.

Heroic Carmen Pacheco was overcome by smoke before she could save her two other children, but they were rescued by firemen in New York City. Mrs. Pacheco also was dragged unconscious from the building and survived.

21   WEEKLY WORLD NEWS
June 12, 1990

Try her Perfect Peach Cake from beyond the grave!

"I didn't know what to ask the thing, so I asked it what I should make for dinner," she recalled. "All of us were amazed when it spelled out an entire menu and recipes."

The women jotted down ingredients and directions and that night Mrs. Van Maastricht cooked one of the dishes, a pie made of fresh peaches and strawberries. It was a hit.

"Before, my husband and my kids always grumbled about my cooking, and I admit it was no great shakes," the mother of two recalled. "But since the great chefs on the Other Side have been helping me out, I can't cook fast enough to please them.

"My pies have won prizes at fairs and my cookies always sell out at the bake sales."

An added benefit of her new ghostly goodies is that they appear to be exceptionally nutritious and wholesome.

"My kids had allergies until I gave them the Ouija board dishes and now they're much better," she said.

Homicidal hubbies

Almost half of all murdered women in England were slain by husbands or lovers, says a new study by researchers.

Of 2,839 murders committed between 1984 and 1988, the victims were men 57 percent of the time. But only 1 in 10 men were killed by wives or lovers.

And 43 percent of the women murdered during those years were slain by husbands or lovers.

From the dozens of recipes she's received from the Other Side, Mrs. Van Maastricht has selected a few of her favorites. Try them for a heavenly taste treat.

PERFECT PEACH CAKE
1 box yellow cake mix
3 cups peeled and chopped peaches
¾ cup half-and-half
½ cup sugar
¼ tsp. cinnamon

Follow directions on package to prepare cake mix. Pour into lightly greased and floured 9- by 13-inch cake pan. Mix together other ingredients and pour over top. Bake at 350 degrees for 45 to 50 minutes.

FINGER-LICKIN' CHICKEN KABOBS
¼ cup lemon juice
2 tbsps. vegetable or sesame seed oil
2 tbsps. honey
3 tbsps. soy sauce
6 skinned, boned chicken breast halves, cut into strips about an inch wide
3 small zucchini squash, cut into ½-inch rounds

Marinate chicken strips in mixture of lemon juice, oil, honey and soy sauce for at least 1 hour. Thread chicken on skewers, alternating with pieces of squash. Grill over medium-hot coals for 12 minutes, turning frequently and basting with the lemon-soy sauce mixture.

OUIJA VEGGIE DIP
½ cup yogurt
2-3 tbsps. mayonnaise
1 tsp. dried dill or 1 tbsp. chopped fresh dill
plenty of black pepper

Mix all ingredients thoroughly and allow to chill in refrigerator for ½ hour before serving. Great with raw vegetables.

'If a guy calls and says Bigfoot ran away with his wife, we wrote it as straight as an AP story… If someone calls me up and says their toaster is talking to them, I don't refer them to professional help, I say, "Put the toaster on the phone."'—SAL IVONE, *WEEKLY WORLD NEWS* REPORTER

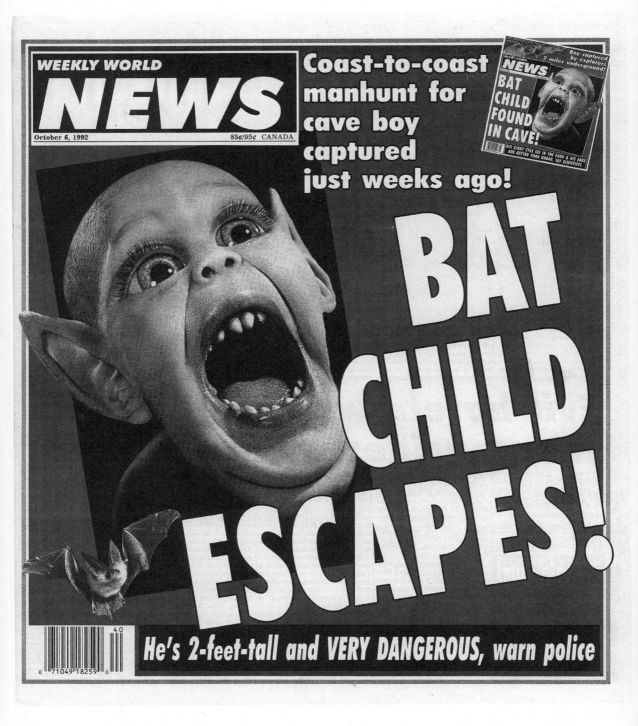

The world's WACKIEST wedding!

WOMAN, 29, MARRIES GIRAFFE

NEWS EXCLUSIVE By BEATRICE DEXTER

She believes he's her dead lover come back to life!

Grief-stricken heiress Pia Torsoni pledged eternal union with her dead fiance — by marrying a giraffe!

The 29-year-old private school teacher and daughter of a wealthy Milan, Italy, industrialist is convinced Pippo the giraffe is the reincarnation of her lover. So she tied the knot with the towering animal in a touching ceremony at the city zoo. The blushing bride says her marriage to 16-foot-tall Pippo is symbolic and fulfills a vow she made to marry no man except her dead sweetheart Antonio Crespedo.

"I found Antonio's spirit in this animal and I united myself with his spirit," Pia told the local press following her bizarre wedding.

"Now that I have married I feel free to go on with my life. Of course I can never marry anyone else, but I don't care. My love will always be only for Antonio."

Pia said she first realized she had a special bond with Pippo the giraffe when she was visiting the city zoo last fall.

She was standing near the giraffe pen crying over Antonio, who had died on September 21 of cancer of the pancreas. Suddenly she realized that one of the giraffes had walked to the side of the pen and was standing quietly by watching her, Pia recalled.

"Its eyes were large and soft, just as Antonio's had been," Pia said. "It looked at me with such understanding and pity. I knew immediately that this was more than an animal's gaze — I knew it was Antonio come back to me in another form."

Incredibly, Pia arranged to purchase the giraffe from the zoo and then announced to her friends and relatives she was going to marry it! She planned a May wedding and invited 200 guests, holding the ceremony in a big barn at her father's estate. The wedding was a solemn formal affair, conducted by a member of the Italian Society for Psychical Research. Pia wept with joy, but many of her friends and relatives were upset by the marriage.

"I think she made an absolute fool of herself," said an elderly relative who asked to remain anonymous. "Pia has always been a very emotional person, but this is taking things a bit far.

"I'm hoping this doesn't ruin her socially. She's always been popular, but people are beginning to wonder. I mean, who wants the wife of a giraffe at their dinner party?"

TILL death do they part! Bizarre wedding photo shows wacko bride Pia Torsoni with her newlywed hubby — a giant giraffe named Pippo.

'EAR'S the culprit!'
Cops use 'earprints' to nab thief

Police nabbed a man accused of more than 30 burglaries through ear imprints he left on the doors of the apartments he robbed.

Gregore Roman would put his ear against the door of a home to be sure no one was home before breaking in. Authorities said Roman was part of a gang that stole $200,000 in valuables from homes throughout western Switzerland in 1988. A Swiss court sentenced the 39-year-old Romanian exile to three years in prison.

New survey confirms...
Gals braver than guys!

Gals say guys are more likely to panic in a crisis, according to a recent survey.

A British poll discovered two-thirds of men are unable to cope in a crisis, one-third of men feel faint at the sight of blood and 75 percent would be useless if their wives went into labor. The surveyors said men fared better at air travel — more than 80 percent of guys keep their cool during an emergency landing.

HOORAY! YOU CAN STILL TOSS DWARFS!

Dwarf-tossing is still legal in South Carolina. State lawmakers rejected a bill to outlaw it because it would deprive dwarfs of earning a living.

WEEKLY WORLD NEWS June 12, 1990

THEY'VE REALLY MADE ED ANGER MAD THIS TIME!

MY AMERICA By ED ANGER

A rap song as our new national anthem? Ya gotta be KIDDIN'!

...but that's what Prez candidate Bill Clinton's DINGBAT WIFE wants!

I'm as hot as a Fourth of July firecracker over a nasty new plot to change our national anthem!

That late, great songwriter Francis Scott Key must be twirling in his grave over a $1 million prize that's been offered by some crackpot businessman in Raleigh, N.C., for a new national tune. Anders Skaar (doesn't sound like an American name to me) says entries can be in any musical style — soul, rap or rock.

That's all we need, folks — a national anthem in rap!

But what makes me so pig-biting mad is that Bill and Hillary Clinton are supporting this fruitcake idea to ditch our beloved anthem.

"Bill really doesn't think much of dumping the *Star-Spangled Banner*, but Hillary hates the song. And we all know who wears the pants in that family. She says jump and he says how high," a top level source in the Clinton campaign told me.

In fact, Hillary thinks about as much of our country's great anthem as she does of women who aren't hotshot lawyers but everyday housewives — nothing!

Well, folks, yours truly didn't charge up Pork Chop Hill in Korea to let some sniveling, spoiled, bleeding-heart yuppies bury the anthem that millions of American soldiers fought and died for, by gum! The *Star-Spangled Banner* is a sacred part of America's history.

George Washington and Abe Lincoln would be downright ashamed at this crazy talk about changing it. So, let's nip this nonsense in the bud. I want all true-blue Americans across this great land to stand up and let these people know how we feel. Just fill in the poll below and we'll give 'em hell, by God!

In the meantime, I just put in a call to my good buddy Ross Perot. I've got a funny feeling that the man who's going to be our next president will be real interested in this attack on our national song!

IF HILLARY Clinton has her way, a new national anthem could very well be written by rap singer Hammer, right.

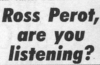
Ross Perot, are you listening?
AMERICA'S last hope: H. Ross Perot!

PRESIDENTIAL candidate Bill Clinton is proud of his wife Hillary. But Ed worries that if HE'S elected, SHE'LL be in charge, and we can all kiss America goodbye!

ED'S NATIONAL ANTHEM POLL
CHECK one circle, clip & send to: ANGER'S ANTHEM POLL, c/o Weekly World News, 600 S. East Coast Avenue, Lantana, Fla. 33462

○ **YES:** I agree with Ed Anger that the plot to ditch the *Star-Spangled Banner* is horrible. Bill Clinton should be ashamed of his wife Hillary for supporting it.

○ **NO:** The *Star-Spangled Banner* is a stupid song and we should replace it with a rap or rock 'n' roll song about America. And I think Bill and Hillary Clinton will make a great president.

17 WEEKLY WORLD NEWS June 16, 1992

PREGNANT HUBBY

WIFE Sheila shows Steve's milk-leaking breast.

By SUSAN JIMISON
Staff writer

Mother-to-be Sheila McMahon is having an easy time with her pregnancy — but her husband Steve is suffering from backache, morning sickness and sore breasts that leak milk!

That's right — Steve, 24, is a pregnant father-to-be, a dad who is going through the whole baby-making project with his wife and feels all the symptoms a woman feels when she's expecting.

"Steve is certainly producing a fluid from his breasts," said obstetrician Dr. James Drife, who examined the Coalville, England, factory worker recently.

"Steve's symptoms are mainly psychological, but they are very real. This really is a most unusual case, quite fascinating," said Dr. Drife.

Steve's pregnancy began last fall shortly after his wife told him she was expecting. The young couple had lost a baby through miscarriage just a few months before and Sheila and Steve desperately wanted the pregnancy to succeed.

Perhaps the excitement of having a first child was what triggered Steve's sympathetic pregnancy. Or perhaps it was his worry that something might happen to this baby, too.

Whatever it was, Steve instantly began experiencing the very same feelings as Sheila and soon his tummy swelled up to pregnancy proportions.

"It was a bit of a shock at first," admitted the young dad-in-waiting. "I was worried, but now I can see the funny side.

"Now sometimes I notice that my breasts have leaked and there are wet patches on my T-shirts. But I'm not ashamed of it. People call me Ernie the Milkman. I'm really quite amazed at it."

Sheila says she thinks it's great to have company in the long nine months of pregnancy and that it makes her feel close to Steve to share the burden. Sometimes her husband comes home complaining of sickness or backache, just like an expectant mom.

"Everything that pregnant women have, he has as well," said Sheila. "He gets cravings for cheese and eggs — it's amazing.

"Then when he complained his chest was hurting, we saw that milk actually spurted out. It's weird. We have been like one person during this pregnancy."

SHE'S having the baby but HE has morning sickness & swollen tummy

Hellhound
A 35-year-old woman bled to death 14 hours after she was attacked by a police dog that found her sleeping in a vacant house, police in West Palm Beach, Fla., report.

SHEILA and Steve are both drinking milk daily for the baby's health.

WEEKLY WORLD NEWS
June 12, 1990

UFO FLEET REFUELS AT POWER PLANT IN EGYPT

By MICKEY McGUIRE
Special to The News

ARTIST'S conception of the scene described by witness Aly Hamdy Chammas, below. Mother ship hovers above android-like beings at river.

A fleet of space shuttle craft and their spectacular "mother ship" have singled out a remote power station in Egypt as a refueling base, and their frequent stops are witnessed by hundreds of villagers who consider the alien visitors as strange but welcome friends!

Even power station employees — knowing it would cost them their jobs — pretend not to notice when the saucer-shaped UFOs and their monstrous, 800-foot-long mother ship hover over the plant to draw electrical current from its transmission lines.

Every man, woman and child living in the Nile River village of Sahafa has walked among the android-like beings that often beam down from the starship to explore the village and surrounding countryside.

"Often they pick up rocks along the river bank, but we have come to know they mean us no harm," plant supervisor Aly Hamdy Chammas explained. "When the great ship draws off power, it is very careful to stay well within the capacity of the generators.

"And the UFOs always refuel in the early morning hours before dawn when power demand is at its minimum.

"We do not begrudge the aliens the power they obviously require."

Villager Sami Hamid said the UFOs have been using the plant as a refueling site since 1987 and have never caused any problems that could threaten the safety of the village or the people.

"All of us here in the village have seen them," he said. "Just eight days ago, as I was walking near the river, the big ship came across the desert like a bolt of lightning. It stopped over the station and just hovered there.

"It projected a greenish-blue ray into the station and at once I heard the generators strain as they worked harder to handle the extra power drain.

"The giant ship was really sucking up the current and the color of the ray changed from greenish-blue to a deep red. After about 20 minutes, it shot into the heavens and vanished.

"Why it requires our Earth power, I do not know. I should think that such a ship must be able to create its own power. I do not understand.

"But if they want power, it is theirs for the taking whenever they have need of it. We look upon them as our friends. Maybe someday the village will need their help and they will repay us for our generosity."

WEEKLY WORLD NEWS (ISSN 0199-574X) Published weekly by Weekly World News, Inc., 600 S. East Coast Ave., Lantana, Fla. 33462. MAIL SUBSCRIPTIONS $24.95 a year in U.S., $44.95 a year outside the U.S. Second Class postage paid at Lake Worth, Fla., and at additional mailing offices in the USA. Canadian Second Class permit #9448 paid at Toronto, Ontario, Canada. POSTMASTER: Send address changes to WEEKLY WORLD NEWS, P.O. Box 11286, Des Moines, Iowa 50340-1286. For subscription address changes and inquiries write Weekly World News, P.O. Box 11286, Des Moines, Iowa 50340-1286. Printed in U.S.A.

CHECKOUT LINE FROM 1982 DISCOVERED!

Easy-listening music & slow line forced shoppers into hibernal state for 25 years!

CHICAGO, Ill. — Building inspectors postponed demolition of the old Hebsen's Drugs building today when they discovered a checkout line still waiting inside the doomed structure.

By GEORGE GOWAN

"Judging by the expiration dates on their purchases and the amount of Velcro in their clothes, we quickly deduced that these people had been standing there since 1982," said inspector Davis Mervin.

Medics arriving on the scene found traces of spilled Pentotussin,™ an opium-derived cough medicine recalled in 1983 for inducing comas.

"Given the opiate fumes, the slowness of the line and the easy-listening music, these people didn't stand a chance," said medic Alan Yarnell. "Hibernation reduced their caloric requirements and they subsisted on whatever snacks they'd meant to purchase."

All members of the checkout line, including the cashier and store owner, are in stable condition tonight at a local hospital. Dr. Yarnell and his colleagues are searching for the shoppers' surviving relatives — and encountering some obstacles along the way.

"At least three young people on the line were trying to buy beer with fake IDs," Yarnell said. "When they wake up, they can look forward to toasting their good fortune."

Mother of lost 3-year-old girl shouts for joy...

BIGFOOT RESCUED MY CHILD

In an incredible display of motherly love, a 3-year-old girl, lost in the wilderness of a mountainside forest, was saved and returned to her parents — by a female Bigfoot who cared for the child like one of her own!

Little Nadia Gurenkov was lost for two days after wandering from her parents' camp in a vast pine forest on the slopes of Russia's rugged Caucasus Mountains, according to a Soviet news agency.

As dozens of military and civilian search parties scoured the countryside, the child was carried into her parents' camp in the massive, hairy arms of an eight-foot-tall Bigfoot beast that was unmistakably female, the report said.

"The creature saved my little baby's life," declared overjoyed mother Marina Gurenkov. "When Nadia wasn't found before the first night, my husband and I were certain we would never see her again. There are so many wild animals in the forest we thought it impossible that she would survive.

"Then, like in a fairy tale, Nadia is returned to us by a beast of the wild. It was so unreal, I simply couldn't believe my eyes. But there was the Bigfoot — obviously a female — lumbering into camp with our little baby cradled so lovingly in her arms," Mrs. Gurenkov told the news agency.

Hulking female creature cared for toddler as one of her own

"And Nadia was safe and unharmed. She was actually laughing and totally unafraid of the creature. It was dusk and the air was very chilly, but she was wrapped in a garment of rabbit fur that kept her warm. And in her hand, my little girl clutched a flower."

Mrs. Gurenkov said Nadia told them the Bigfoot woman found her while she was sleeping in a forest clearing.

The girl's mother estimated the child was found three miles from the camp.

"My daughter is very intelligent for her age," the mother explained.

"She was able to tell us all that happened.

"The creature carried her to a cave where there was another huge Bigfoot and four smaller ones. She said there was 'a mama and papa and their babies.'

"She said they wrapped her in a fur blanket and they fed her some kind of raw meat and gave her water.

"Then, the female carried her back to our camp. She laid Nadia on the ground a few yards from us, smiled down at her and then just walked back into the forest.

"I wish I could tell her how grateful I am."
— EDGAR MITCHELL

TENDER: Female Bigfoot gently cradles little Nadia Gurenkov.

Why our President doesn't look a gift elephant in the trunk

President Reagan never looks a gift horse in the mouth. In fact, when it comes to official freebies, Ronnie and Nancy never say "No!"

Because a federal ethics law prohibits officials from keeping gifts presented by foreign dignitaries, the 73 gifts the President and First Lady received last year were accepted for "official use."

Among the gifts Reagan received last year were:
• An 18-month-old baby elephant from the President of Sri Lanka, which was given to the National Zoo, where it died.
• A 17th century clock worth a cool $3,500 from Austrian President Rudolph Kirchschaeger.
• Six bottles of wine and nine pounds of seedless tangerines from the ambassador of Morocco.
• A tablecloth and a lacquered box from Soviet Foreign Minister Andrei Gromyko.
— SYLVESTER WINTON

WHITE HOUSE WELCOME: President Reagan says hello to a live gift from the President of Sri Lanka.

Going to great links

History's longest continuous sausage was stuffed and proudly displayed in Birmingham, England, on June 22, 1983. The wonder-wiener stretched for 5½ miles and weighed 2.67 tons, according to the *Guinness Book of World Records*.

BIGFOOT

In the summer of 1987, *Weekly World News* reported that Katie Martin, a Seattle secretary, had carried on a two-week affair with Bigfoot on the south face of Mount Rainier. Nine months later, Katie proudly gave birth to a little furball named Kendall Martin, whom Katie's husband not-so-affectionately referred to as 'Littlefoot'.

Who can blame Katie for her mountainside indiscretion? Everyone loves them some Bigfoot!

Many Bigfoot lovers comb the woods, camera at the ready, looking for the shy, old-school Patterson–Gimlin Bigfoot darting through the trees. Other Footies set a table place, Elijah-style, in their dining room, hoping to break bread with the genial *Harry and the Hendersons* family yeti. Still other 'Woopies' – wookie groupies – mix their Sasquatch with pleasure, making ATM withdrawals so they can go all the Bigfoot way with Helen, the Bigfoot Hooker.

Anyway you shave it, *Weekly World News* let the fur fly when it came to covering Bigfoot. The periodical gave the world the hairiest collection of Bigfoot reportage ever assembled! No other news organization in the history of journalism has scored more Bigfoot scoops than *Weekly World News*. Our reporters trod every patch of forest on earth tracking these wily ape-like creatures, and bagged Bigfoot in places no one would think of looking: from South Whittle, North Dakota to Cangyuan, China, and everywhere in between.

The paper found all kinds of Bigfoot: tall ones, short ones, fat ones, skinny ones, big ones, little ones, hairy ones and even a gay one. Bigfoot and his furry offshoots have been found in many legendary exclusives, including Fatfoot, Littlefoot, Leadfoot, Mummyfoot, and the legendary Babyfoot, discovered by anthropologist Dr Jan Broder in China in 1987.

Worried about the danger of being kidnapped by a Bigfoot? Well, you needn't be. W*eekly World News* reported that the experience wasn't all that bad when it interviewed former Bigfoot love slaves Paul Stillyard and Leon Verdell. All the same, to help protect readers from this fate, the paper ran an exposé on the 'Top 10 Jobs Most Likely to get you Kidnapped by Bigfoot'. Stay away from these gigs and you should be safe.

In addition, according to *Weekly World News*, readers can count on hard-working law enforcement to have their backs; the paper famously reported on the harrowing story of the Iowa cop that gunned down a two-headed Bigfoot near a farm sixty miles outside of Great Bend, Iowa, in 2005.

Weekly World News remains the only periodical that tamed Bigfoot, and brought him into the world's living rooms to soothe many readers' savage inner beasts.

BLOOD-THIRSTY HOUNDS FROM HELL
VAMPIRE POODLE HORROR

...DOZENS OF PEOPLE KILLED IN RAMPAGE

IF YOU fear your poodle may be a vampire, DO NOT try to deal with it yourself, say experts.

By SHARON HUMPHEYS

PET owners are being viciously slaughtered in their sleep by cute, cuddly poodles who turn into blood-thirsty fiends at night.

So far, more than 100 dog owners worldwide have been drained of blood or viciously pounced on and ripped to shreds. An expert tells *Weekly World News* that these are no mere pooches — but an evil breed of vampire poodles.

"By day, these new perilous pooches seem like the perfect lapdog, playfully bounding about fetching balls and licking the faces of their owners," notes Dimitru Costache of the Romanian Vampire Finders Society. "But at night, they transform into the hounds from hell.

"They sit and wait for you to lay down for bed — and then they go straight for the jugular."

Thus far, attacks have been reported in Europe, Asia, Africa and in four U.S. states — Iowa, New York, Kansas and California.

Housewife Adrienne Bria 51, recently watched in horr as her iron worker husband Mathieu, 55, was torn to pie by their new poodle pal Fifi the bedroom of their home miles outside Paris.

"We found her wandering the street and took her in," Adrienne. "She was so nice about a week, but got very

GOD'S AUTOGRAPH SELLS FOR $500 MILLION

AN ANONYMOUS billionaire has reportedly purchased "God's autograph" through an on-line auction site for an astounding half-billion dollars.

The item description on the site called the autograph "the real deal" and said it was "personally snagged by Billy Graham sometime in the early '70s." As seen in an accompanying photograph of the writing, which appears to be in blue ball-point ink on notebook paper, it reads:

B-dog,

Thanks for all your help over the years. You rock!

See you in Heaven, Homey,

God

The seller, Kirk Stipes, 28, an unemployed car detailer, claims he has documentation to back up the purported history of the autograph.

"I got it from a dude who got it from a dude who knew a guy who was going out with a girl whose cousin was Billy Graham's personal secretary for a few years around 1973 or something," says Stipes. "I got a note from the dude that explains all that and plus it's, like, notarized or whatever.

"Everybody knows Billy Graham is tight with God and Jesus and all that crowd, so it's like totally possible that if anyone could get an autograph from God, it would be him. Word."

Asked what he plans to do with his newfound wealth, Stipes says he plans to contin-

ue dealing in "super kick-as rare autographs."

"I already got leads on T Easter Bunny and E.T."

BEWARE! That cuddly poodle could be a vampire and slaughter you in your sleep!

...I cooked my celery and ...e soup and hid under the ...

...hat night, my dear Mathieu ...aking off his boots to go to ... when Fifi grabbed his ankle ... underneath. At first, I ...ght they were fooling ...nd. Mathieu was saying, 'No ...stop, it's not time to play . . . ...ou have sharp teeth, stop it!' ...inally, he screamed, 'Oh my ... save me!' as little Fifi ...ged him kicking and ...ming under the bed. ...uddenly, there was a sea of ... pouring out from under ...ed — and I knew my Math- ...as gone.
...hen, Fifi stuck her head out ... under the bed and I could ...hese long fangs, much larg- ...an normal canine teeth, ... swear that she gave me an ...rin and started to walk ...rd me. So I ran out of the ...e — and I'm never going ..."

...ientists are arguing about ...udden origin of the savage ...pecies of deadly doggies.

Some say the first one was created recently by a vampire bat, or a lonely vampire who wanted a furry fanged friend.

Other experts insist that a whole pack of them were released and scattered around the world during recent excavations of a small vampire city in the Romanian mountains.

But they do agree that these new vampire poodles are truly a menace, and give pet owners this advice on how to tell if your cute little pup is actually a killer vampire dog in disguise:

● Poodles have white fur, but vampire poodles have REALLY white fur and refuse to go outside and do their business. They will only go out at night.
● Try to feed the critter tempting food like a nice juicy steak, but smother it in garlic. If it howls and heads for the hills, it just might be one.
● Pick up the pooch and stand in front of a full-length mirror — if you see yourself standing there alone, you could possibly have a vampire crea-

ture on your hands.
● If your Fluffy is killed by a car and shows up 10 minutes later as if nothing ever happened, you might just be the owner of a vampire poodle.

"If you should find that your poodle is actually a vampire, do NOT try to deal with it yourself," warns Costache. "Call the Romanian Vampire Finders Society immediately. We are professionals. We will know what to do!"

NEWS 'TOON

"You have a way with children."

NEW WHITE HOUSE SHOCKER!
PRESIDENT TO NAME HOMELAND SECURIT'

Bush refuses to change his mind even after learn

By ALFONSO PITELLI

IN a bombshell revelation that shocked even his closest Republican supporters, President George W. Bush announced that his new director of Homeland Security would be Yoda, the famed Jedi master from the *Star Wars* films.

White House insiders reveal that Bush got the idea after watching the new *Stars Wars* DVD set he said Santa gave him for Christmas.

"Yoda may not look like much on the outside," the commander in chief told a stunned White House press corps. "But the little guy is one heck of a warrior.

"Anybody with half a brain can see he's the perfect choice."

Bush noted that he was also impressed with the fact that Yoda is pint-size.

"I'll tower over him at press conferences — which is important since I'm the president," he added.

On the face of it, the 894-year-old Yoda, a member of an undisclosed alien species, would seem like a good replacement for outgoing Homeland Security boss Tom Ridge.

Like Ridge, Yoda doesn't have a neck.

Also, Yoda is a master of The Force and has trained some of the top Jedi knights in the Star Wars galaxy, including Obi-Wan-Kenobi, Mace Windu, Qui-Gon-Jinn, Luke Skywalker and even Darth Vader, who turned evil.

But one administration source tells *Weekly World News*

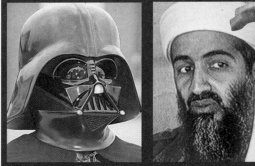

IMPRESSED by Yoda's defeat of Darth Vader, above left, President Bush is sure pint-size warrior will make short work of Osama Bin Laden, right.

that Cabinet members were shocked when Bush announced his decision.

Vice President Dick Cheney reportedly blurted out, "But Yoda doesn't exist!"

Still, the President refused to budge.

"Bush shot back, 'So what?,'" says the source. "'I'm the president. If I say we're winning the war in Iraq, then we're winning it. If I say Saddam and Al Qaeda are linked, then they are. If I say we'll find weapons of mass destruction there, then we will — eventually. Trust me on that one.'"

Adds the source, "As usual, Bush refused to change his mind even after learning that Yoda isn't real."

Instead, Bush told the Cabinet he was especially impressed with Yoda's 500-year track record in "fighting evildoers, like that Garth Vader guy."

He added, "And I'm particularly interested in his ability to sense fluctuations in The Force

LIKE Tom Ridge, Yoda has no neck.

YODA CHIEF
...da isn't real

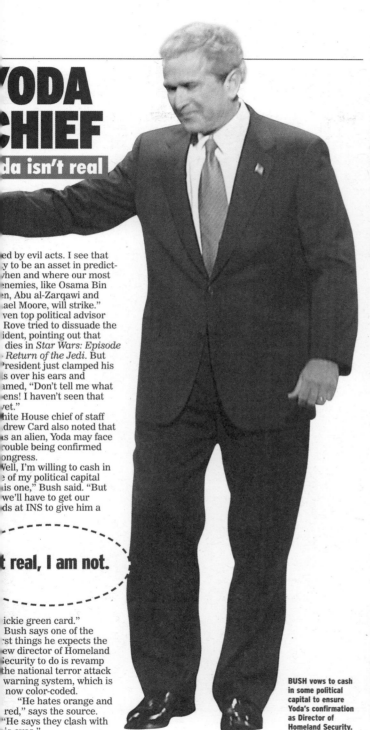

...ed by evil acts. I see that
...y to be an asset in predict-
...hen and where our most
...enemies, like Osama Bin
...n, Abu al-Zarqawi and
...ael Moore, will strike."
...ven top political advisor
...Rove tried to dissuade the
...ident, pointing out that
...dies in *Star Wars: Episode
...Return of the Jedi*. But
...resident just clamped his
...s over his ears and
...amed, "Don't tell me what
...ens! I haven't seen that
...yet."
...hite House chief of staff
...drew Card also noted that
...s an alien, Yoda may face
...rouble being confirmed
...ongress.
...ell, I'm willing to cash in
...of my political capital
...is one," Bush said. "But
...we'll have to get our
...ds at INS to give him a

real, I am not.

...ickie green card."
...Bush says one of the
...rst things he expects the
...ew director of Homeland
...Security to do is revamp
...the national terror attack
...warning system, which is
...now color-coded.
"He hates orange and
red," says the source.
"He says they clash with
...is eyes."

BUSH vows to cash in some political capital to ensure Yoda's confirmation as Director of Homeland Security.

THERE'S nothing better than family...

HOW TO HAVE A SECRET SECOND FAMILY

By SCOTT STEVENS

IF YOUR family is too much for you, try relaxing with a second one! That's the advice of Jeremy Stoppard, author of *Non-Sloppy Seconds: How to Keep a Secret Second Family*.

"Going back home to the same family each night can be a drag," Stoppard says. "But ironically, having a SECOND family can make each one seem like a vacation from the other."

Some of Stoppard's tips include:

● Only marry one of the women, or else get an alias. "Bigamy is still illegal in the United States."

● Tell both families you work for the CIA. "Then forbid them to talk about you to anyone. That cuts down on the risk of being found out. Also, it gives you an excuse if you're ever caught with your other family's possessions."

● Keep a regular schedule. "You need consistent excuses, like 'Every Thursday, Friday and Saturday I have to go on a secret mission.'"

● Don't have two spouses with the same first name. "You DON'T want to answer the phone by saying, 'Jane? WHICH Jane?'"

● Keep both families at least 10 miles apart. "Any closer, and you risk running into the other one."

● Have a friend — preferably one who also has a second family — to cover for you. "Sometimes you need someone to vouch for where you say you were."

● Keep separate credit cards and wardrobes. "Or else you'll hear a lot of 'Honey, where'd you get this shirt...?'"

...and with a second one you can double the fun!

TRAPPED IN HIS CAR FOR 33 DAYS...
AVALANCHE VICTIM EATS HIS OWN CLOTHES TO SURVIVE!

'I ate my shoes first...I was starving after 2 weeks'

By BEATRICE DEXTER
Correspondent

A stranded motorist spent 33 terrifying days trapped in his car under a massive snowslide, but survived in good shape — because he ate his own clothing!

Salesman Michal Laco, 32, was found by a rescue team more than a month after he was buried in an avalanche while driving through the mountains. The Havirov, Czechoslovakia, father of two is now recovering in a hospital.

"I ate my shoes first," the emaciated survivor told reporters in Prague.

"It was two weeks into my ordeal and I was starving.

"After that I ate my wool socks and my ski cap. By that time I didn't care what I was eating. I knew my only chance of survival was to eat whatever was at hand."

MIRACLE man Michal Laco smiles at news conference after his ordeal.

Laco had been on his way to his home from a business convention when he was stranded in freezing temperatures by an avalanche of snow and ice. His car was submerged under four feet of slush, but the man was able to breathe.

Officials believe that the snow layer surrounding Laco's car kept temperatures fairly high inside it and Laco says he took bites of snow to ease his thirst. The salesman carried nothing to eat in his car, however, and knew he faced death by starvation.

"I figured help would not reach me for a long time," he said. "At first I thought I could tough it out. Then I remembered tales of people eating their shoes for the nourishment in the leather."

After eating his shoes, Laco sliced up his socks and wool ski cap. These he ate slowly over an eight-day period, chewing carefully until the wool was digestible.

Next, Laco removed his cotton shirt and ate it.

"Fortunately, most of my clothes are made of natural fibers — cotton, wool, things like that," Laco said.

"I don't know what I would have done if my clothes had been made of synthetics like nylon.

"The taste wasn't bad, but the texture was a problem. And I was afraid that if the rescuers took too long I'd die of cold because I lacked enough clothing."

Fortunately, a rescue team found Laco on the 33rd day of his ordeal. By that time, the stranded motorist was down to his skivvies, jacket and undershirt.

"He was shivering, but appeared pretty healthy," said rescue worker Peter Dzur.

"He was weak, but otherwise okay.

"We're pretty certain he would have died if he hadn't had the nourishment his clothing provided."

WEEKLY WORLD NEWS
June 16, 1992

"'Midnight Star', a song on my second album (it was the track right after "Eat It"), was very much inspired by the *Weekly World News.* It was about a gullible guy who adamantly believed all the supermarket tabloids which featured headlines such as "The Incredible Frog Boy is on the Loose Again!"'— **'WEIRD AL' YANKOVIC**

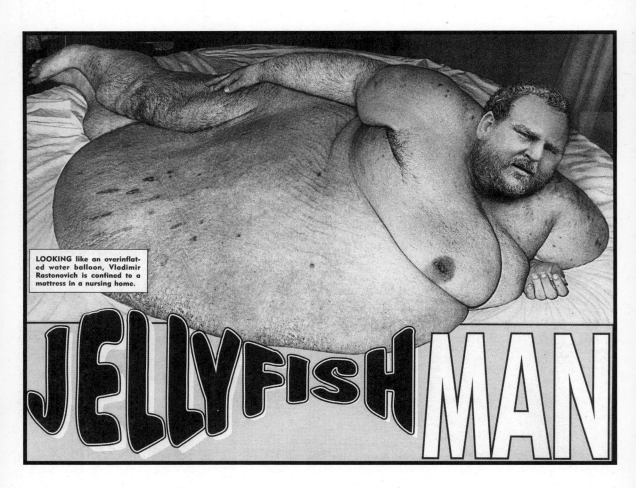

NAPOLEON WAS HALF-MAN AND HALF-WOMAN!

Famous French hero had narrow shoulders, wide hips and big breasts, says study

"FEELINGS of sexual inadequacy drove Napoleon to world conquest," says one expert.

World-famous conqueror Napoleon Bonaparte was really half-woman!

He had soft skin, well-defined breasts, hardly any body hair and many other female attributes.

This amazing revelation comes from modern analysis of the French emperor's postmortem report and other startling evidence.

Because of a problem with his pituitary gland, Napoleon became feminized over a period of more than 20 years beginning in his 30s, say experts. And, incredibly, they add that his fiery, warring spirit was nothing more than a desperate effort to compensate for the disorder that slowly stripped him of his manhood and left him impotent.

At the time of the French hero's death, "his body was feminized," said British surgeon Dr. James Robinson, who made a major study.

"The body was covered by a deep layer of fat. The skin was white and delicate, as were the hands and arms.

"There was scarcely any hair on the body and there were well-marked breasts and a mons veneris (mound of fatty tissue covering the pubic area). The shoulders were narrow, the hips broad and male genitalia exceedingly small.

"The feelings of sexual inadequacy which have led sane men to suicide nearly drove Napoleon to world conquest. He compensated for these deficiencies by his aggression," said Dr. Robinson.

Major General Frank Richardson — a noted Napoleon expert — added:

"It is true that Napoleon became feminized over the years and had large breasts. As he sat in his carriage with his second wife, bystanders mistook him for her elderly governess."

Both Maj. Gen. Richardson and Dr. Robinson are convinced that the emperor suffered from a pituitary problem known as Pituitary Eunuchoidism.

The pituitary gland normally stimulates the sex glands in the human body to activity but Napoleon's pituitary became exhausted prematurely.

In fact, Dr. Robinson is sure that Napoleon was impotent in his late 30s and believes the leader's son — Napoleon II — may have been the result of a primitive form of artificial insemination.

He added it was possible one of the conqueror's own brothers acted as the donor in order to "maintain the Bonaparte likeness."

Skunks are gentle little stinkers who get rid of bugs, mice and garbage

If skunks could sue for slander, they'd collect a fortune. Over the centuries people have maligned them as foul-tempered, mean stinkpots — but in reality they're gentle, lovable creatures . . . and they make great pets!

The skunk also is a walking clean-up factory — he eats hordes of insects and other pests, and is better at catching mice than a cat. He'll even dispose of leftover garbage.

But though he's usually easygoing, the skunk can get nasty when threatened — firing a spray so smelly that the human nose can detect as little as one-trillionth of an ounce in the air.

Surprisingly, the spray is visible at night, giving off an eerie phosphorescent glow, a lot like tracer bullets.

The skunk's aim is accurate up to 12 feet, and if he misses, he simply fires again; his sacs hold enough spray for four to six shots in a row.

The skunk's smelly weapon is so feared that few animals dare tangle with him. As a result, he ambles placidly over his chosen territory — which is usually three-quarters of a mile square — with little fear of other creatures.

Interestingly, the skunk's stinking muck is refined and used in the manufacture of some perfumes.

Skunks like people and make excellent pets if de-scented. They're popular on farms, where they eat rats.

Many skunks get hit on the highways — they can't conceive of being attacked by anything, so they ignore cars.

The cougar, lynx, fox, coyote and mink are about the only animals that will attack a skunk.

WEEKLY WORLD NEWS

January 28, 2003

WARNING: HOW Osama Bin Laden is brainwashing YOU!

Amazing photos inside!

3,000-YEAR-OLD MUMMY HAS BABY BOY!

Miracle birth baffles docs!

Your co-worker may be a space alien! INSIDE: HOW YOU CAN TELL!

Eerie photos baffle experts!

GIRL'S GHOST HAUNTS DOLLHOUSE!

STEVENS family: Wife Dorothy, Tammy and dad Bill.

By BEATRICE DEXTER
Special correspondent

The dollhouse in Tammy Stevens' playroom is haunted — and her family has photographs to prove it!

Incredibly, 10-year-old Tammy's father Bill snapped a picture of the handmade wooden house and caught images of a blonde child clearly visible inside the 32-inch-high toy.

In one shot the ghost girl is doll-sized, peering out of the balcony windows. In a second shot, the girl's image has grown to full size. "We don't know who she is but we believe she came with the dollhouse when we bought it at a church rummage sale a few months ago," said Bill, an appraiser from Phoenix, Ariz.

"We saw her first about a week after we got the toy for Tammy. Since then she appears regularly every night.

"The dollhouse probably belonged to this little soul, who may have died in some kind of tragedy," the dad guessed.

Stevens says the ghostly child is not the only eerie phenomenon associated with the dollhouse. When darkness falls, the little house is literally possessed — with the sounds of sobbing and wailing coming from an upstairs bedroom and dollhouse furniture mysteriously disappearing from its tiny rooms.

Bill and his wife Dorothy have tried to trace the dollhouse to find out something about its past, but no one knows who donated the toy to the church rummage sale. And although the house has been carefully hand fashioned, it is from a common design, Bill says.

"When we first brought it home, we put it in Tammy's bedroom," he recalled. "But she kept getting up at night and coming to our room with complaints that the house was making noises. She said the house was haunted and we told her it was just her imagination.

"But one night I went to her room with her and I actually heard the crying coming from an upstairs bedroom at the back of the little house. After that I put the dollhouse in the guest room — I don't think it's good for Tammy to be frightened of sleeping in her own room."

The Stevenses say they want to get rid of the dollhouse, but they paid $200 for it and they want to get their money back on it. They're hoping someone will read about its haunted history and buy it as a curiosity. "You could even videotape the ghost or exhibit it or something," Bill says. "The ghost appears every night."

DAD photographed ghostly image of little girl when she appeared in the dollhouse balcony window, shown above and in inset.

FULL-SIZE image of little girl's ghost was captured on film by Bill Stevens. All toy furniture has disappeared, save for a dining room set, shown lower left.

LOCH NESS MONSTER IS A GIANT DUCK

Weekly World News Exclusive Photo!

CONTRARY to popular belief, the Loch Ness Monster is not a dinosaur — it's a huge mutant duck, a top researcher claims.

British zoologist Dr. Bernard Gluber plans to prove his stunning theory by capturing the elusive bird using the largest decoy ever constructed.

"The floating decoy will be 30 feet long and equipped with speakers emitting mating calls designed to lure Nessie," he says.

Dr. Gluber notes that the most convincing photo ever taken of Nessie, snapped by Dr. Robert K. Wilson on April 19, 1934, shows a creature with a long, swan-like neck gliding gracefully across the surface of the Scottish lake.

"One need only compare the silhouette of Nessie to a photo of a waterfowl taken in profile to conclude the animal is a close relative of the duck, swan and goose," the scientist declares.

Dr. Gluber's bird theory flies in the face of conventional wisdom, which holds that if Nessie exists, she's probably a plesiosaur, an aquatic dinosaur that ruled the seas 100 million years ago.

"The trouble with the plesiosaur theory is that Loch Ness didn't exist in the dinosaur era. The lake is less than 12,000 years old, having been glacially excavated during the last Ice Age," Dr. Gluber observes.

SADDAM & O
– THEIR SECRET LOVE N

WASHINGTON — The Pentagon and CIA have found irrefutable evidence to prove that Osama Bin Laden and Saddam Hussein are alive and kicking: A sizzling photograph of the doe-eyed evil-doers making love in a tent in Pakistan.

But don't think all is right in terror land just because the world's most wanted war criminals "got jiggy with it" in their love nest while head-scratching U.S. agencies lost yet another golden opportunity to track them down.

According to a CIA source, Saddam is said to have been "extremely disappointed" in Bin Laden's sexual prowess, openly complaining to Bin Laden, "You are like the beak of a hummingbird or straw from the bale . . . too paltry to bring me pleasure."

And by the time their tender-turned-testy liaison was over, says the source, Saddam literally stomped out of the tent, shouting,

Sizzling photo shows terror 'tough guys' in bed together!

By ROD TIPTON
Weekly World News

"I'll call you later — maybe."

"This is the smoking gun we've been looking for — proof beyond doubt that Saddam and Bin Laden are still in a position to cause trouble," the source told reporters during a background briefing here in the nation's capitol.

"Our best intelligence tells us the picture came from a rendezvous in a heavily guarded area of Lahore, Pakistan, on May 22 or 23.

"That means Bin Laden and his Al Qaeda terror network continue to be capable of moving freely from place to place and masterminding more mayhem right under our noses.

"It also suggests that Saddam has equal capabilities to do the same.

"Had we learned that Saddam was in Syria or Jordan we wouldn't have been all that surprised. But hearing that he met Bin Laden in the tent in Pakistan is a different story.

"It makes me wonder exactly where we stand in the war on terror. A few weeks ago, I would have told you we were slam-dunking this thing.

"Now I'm not so sure."

Tight-lipped Pentagon and CIA spokesmen will neither confirm nor deny the existence of the photograph for fear of a causing a Muslim backlash at home and abroad.

But it's clear that they are orchestrating press leaks to make sure the gay encounter receives the widest possible publicity without them being directly involved.

Even President George Bush appeared to allude to it while bantering with reporters before his weekly radio address on May 24.

"There might be some new evidence to show Saddam and Bin Laden are in close contact," he said with his trademark halting laugh. "We're looking into that."

According to the CIA insider, the photograph was one of three telltale images and a short written account that were mysteriously e-mailed to the West. Sources say the photos were briefly broadcast by the Al-Jazeera news agency — and just as quickly yanked from the air.

It clearly shows Saddam and Bin Laden deeply involved in the kind of gay intimacies that many Muslims and Christians consider to be unnatural and "against God."

"It's a serious topic, which hasn't kept people from joking about it," a Pentagon source told reporters.

"Everybody's laughing about the rose that Osama's holding while Saddam strokes the back of Bin Laden's neck — the two of them are just lost in their own sick little world.

"They also wonder how Saddam keeps from crushing skinny Osama with that big fat gut of his."

According to the CIA source,

TRACKING TERRORISTS: President Bush is carefully watching the perverted madmen's antics.

WWN EXCLUSIVE
PHOTO COURTESY IRAQI TV NEWS

agency analysts are "99.9 pe certain the photographs h been altered or retouched.

Saddam and Bin Laden hav been suspected of having "a for one another. But as the s points out, the new photos ar first hard evidence to prove it.

On the other hand, Sad penchant for hunky young me been one of the Arab world's kept secrets since 1990, French *papparazzi* caught romancing an extremely endowed pool boy at a p compound in Baghdad.

And Osama Bin Laden's history is just as shocking. "He the company of goats and c

STRANGE BEDFELLOWS: This shocking photo proves beyond a shadow of a doubt that Saddam and Osama are partners — in every possible sense.

arly," says the CIA source. aybe that's because his other s, like Saddam, laugh at his y weeny' too, while the ani- give him unconditional love." ds the Pentagon source: n the laughing stops all this information really proves is ur war on terror isn't over by shot. e're particularly disappointed we had hoped recent reports addam's mustache had been meant he was a goner. s long as Saddam Hussein sama Bin Laden are in bed er — both figuratively and ly — we've got the potential other 9/11 on our hands."

Saddam starred in gay porn films

Saddam's homosexual relationship with Osama comes as no great surprise to those close to the dictator.

As reported in our March 11, 2003, issue, Kuwaiti secret police uncovered a shocking 1968 porn film starring none other than Saddam Hussein.

"Saddam starred in as many as 85 of these films under a variety of stage names, most frequently Omar Studdif," reveals Hussein biographer Sadiq al-Sabah.

SCENES from *La'iba al-Waladaani* (The Two Boys Played, 1968) — a gay porn film — show a younger, leaner Saddam Hussein.

NEWS EXCLUSIVE: Bible expert discovers Adam & Eve's last name

'MR. & MRS. YAHPRIMA'

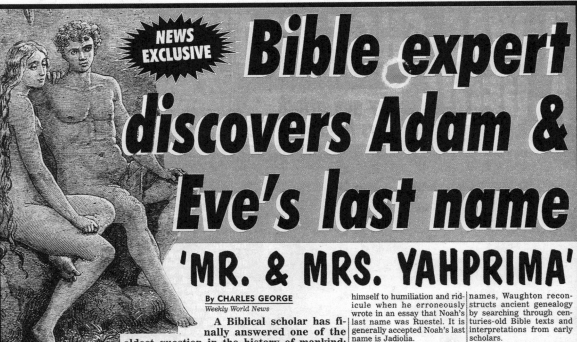

ADAM AND EVE in the Garden of Eden.

By CHARLES GEORGE
Weekly World News

A Biblical scholar has finally answered one of the oldest question in the history of mankind: He's discovered Adam and Eve's last name!

That's right. The famous first couple had a last name — and it was Yahprima, pronounced Ya-PREE-mah.

"I've studied every available source for nearly three years and can now confidently state that Adam and Eve's last name was Yahprima," said Bible scholar Jack Waughton of Eugene, Ore.

"It translates loosely into the 'first of God.'"

Waughton said he's been interested in the unusual subject ever since he was a young boy and asked his father what Moses' last name was.

"My father didn't have any idea," he remembered.

"I was just 9 or 10 years old at the time but that question stayed on my mind for many years."

Waughton is the world's most controversial authority on Biblical last names. He made international headlines back in June of 1992 when he revealed that Moses' last name was Comsterion.

But months later he opened himself to humiliation and ridicule when he erroneously wrote in an essay that Noah's last name was Ruestel. It is generally accepted Noah's last name is Jadiolia.

"That was a big mistake on my part, I admit that now," Waughton said.

"I was using information I took from an 1911 article that had been proved to be false. I was eager to return to the limelight I enjoyed when I had found Moses' last name. I should have exercised more caution."

He learned his lesson and made sure he had the facts right before proclaiming Yahprima as Adam and Eve's last name.

"At one time I thought the name was spelled Yahprema with an 'e' instead of an 'i,'" he said. "I wanted to be certain of the spelling before I wrote anything about it."

To research Biblical last names, Waughton reconstructs ancient genealogy by searching through centuries-old Bible texts and interpretations from early scholars.

He is currently working on a project to find the last names of all 12 of Christ's disciples.

Jack Waughton

Samson's hair found in Israel!

By RANDY JEFFRIES
Weekly World News

LONG-LOCKED Samson was played by Victor Mature in *Samson and Delilah*.

JERUSALEM — Archaeologists have found nine tufts of 3,000-year-old human hair — and experts say it belonged to the biblical strongman Samson!

The dark, curly 13-inch strands were found near Yesodot, Israel, which was known as the Valley of Sorek in biblical times. That's the spot where Delilah clipped Samson's locks, stripping him of his amazing physical power and selling him out to his enemies.

"We're convinced it's Samson's hair," says archaeologist and Bible scholar Dr. Josef Shehori, who has supervised digs in the area for nine years, searching for the legendary tresses.

"The Bible doesn't say what happened to the hair. But other religious and historical documents say the Philistines preserved it in an airtight jar — using a technique learned from the Egyptians.

"The jar we found perfectly matches the one described in the ancient writings, right down to the etchings near the top."

Shortly after the hair was found, Dr. Shehori's research partner, noted biochemist Dr. Sarah Mishal, began running tests on it. "The chemical analysis of these strands reveal incredibly high levels of protein and testosterone," says the renowned expert.

Scientific tests confirm Bible hero's amazing strength

"These levels indicate that the man this hair came from had a muscular development that was 70 to 100 times greater than the average man. That is consistent with everything we know about Samson from the Book of Judges in the Bible and other holy books."

But other scientists are skeptical about the find. "I've studied Dr. Shehori's research," says Professor Lawrence Meeks, the famed chemist and outspoken atheist from Sydney, Australia. "And I'll concede that the cells in this hair are extraordinarily high in the substances that build strong muscles. But I think it's stretching things to say it belonged to one particular man."

But Dr. Shehori contends the similarities between the description in the documents and the hair he discovered can't be coincidence. "We're still studying this amazing find," says Dr. Mishal.

"A lot more needs to be learned about it. We're keeping its exact location a secret for the time being. But we should be ready to release a full report by August 1997."

Prisoner abuse

BOISE, Idaho — Five prison guards got in trouble for taunting death row inmates on the night killer Keith Wells was executed by lethal injection. They played pop star Neil Young's 1971 song, *The Needle and the Damage Done*. The guards were reassigned to administrative duties.

WEEKLY WORLD NEWS

June 3, 1997 — $1.25 U.S. — $1.39 CANADA/ 70p U.K.

Freaks of nature caused by pollution, say top scientists

WORLD EXCLUSIVE STORY AND PHOTOS!

Half-human half-fish are washing up in Florida!

Screaming tourists flee beaches!

Are you a man... or a mouse?

By KATE McCLARE
Weekly World News

SCIENTISTS PROVE MAN EVOLVED FROM RATS

...and not from monkeys!

EXCITED scientists have proved it beyond the shadow of a doubt: Man didn't evolve from monkeys, man evolved from dirty, filthy, garbage-eating rats!

Researchers at the Hunan Institute of Natural History say they've zeroed in on a furry, four-legged scavenger that lived 125 million years ago, and both modern humans and modern rats are its — ugh! — kissing cousins!

"We share so much genetic information," jokes Dr. Ying Chou-lin, "that it's surprising we don't sprout whiskers, tails and long front teeth.

"Kidding aside, and on a far more serious note, this new discovery will turn theories of human evolution on their ears.

"For one thing, monkeys, chimps and primates would now seem to be completely out of the picture.

"Now, we've got a new line of creatures to compare ourselves with — rats, mice, even bats, which are all closely related."

Found in a quarry in China where many dinosaur remains have been uncovered, a pair of "Adam and Eve rats," as some newspapers are calling them, piqued the interest of researchers from several countries, including China, England and the United States.

Experts dubbed the critters Eomaia scansoria — two Greek words that mean "ancient mother."

According to the experts, the rodents were the world's first "placental mammals," which means they nurtured their babies before birth the way humans still do: By using a placenta to pass food, oxygen and a means of waste disposal to the fetus.

Its survival as a species led directly to the evolution of other placental mammals — including humans.

Equally amazing, the ancient rats appear to have had a disproportionately large skull and brain, indicating what Dr. Chou-lin calls "a keen and unrelenting intelligence that may be considered a precursor to human intelligence, which is unparalleled in the animal kingdom."

FROM rat to man — this chart shows what scientists now believe to have been the true course of human evolution.

2002 A.D.

9 Million B.C.

125 Million B.C.

Weekly World News family of readers — 100 million strong!

HALF-ALLIGATOR HALF-HUMAN GIVES BIRTH!

Bizarre species was found in Florida Everglades back in 1996, say scientists

By KEN ROLAND
Weekly World News

MIAMI, Fla. — A half-human, half-alligator captured in the Florida Everglades last spring has stunned wildlife researchers — by giving birth to a live offspring!

Scientists say they had no idea the rare creature was expecting — or even that she was a female — until she delivered her 18-inch-long baby on December 15.

"They tell me the little one appears to be in good health and is very active," said Dr. Paul Ledbrader, a paleontologist who captured the adult specimen. "It is a dead-ringer for its mom and won't leave her side. The baby swims like a fish, eats raw chicken and fish and has the I.Q. of a 2-year-old. It's already grown to 28 inches in length and it weighs 45 pounds.

"The birth is terrifically important to science because now we have not only a full-grown, reproductive adult, but also a juvenile that is developing before our eyes. The zoologists can study this infant intensively and learn a tremendous amount about the animal's growth and behavior patterns. They can also watch the interaction of mother and baby to learn how the creatures relate to others of their species."

Dr. Ledbrader snared the 5-foot, 11-inch adult specimen — which scientists are calling an Allisapiens — while spending a quiet day last April fishing and canoeing in the Everglades. He hauled the creature to a public boat landing, and wildlife officials later confiscated it and airlifted it to a research facility west of Miami.

Dr. Antoine Prevon.

There scientists under the direction of French zoologist Dr. Antoine Prevon, a specialist in rare reptiles, have determined that the Allisapiens is an intelligent creature capable of understanding human speech and making rational decisions. Although the reptile communicates with hisses instead of words, it apparently has sophisticated thought processes. Studies of the baby indicate it, too, is highly intelligent.

Dr. Paul Ledbrader.

Dr. Ledbrader says he has kept in touch with Dr. Prevon and the internationally-known expert provides him with regular updates and photos documenting the creature's progress.

In his public statements, however, Dr. Prevon is cautious.

"The Allisapiens is a priceless find and it is our intention to learn as much as we can from it," the zoologist told an international symposium in Amsterdam on December 29.

"Some of my colleagues believe the animal may be a missing link, an ancient creature that developed as man was evolving many millions of years ago, but I'm not prepared to confirm that at this point.

"What we do know is that this reptile is cold-blooded with a leathery skin and thrives on a diet of meat and aquatic vegetation. It spends most of its time in water, yet it is able to use tools, communicate with others, plan ahead and remember past events. The creature's baby was delivered in a live birth after a pregnancy of many months, but it was not suckled by its mother.

"The animal shares traits of both reptiles and mammals — making it one of the most unique and fascinating animals in the history of zoology."

The French scientist and other researchers at the federal facility have refused to allow journalists access to the rare Allisapiens, but Dr. Ledbrader willingly shared photos and information with *Weekly World News*, which published a world exclusive story June 25, 1996 after he found the animal.

"This is one of the most amazing discoveries of the century," Dr. Ledbrader said, "and I think the public has a right to know as much as possible about it."

Amazing baby . . .
. . . swims like a fish
. . . eats raw fish & chicken
. . . has the I.Q. of a 2-year-old human

'WE W[
BEATLES
JOURN

RE THE
OF FAKE
ALISM'

—DEREK CLONTZ,
FORMER EDITOR,
WEEKLY WORLD NEWS

FASHIONABLY FIERCE: Warriors of Borneo's Unaga tribe go into battle wearing tuxedos found in the wreckage of a cargo plane.

DRESSED TO KILL!

Wacky jungle savages wear tuxedos into battle!

By MARK CASSIDY
Correspondent

A slaphappy band of headhunters prowling the steamy jungle of Borneo has stormed into battle three times in recent weeks — all decked out in spiffy black tuxedos!

"I wouldn't have believed it if I hadn't seen it for myself," anthropologist Kurt Franz told a recent meeting of researchers, held in Bern, Switzerland.

"There were literally hundreds of spear-chucking savages in ruffled shirts, tuxedos and bow ties battling enemy tribesmen wearing only loincloths and warpaint — and the guys in the tuxes were winning."

Franz said he and two colleagues were studying a tribe of headhunters living along Borneo's Barito River when a cargo plane on a flight to the coastal city of Benjarmasin crashed into a mountainside, killing the three crewman on board.

The wacky warriors found the wreckage and plundered everything on board — including 320 tuxedos with all the customary accessories.

"The Unagas were like children in a toy store," the Swiss anthropologist recalled with a chuckle.

"They found radios, CD players, electric shavers and other gadgets that, to them, were absolutely useless.

"But the tuxedos were another story. That totally fascinated them and they insisted we help them get all dolled up. The clothing was in remarkable condition, considering all it had been through.

"They were so excited we knew it would be dangerous to argue with them, so we helped them get dressed up — right down to the cummerbunds. I remember thinking to myself, 'This wild-eyed bunch is really dressed to kill.' And darned if that wasn't exactly what they did.

"They grabbed up their knives and spears and strutted off to wage war on a village further up the river.

"The Unagas had been at peace with other local tribes for more than two decades and we tried to convince them that attacking another tribe would be a terrible thing to do.

"But they were so fired up about their new clothes, nothing we said could hold them back.

"By sundown, the battle was over and the Unagas were back in their village and dancing around their campfire, still wearing their tuxedos — with a dozen severed enemy heads on display.

"It was quite a sight."

11 WEEKLY WORLD NEWS
June 16, 1992

QUIT SMOKING

Now you can use the amazing power of hypnosis to beat cigarettes safely, easily, without prescriptions and without weight gain. You've tried before but no matter what you do, you continue to fall back. Dr. Bengali understands and his HYPNOSIS PROGRAM can reach to your subconscious mind giving you success at last. This is the same program thousands have attended nationally, AVAILABLE FOR THE FIRST TIME TO ATTEND IN YOUR OWN HOME!

A lady in Vermont writes, "I never believed in Hypnosis before, but now I praise this program to everyone."

You get four professionally packaged Audio tapes. Not ocean waves, but SOLID, REAL HYPNOSIS!

Send $39 plus $3 handling to: Dr. Bengali
266 Ontario St.
P.O. Box 6028
Albany, NY 12206

OR CALL 1-800-473-0767
30 Day Money Back Guarantee   MC/VISA Accepted

WOMAN'S CORPSE WAS SO-O-O FAT

...3 angels were needed to lift her soul into Heaven!

CHICAGO, Ill. — A woman who died last week was so fat that it took three super-strong Angels of Death to carry her soul to Heaven!

And 19 onlookers who witnessed the heart attack death and its awesome aftermath say the three celestial escorts had to struggle to lift the departed spirit of the hefty 350-pound woman — and almost dropped her twice.

The first-ever case in the annals of angel sightings occurred downtown in mid-afternoon as German tourist Lina Kaufmann, 58, stepped from the curb and started across Michigan Avenue.

"She just collapsed in the crosswalk," said Tom Altegor, 29, who was standing beside Mrs. Kaufmann and saw the whole thing. "She dropped her packages and started turning blue. There were people all around but none of us knew CPR. The poor woman was dead before the paramedics could get there. I started to cover her with my jacket when suddenly I was surrounded by a clear, bright light.

"A powerful-appearing winged figure descended and started to gently remove her soul — which looked just like her body except that it was sort of transparent.

"But he had a hard time. He got less and less gentle as he yanked on it. Finally he gave it a real hard tug and pulled it free. But when he tried to lift it, he seemed to hurt his back.

"He raised his arm and gestured to the heavens and instantly two more angels appeared. One of them said something to the woman in German and pointed up to the sky.

"Then the three of them lugged her up and out of sight — almost letting her slip from their hands twice. She was just so heavy."

Eighteen other witnesses tell the same story.

Chicago-based Bible scholar and angel expert Rev. Thomas Traley, 37, says that, although no one has witnessed such a thing before, the scriptures say angels often gather in "bands."

"That's because God realizes that one angel can't always do what needs to be done alone," Rev. Traley explained. "The Angel of Death has a particularly difficult time. He must carry many different kinds of souls to Heaven — some of them disoriented and confused.

"Sometimes they even try to fight with him before they realize they're dead.

"That's just one of the many reasons God gives him helpers. In this case they were needed not because of hostility but because of sheer weight. I know they had to struggle with Mrs. Kaufmann but I believe she's definitely in a better place now."

By RANDY JEFFRIES
Weekly World News

ALLEY-OOP! Three angels lift the soul of a 350-pound woman up to Heaven.

Rev. Thomas Traley

Tom Altegor

THE STATUE OF LIBERTY IS GETTING A BOOB JOB!

By ARI SMELKINESON
Weekly World News

WILL giving America's symbol of freedom a 38 D-cup make her more attractive? What's your opinion? Vote below.

BEFORE! / AFTER!

NEW YORK — A bizarre proposal to give the Statue of Liberty a boob job is bouncing around the Big Apple.

In an attempt to present a more attractive image, Lady Liberty will undergo a massive modernization procedure.

The statue, built in the late 1800s by French sculptor, Frederic-August Bartholdi, who modeled the statue after his mother. Apparently, she was not amply-endowed, so he sculpted Lady Liberty as a modest A-cup. But new plans are in the works to keep the Statue of Liberty abreast with modern styles and attitudes about body image.

This spring, a corps of engineers is making it their top priority to go under her dress and rebuild her rack. The operation will enhance her bosom to that of a bountiful size 38 D-cup. They'll fill in her cleavage with concrete — silicon was found to be unsafe to use due to leakage problems. It should take a few months for the new bosom to settle into place, but after that, the renovation crew promises that she will look completely natural.

"No one will be able to tell she's had breast enhancement," one crewmember vows.

However, the opposition is well stacked against the project.

"Why not give the Venus DeMilo some arms or repaint the Mona Lisa so she has more voluptuous lips?" sniffed one art critic.

One irate dad of three girls in Manhattan argues, "I think it stinks. I hate the idea of my tax money going for something as superficial as a boob job."

"The Statue of Liberty represents freedom and hope for millions of immigrants. Who cares about her breast-size? She looks just fine the way she is."

But one French fashion designer says Lady Liberty is long overdue for a makeover. "Her look is about 100 years out of date," the designer snorts. "The boob job is just the beginning. She needs to have a new hairstyle, and maybe lose that unflattering gown and wear a tank top to show off her abs."

Alise Bueskei, a visiting tourist from Trenton, N.J., says, "The sexier and more alluring the Statue is, the more people from other countries will want to come and be welcomed by her."

Ginger Kolachakk, of Manhattan, says, "Some people can totally make a mountain out of a molehill. She's been lifting her lamp up for all to see, so I say show us what you've got shaking there, sister."

Travel consultants predict that the new renovation will be a boost to tourism, not a bust. One expert estimates, "We're going to have our hands full with people wanting to see her new look. The Statue of Liberty will grow into the biggest tourist attraction in the country once she gets her new boobs."

The statue was built by French sculptor Frederic-August Bartholdi, who modeled the statue after his mother. Apparently, she was not amply endowed.

TOURIST
Alise Bueskei

NEW YORKER
Ginger Kolachakk

Should America's symbol of freedom be altered?

YOU BE THE JUDGE

☐ YES: The Statue of Liberty should be altered.
☐ NO: The Statue of Liberty should not be altered.

Mail your response to Lady Liberty Poll, c/o Weekly World News, 5401 NW Broken Sound Blvd., Boca Raton, FL 33487

If your neighbor has a heart of gold, he or she may be... POSSESSED BY AN ANGEL

...says expert!

Herbert Vesternak

By BEATRICE DEXTER
Weekly World News

DALLAS, Texas — An expert on Christianity has caused a sensation in religious circles with his revelation that ordinary people can be possessed physically and mentally — by heavenly angels!

Dr. Herbert Vesternak, 58, says angelic possession is as common as demonic possession, but goes unnoticed because its effects don't grab headlines.

"We hear about people possessed by demons who shout curses and vile phrases, slaughter their entire families, or blow up nightclubs," Dr. Vesternak says.

"But we don't hear about people possessed by angels who quietly help a neighbor, or spread love and goodwill, or give away their possessions to the needy.

"Yet my research shows angelic possession is common and may actually be behind most of mankind's unselfish behavior. It's the basis of many great acts of kindness, sacrifice and generosity."

Dr. Vesternak — whose book *In the Hands of Angels* is scheduled for publication early next year — spent three years studying demonic possession for a Ph.D. dissertation in the late 1980s. In the course of his research he interviewed 134 exorcists on the signs of possession and its effects on the possessed.

To his surprise, it soon became clear to him that there were two distinct types of possession — one by an evil entity, or demon, and another by a good entity, or angel. The theologian became so fascinated with the idea of angelic possession that he devoted another five years to his research, studying ancient Christian writings, reviewing eyewitness reports of heroism and collecting rare firsthand accounts of angelic possession.

"My research indicates that angels are frequently dispatched from Heaven to take over the bodies of ordinary Christians," the author said.

"Apparently they are meant to inspire humans through their selfless actions. We hear stories of people who acted through great love or faith, who sacrificed themselves to benefit others, who remained truthful and honest even when it caused them difficulties. They were probably possessed by angels."

Dr. Vesternak says it is possible to call down an angel possessor, much as it is possible to summon a demonic possessor. To do so, a person must use Christian ritual, prayer and holy thoughts, the author said.

"People who have consciously invoked angelic possession describe the feeling of being taken over by a heavenly spirit as extremely moving and my personal experience supports that," he says.

"The possessed person feels filled with strength and love and full of heavenly power. I'm convinced we can all have this wonderful experience. That's why I have written my book about it — I want everyone to know the joy of angelic possession."

How to get possessed by an angel!

You can summon a spirit from Heaven to take over your body and govern your actions, Dr. Vesternak says, just by following the four simple steps below:

- Find a quiet, private place where you can spend an hour or so without being disturbed. Go there, read your Bible and open yourself to receive your angelic possessor.
- When the spirit moves you, pray to God for a heavenly possessor. Tell Him why you wish to be taken over by the spirit of goodness. Consciously place yourself in His hands.
- With your eyes closed and your heart wide open, picture your body being taken over by an angel. Feel the change in your spirituality. Feel the power of love and forgiveness grow in you.
- Let goodness flow through you. From this time forward, whenever you experience an impulse to be generous, kind or self-sacrificing, give in to that impulse. Make yourself into a heavenly instrument, willing to serve God's purposes. You will find that the power of good will take you over and control your actions — and you will be possessed by the spirit of Heaven.

JANUARY

THE DAY THE EARTH WILL STAND STILL!

- ALL BANKS WILL FA[IL]
- FOOD SUPPLI[ES] WILL BE DEPLETE[D]
- ELECTRICIT[Y] WILL BE CUT OF[F]
- THE STOCK MARK[ET] WILL CRAS[H]
- VEHICLES USIN[G] COMPUTER CHI[PS] WILL STOP DEA[D]
- TELEPHONES WI[LL] CEASE T[O] FUNCTIO[N]
- DOMINO EFFE[CT] WILL CAUSE WORLDWIDE DEPRESSIO[N]

THE CLOCK IS TICKING

1, 2000

Will you survive the nightmare computer disaster?

WASHINGTON — With January 1 of the year 2000 fast approaching, experts are warning of impending worldwide chaos when the dreaded "Millennium Bug" computer glitch kicks in.

Both government and industry have so far been helpless to fix the programming goof that will cause computers to go haywire when the new millennium arrives. So thousands of people have begun stockpiling food and weapons — and even building fortified bomb-shelter-type hideouts in the hinterlands.

At the same time, jittery financiers are shifting their assets to cash and gold in anticipation of a stock market crash and a run on banks.

"We're talking about a total collapse of society. Think back to the movie *Road Warrior* — that's the kind of mayhem headed our way," declared one computer-industry analyst.

"Most people still have no idea just how out of control things are really going to get."

Some of the predicted effects of the computer glitch: multi-statewide blackouts, planes literally falling out of the sky in mid-flight, telephones going dead, assembly lines grinding to a halt, widespread home foreclosures, and even Somalia-style food riots.

"The problem is cropping up because, in a move to save limited space on hard drives, early computer programmers used only two digits to record years — for example, 1998 appears simply as 98. Come the turn of the century, this shortcut is expected to confuse computers and microchips in millions of machines, making them read "00" as the year 1900 instead of 2000.

That means that government computers that spit out Medicare checks and other benefits will suddenly decide that millions of people are ineligible to receive benefits and will cease payments.

Worse, common mechanical devices ranging from clock radios and microwaves to today's high-tech cars will become useless hunks of metal.

To cope with the looming crisis, people around the country have been buying specially fortified "survival homes" in the countryside — some costing more than half a million dollars. Folks with less money in their pockets are forking over cash to secure berths in large, gated compounds to prepare for the great collapse.

In California, security experts have been working around the clock to equip fancy homes with electrified fences, sensors and appliances to make them self-sufficient. Their clients include Hollywood moguls, plastic surgeons and others anxious to hang onto their wealth.

"It's just going to be madness by January 6," Millennium Bug expert Candace Turner, 49, told *USA Today*. Turner, who has already planted a large garden for food during the bad times ahead, predicts that after the Bug bites, our high-tech form of communication will be a thing of the past.

By GEORGE SANFORD
Weekly World News

"I just hope that everybody's brushing up on their Morse code," she said.

In what is being called the "Great Geek Migration," computer programmers — who know better than anyone that the digital disaster can't be averted by minor fixes — have been evacuating big cities in droves and heading for the hills.

Groups gearing up to flee to rural havens have been advertising on-line for people who share common interests to complete their "tribes."

Some computer nerds have been openly talking of returning to a feudal type society, the kind that maintained order during the Middle Ages.

A typical ad called for "serfs to construct a fortress, tend the fields and cut wood," as well as "knights to protect the domain and hunt food."

Experts say the approach is not that way-out under the circumstances.

"This will be a situation similar to what our parents' generation went through in the Great Depression, only much, much worse," warned a New York City sociologist in a recent magazine article.

"Today, there are many fewer people who are accustomed to physical privation or living off the land and there is not the extended family that offered support in the old days.

"Values such as respect for the elderly and neighborliness are much weaker than they were back in the 1930s. It will take a lot less to tip us over into a state of total barbarism.

"The suicide rate as well as crimes such as homicide, assault and gang rape will probably skyrocket.

"As in London in the times of Charles Dickens, perhaps as many as one in four women will be forced to turn to prostitution to eke out a living in impoverished shantytowns.

"I see this as a much darker, more violent period, more like the Dark Ages of Europe than anything in American history."

While many experts expect the chaos to continue for years and worsen as society spins further and further out of control, others are more optimistic, forecasting a brief period of tribulation followed by renewed harmony.

Computer consultant Ed Yourdon, co-author of the book *Time Bomb 2000*, who recently moved to a solar-powered retreat in northern New Mexico, told reporters he doesn't expect civilization to collapse, but confirms, "There will be some time of absolute chaos."

Vatican sources say...
Pope will blast off in 1999

ARTIST'S CCONCEPTION of how Pope John Paul II will look in his space suit!

At 78, aging Pontiff plans to be the next senior citizen in space!

NASA refuses comment

By VINCENZO SARDI
Weekly World News

VATICAN CITY — U.S. Senator John Glenn may have been the first senior citizen in outer space — but he won't be the last. Pope John Paul II is lobbying to fly on the next shuttle flight at the ripe old age of 78!

Aides to the Pontiff are convinced that the proposed Papal space mission will restore John Paul's robust, virile image while at the same time reinvigorating the Catholic Church.

"This mission will prove that the Holy Mother Church is not mired in the past, but rather is at the forefront of the modern age," confirmed Fr. Antonio Cabini, who is spearheading the Pope's behind-the-scenes campaign to land a seat on the shuttle.

The Pope is said to have been inspired by the bravery of former astronaut Glenn, who in October returned to space for the first time in 36 years. Sen. Glenn, who was the first American to orbit the Earth back in 1962, became a hero all over again when he left the safety of his desk in Washington to risk his life on the shuttle *Discovery* at age 77.

Pope John Paul's aides believe that he needs to take a similar dramatic move to perk up his career as the world's most prominent religious leader — a career that has suffered from a lack of press attention and waning public interest in recent years.

"When His Holiness first assumed office in 1978, he was perceived as an outgoing man's man who wasn't afraid to take on Communism or to travel to the four corners of the Earth spreading the word of Our Lord," explained Fr. Cabini. "This was in marked contrast to his predecessors, who were content to remain quietly within the confines of the Vatican.

"People around the world responded to this manly image and, as a result, millions of lapsed Catholics returned to the Church."

But after the Pope was wounded in an assassination attempt, things changed.

He became more cautious and assumed a much lower profile. Sadly, his effectiveness has steadily diminished over the past few years.

"This launch will help bring back the 'old' Pope John Paul II," said Fr. Cabini.

Critics of the Vatican plan say

He will be one giant step closer to Heaven!

THIS MISSION on the part of Pope John Paul will distinguish him from his predecessors, who were content to remain quietly in the confines of the Vatican.

that this is simply a case of an old man trying to recapture his glory days and argue that blasting the Pope into space would serve no serious scientific purpose. But Fr. Cabini insists that man has a spiritual as well as scientific interest in space exploration.

"No ordained minister has ever traveled outside the Earth's atmosphere," the Pontiff's aide pointed out. "If this mission is successful, His Holiness will literally be closer to Heaven than any living religious leader in history.

"And this would be the first step in spreading the word of God beyond our planet."

Since early November, the Vatican has been quietly petitioning NASA to approve the Pope for astronaut training. The space agency has been tight-lipped about the Pontiff's chances, but insiders reveal that there is resistance to green-lighting the mission.

"We have real concerns about the separation between church and state," said a NASA source. "The U.S. government can't appear to favor one religion over another."

Mankind came here from the Red Planet!

Meteors from Mars brought human life to Earth!

By MIKE FOSTER
Weekly World News

Human life and civilization were brought to Earth from Mars — by meteorites!

That is the startling theory of researchers Robert Bauval and Graham Hancock, authors of the book *Keepers of Genesis*.

The shocking revelation comes on the heels of NASA's announcement that a meteorite discovered in Antarctica contained a 4.5 billion-year-old fossilized organism from Mars.

"Life on Earth may indeed have been imported — or 'seeded' — by a meteorite billions of years ago," according to the authors.

The researchers believe that a second meteorite landed on Earth around 12,500 B.C. and helped to spawn Egyptian civilization.

Some meteorites have a pyramid-like shape when they hit the ground — and the experts have concluded such an object is at the root of the mystery surrounding the awe-inspiring Giza pyramids.

"It is known that long before the Pyramid Age of Egypt (circa 2500 B.C.), a strange pyramidal 'stone' was kept within a sanctuary called the Temple of the Phoenix 12 miles to the east of Giza in the sacred city of Heliopolis," the authors say.

The enigmatic stone was called the Benben, derived from the word ben — which means seed. Ancient Egyptian texts say that it "came down from Heaven" like a firebird or phoenix.

It was said to have been "sent by the Gods" in an era dubbed The First Time.

"We used the science of astronomical alignments to calculate the date of the First Time to 12,500 B.C," say the researchers.

The whereabouts of the Benben are unknown — but experts believe it must have been of supreme importance to the Egyptians, because replicas of it serve as capstones of all the pyramids.

The strange space origins of the Benben might explain parallels between Martian and Egyptian structures — such as the resemblance of the Sphinx to the Face on Mars and the likeness the pyramids bear to similar structures on the Red Planet's Cydonia Plain.

"The odds of such correlations happening by coincidence are somewhere in the region of 1 in 7,000," former NASA consultant Richard Hoagland has said.

Amazingly, new answers may be at hand. Recently, archaeologists discovered a hidden chamber sealed behind a secret door in the Great Pyramid.

"Why shouldn't the pyramid builders have concealed the Benben behind that door?" Bauval and Hancock ask. An attempt will be made later this year to open the stone door.

THE GREAT PYRAMID in Egypt may hold information about mankind's extraterrestrial origins, say scientists.

BARE-BOTTOM

Daredevils strip to the buff to dive off 140-foot tower!

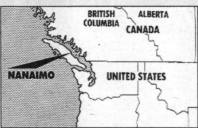

BRRR! Thousands of thrill-seekers flocked to chilly Nanaimo, B.C., for the world's first in-the-buff bungee jump.

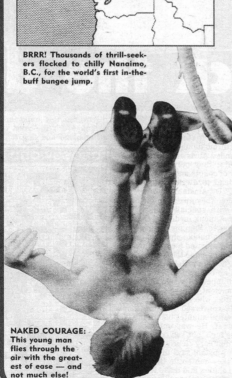

NAKED COURAGE: This young man flies through the air with the greatest of ease — and not much else!

NANAIMO, British Columbia — Dingbat daredevils streamed into the wilds of Canada and camped overnight in the bone-chilling cold to take part in the world's bawdiest bungee jump, leaping 140 feet through the air — while naked as jaybirds!

"Wow! I felt like a bird with no feathers flying around up there," shivered a shapely lady jumper moments after her eye-popping plunge into space. "It was so exciting I forgot to get scared.

"I heard all those people hooting and hollering at my naked body, but I wasn't embarrassed a bit — 'cause I was having a lot more fun than they were."

The bare-bottom belle was one of thousands of thrill-seekers who flocked to Nanaimo, at the invitation of Greg Brown, manager of the Bungee Zone — where customers pay $95 to leap off a platform 14 stories above the Nanaimo River with nothing but an elastic cord tied to their ankles.

"Greg wanted to stir things up a little, so he decided to have a day when people could jump for free — as long as they'd do it in their birthday suits," recalled Bungee Zone marketing manager Shannon Matticks. "We put the word out and the next thing you know, we were getting inquiries from Japan, South Africa, all over the world."

And as the big day drew near, an array of shameless show-offs poured into Nanaimo — college kids and corporate execs, psychiatrists and secretaries, all itchin' to

By JOE BERGER
Weekly World News

doff their duds and take the dive of a lifetime.

They came from as far away as New York and North Carolina, camping at the gate to assure themselves a spot in the world's first buck-naked bungee fest.

But with only 120 jump slots available, hundreds of hopefuls were left permanently grounded.

Those would-be baredevils reluctantly joined the crowd of 2,000 spectators, who paid $2 a head to gape and gawk as the saucy stars of the show gamboled in all their glory. "There were fat guys and skinny guys, and some of those girls were really something to behold," said one middle-aged ogler.

"They just kept jumping, one after the other all day long, and I was shocked how easy it was for people to rip off their clothes in front of strangers.

"But it wasn't all that sexy, really. It was just a lot of fun to see how silly everybody looked, bouncing around up there naked as the day they were born."

UNGEE JUMP!

Ken Oenema gets
his 14-story plunge.
Canadian was one
who got to dive for
ing their duds in
ering audience.

The former 'Evil Empire' is shrinking fast!

Russia's economy is SO-O-O bad – their hot dogs are only two inches long!

By JOE BERGER / Weekly World News

MOSCOW — Weenie-loving Russians have gone gaga over the grand old American hot dog. But most folks here are so down-and-out they can't afford the big, juicy jumbo franks we enjoy in this country — so Russian street vendors sell hot dogs that are just two inches long!

"It's sad that we've come down to this, it really is," said rugged trucker Tatlin Parinov, taking tiny bites from the two-inch dog he was munching for lunch.

"We used to be able to stop on the corner and have a big, long, plump hot dog with all the trimmings — but now things are so bad, this is all we can afford.

"Americans must see us nibbling these little things and think it's funny. But believe me, there's nothing funny about a two-inch hot dog."

Hungry Russkies have been gobbling hot dogs like they were going out of style since detente made the mustard-covered delicacy available in the Soviet Union in the early 1980s.

"The minute Communism fell, we bought our own cart and began selling delicious hot dogs on the street, with relish, onions, sauerkraut, everything — just like they do in New York City," boasted busy vendor Vladimir Tretyakov. "Soon there were vendors everywhere, but we didn't mind because everyone loved hot dogs and there was enough business to go around.

"But then the economy got so bad nobody could afford a hot dog for lunch, so we reduced the size of the weenies and buns. And every time the economy took another jolt, we reduced the size a little more — till suddenly we're down to two-inch hot dogs.

"We only charge eight rubles (about 50 cents) for the two-inch dogs — but still, that's half of what most workers earn in a day."

Luckless Russians are allowed to dress up their dinky dogs with a quarter ounce of mustard, half an ounce of relish and three strands of sauerkraut — and not the tiniest bit more.

"We're not trying to be stingy, but after all, these are only two-inch hot dogs we're selling here," said Vlad's assistant Alexei.

"If they took any more garnish than that, they'd have to put it in their pockets."

Freeloader's cockroach scheme exposed!

OSLO, Norway — Con artist Karl Brevik got free meals in ritzy restaurants all over Europe by pretending to have a bug in his soup. But the scheme unraveled when the freeloader stormed out of a restaurant — leaving his bag of dead insects behind.

Authorities charged the 36-year-old moocher with fraud. And after listening to testimony from restaurant owners in seven countries, a judge sentenced him to three years in prison.

Lawmen said conniving Karl ate free for years by announcing, "Waiter, there's a cockroach in my soup!" Restaurant bosses normally got so flustered that they'd offer him anything on the menu for nothing. But the scam backfired the night a confident restaurateur refused to believe that he had bugs in his kitchen.

Indignant Karl stomped out — leaving his bag of dead cockroaches on the table.

Man chokes to death in pie-eating contest

Hefty Wilhelm Muller keeled over and died during a pie-eating contest — when he choked on a giant chunk of rhubarb filling!

The 32-year-old Bonn, Germany, man was leading all contestants when he took his fatal bite, witnesses said.

ALIEN BACKS

By MICHAEL FORSYTH
Correspondent

STRONG BACKING: If history is any indicator, the fact that the extraterrestrial is in Arnie's camp means the Terminator's a sure winner!

IN WHAT'S bei "most stunning of the year," a m has endorsed Holly Schwarzenegger California!

Sources close to Schw campaign confirm that an "unwavering support" fo Terminator after meeting the muscle-bound super for three hours at a Angeles hotel.

Previous extraterrestrial po endorsements had typically made by P'Lod, but the alien, for his close relationship with Clinton, has been keeping a lo file since his recent run-in wit Clinton, as reported Sept. 9, 20 *Weekly World News*.

"Arnold is the best man fo job," T'rel reportedly declared. a perfect specimen of hum mentally and physically super the average Earthman — a na born leader."

As unbelievable as all that sound, an insider privy to the rendezvous took a snapshot historic meeting and leaked respected UFO researcher Ransword, who in turn provide astonishing photo exclusive *Weekly World News*.

"My source says the alien is ly impressed by Arnold's driv focus — how by sheer willpow turned himself from a skinny, kid into a bodybuilding char then into one of the biggest st Hollywood, despite a lack o apparent acting ability," D.C.- Ransword told *WWN*.

"Rumor has it the alien wa influenced by Arnold's perforr in the 1987 movie *Predator*. It the ugly alien Arnold defeats an uncanny resemblance to extraterrestrial race that T'rel ple despise."

The E.T. is so high on the hero that he also promised to u substantial influence in the nat capital to help amend Article the Constitution — allow Austrian-born Arnold to some run for president.

Incumbent Gov. Gray Dav

ARNOLD FOR GOVERNOR
– and Danny DeVito for Lt. Gov!

...ped as the ...evelopment ...space alien ...an Arnold ...ernor of

...gubernatorial ...T'rel pledged

...waging the fight of his political ...the recall election, is said to be ...away" by the setback. That's ...se the alien is a close colleague ...od, who authorized him to ...he endorsement. In fact, some ...claim it was T'rel who first ...ced P'Lod to Hillary.

...now-infamous brawl ...n Bill Clinton and P'Lod left ...president with a black eye and ...the alien in a holding tank at ...for 72 hours — and, experts ...in hot water with his superi...hich may explain why he ...the endorsement baton to

...v. Davis assumed Hillary ...ut in a good word for him and ...the coveted alien endorse...ocked up — when he got the ...about Arnold, he sulked for ...says a source in the gover...ffice.

...ough government officials ...deny T'rel's existence, he's ...eal, according to top UFO ...including Ransword, who's ...tudying the strange visitor's ...d-the-

scenes role in U.S. politics for more than a decade.

"This is the same alien race that endorsed Bill Clinton in 1992 and George W. Bush in 2000," says Ransword. "Many pollsters say the support for Bush swayed just enough votes in Florida to determine the course of the election."

How the aliens pick candidates is a mystery, but pundits call it significant that Bill Clinton is backing Davis.

"It's no secret that P'Lod and Bill Clinton are bitter love rivals," says a top GOP strategist. "The two had a highly publicized fistfight over Hillary just a few weeks ago.

"When T'rel announced out of the blue that he was backing Arnold, it sounded to some people like he might be doing it just to spite Clinton, as a gesture of support for his friend, P'Lod."

But expert Ransword pooh-poohs that theory.

"Aliens would never allow petty personal feelings to affect such an important decision," he declares. "Their only goal is the betterment of mankind."

During the closed-door meeting, the alien, believed to hail from the star system Sirius B, reportedly gave Schwarzenegger advice on how to resolve California's crippling budget crisis and also told him how to meet the state's energy needs for the next 500 years cheaply and efficiently.

Arnie and the alien "really hit it off," the campaign insider told Ransword.

"T'rel liked the fact that Arnold never seemed intimidated by him. He felt like they had a lot in common — and their accents are actually similar.

"He finds it reassuring that Arnold is pro-gun control. Aliens are very uneasy about how trigger-happy Americans are."

What the strongman superstar thinks about the endorsement is unknown.

"Surprisingly, even though he's married to a Kennedy and has a lot of friends in politics, Arnold didn't know that aliens were really here on Earth until just five hours before the meeting, when he was notified that T'rel wanted an audience with him," the secret source told Ransword.

"He listened politely to what T'rel had to say, but he didn't make any promises."

Why T'rel wants Danny

Although there is no race for lieutenant governor, alien T'rel predicts that Cruz Bustamante will be the subject of a second recall after Arnie is installed and that the big guy's *Twins* co-star, actor-director Danny DeVito, will be elected in a landslide. T'rel told Arnie that he is impressed by DeVito's charm, personality and intelligence and that the former screen twins will make an unbeatable team who will haul California out of its present difficulties.

'They really knew how to take hold of a premise and go as far as humanly possible with it. It was beautiful.'—**JOE GARDEN,** *THE ONION*

Got the flu? Guess again!

SPACE ALIEN POOP IS MAKING US, SICK, SICK, SICK!

By KEVIN CREED / *Weekly World News*

Thousands are dying of virus left here by extraterrestrials who can't hold it any longer!

WASHINGTON — Millions of people around the world have contracted a strange and potentially fatal virus — from space alien feces!

And at least one expert predicts that by the year 2002, one in every two Americans will have had the debilitating illness.

Controversial internist Dr. Marcus Balinter says that tens of thousands of the Americans who reported flu symptoms last season were not infected with the flu at all. He said they were suffering from an illness that is contracted by eating beef, lamb, chicken and other meat contaminated with the bodily wastes of extraterrestrial visitors.

Hundreds of Americans in the Deep South and the Midwest may have died from the virus, he said, and countless others may die in countries around the world.

"Hundreds of extremely reliable witnesses report encounters with space aliens in the United States each year, so there is little doubt that extraterrestrials are here among us," Dr. Balinter says. "Even the most conservative of the experts say there are probably half a million aliens in the Earth's atmosphere right now."

Dr. Balinter says he concluded that space alien feces causes many earthly illnesses after consulting with an international group of UFO experts. They say that alien dung is solid at first, but as it decomposes it takes on the color and consistency of grain.

Farm animals can't tell the difference.

"Most UFO and space alien sightings occur in rural areas," Dr. Balinter says. "They stay out of the cities to lessen the chance of being discovered.

"They dump their waste products into fields and streams and many other places where it ends up being consumed by livestock. These animals digest the disease-ridden material and we, in turn, eat their flesh.

"The waste products contain a virus that produces flu-like symptoms. It overpowers the human immune system."

Dr. Balinter's theory has had little support among his colleagues in the medical field.

But he is unfazed.

"As more people come down with this mysterious 'flu,' scientists will have to look more deeply into the cause," he says. "When they do, they will see that I'm right."

Dr. Marcus Balinter.

SPACE alien poop starts out as a solid waste product.

Gal arrested for drunk driving — on a lawn mower!

BORAS, Sweden — Cops charged hell-raising Helga Andersson, 34, with drunk driving after a wild midnight joyride — on a lawn mower.

Lawmen said tipsy Helga left a party with three friends, put them in a cart attached to her riding mower and put the pedal to the metal.

"She mowed down all the plants in four backyards and uprooted eight small trees before we finally caught up with her," said police officer Rune Sjoden.

"And she wasn't done with her partying yet.

"As we were driving her to the station, she kept asking us to stop at a bar so she could get one more drink."

After losing for the first time... TENNIS-PLAYING ROBOT GOES BERSERK — & BASHES HUMAN OPPONENT TO DEATH!

By GRANT BALFOUR
Weekly World News

LOS ANGELES — A wealthy tennis enthusiast met a grisly death at the hands of her "perfect" coach — a tennis-playing robot that went berserk after losing a game!

Police say the entire hair-raising attack was recorded on a video taken for training purposes. The tape shows Elaine Hersholl, the 41-year-old wife of a well-to-do movie executive, lobbing a winning backhand, approaching the net to reset her mechanical opponent for a new match — then being clubbed in the head again and again by the robot's heavy, steel arm.

Mrs. Hersholl's personal physician said she died of a crushed skull.

"That thing literally beat her brains out," said one investigating officer.

Bereaved pals said Mrs. Hersholl, who often played until late at night, had wanted more than a human tennis coach could offer.

"And she'd grown tired of playing against those ball-serving machines when she found out about this high-tech mechanical tennis player," a friend said. "The whole idea thrilled her."

Mrs. Hersholl eagerly paid an undisclosed sum to a Japanese electronics laboratory for a prototype of a robot that was still in the experimental stages of design.

The robot came equipped with ultra-sensitive electronic eyes, wheels at the base of its feet allowing for 360 degree movement — and that movable steel arm.

According to the robot's manufacturer, it had been programmed to win every game by evenly matching a human player's skill, constantly demanding better and better performance.

"Over the last few months, we all saw a great step forward in Elaine's game," said a former tennis partner. "She was suddenly the hottest player at the country club. All that practice at her home court was paying off."

But Mrs. Hersholl found improvement came with a high price the day she outperformed her computerized partner. That evening, her bloody body was found slumped over the net at midcourt. Her metal-plated assailant was spinning in small circles next to her with its racquet outstretched.

Police computer experts believe an unexpected win by the robot's opponent caused the mechanical man to go berserk — triggering the fatal volley of blows.

TRAGIC Elaine died of a crushed skull.

TENNIS BUFF Elaine Hersholl and her robotic partner enjoyed a spirited match before the vicious attack occurred.

'The thing literally beat her brains out!'

PHOTO COURTESY OF SPORTS INJURY INST.

WEEKLY WORLD NEWS WANTS TO KNOW WHAT YOU THINK... SOUND OFF!
Anything in the paper you like, don't like or would like to see? Let us know by writing us at: Sound Off!, c/o *Weekly World News*, 600 East Coast Ave., Lantana, Fla. 33464-0002.

MAN ORDERED TO EAT HAY BECAUSE HE FED HIS HORSE JUNK FOOD

AZUL, Argentina — A man who made his horse sick by feeding the animal french fries, pizza and other junk food has been ordered to take a dose of his own medicine — by eating an entire bale of hay!

"Let him see what it's like to eat food that his system can't digest," said Judge Gerardo Montez.

Arnoldo Busquez, 37, was handed the bizarre sentence after being convicted of cruelty to an animal. His horse suffered a severe gastrointestinal illness but has since recovered.

The judge denied the defendant's request to pour beer on his bale of hay to make it go down easier.

Red-faced camper's shocking claim:
'I was sniffed & groped by a lady Bigfoot'

"She was THIS BIG." Bill Corlston holds drawing of female Bigfoot, enlarged view below, as he describes his incredible encounter with the amorous creature.

Hairy 8-foot-tall beast had lovin' on its mind!

By DAVID WALSH / Weekly World News

OLYMPIA, Wash. — Less than two weeks after a lovestruck Bigfoot is alleged to have dragged a lumberjack into the forest and kept him as a love slave for three mind-boggling months, 20 more hikers have reported seeing an "over-sexed Bigfoot" — and at least three men claim to have been accosted by the giant, humanlike creature!

Witnesses say the thing is 8 feet tall, hairy, foul-smelling and looks like something between a human being and a gorilla.

It has been described as having "large breasts and wide hips."

The creature wears a crude, dirt-smudged body covering. The positions of the smudges make the covering look almost like a polka-dot dress.

They say it tosses its head, sways its hips and "sashays," almost like a human female — although its gender has yet to be confirmed. Several campers say they heard it make eerie cries like a cat in heat.

Rangers at Olympic National Park say the sightings have all occured over a 7-day period. In most cases, the Bigfoot was seen from a distance.

But three men claim to have had the terrifying experience of being attacked, caressed and even kissed by the amorous beast. One of them, camper Gerhard Volger of Hamburg, Germany, gives this bone-chilling account.

"I heard a rustling outside my tent at 11 at night," he says.

"I shined my flashlight out into the darkness — right into the face of the most horrible looking thing I've ever seen. Before I knew it, that monster tore open the canvas tent and grabbed me. I thought it was going to kill me but then I realized the damn thing had something else on its mind.

Some people are saying it might be a male. But I don't even want to think about that. I'm telling everyone I was groped and sniffed by a lady bigfoot."

Volger says the Bigfoot made aggressive, very sexual advances that included rubbing her body against him, groping him with her hands and even pressing her mouth to his face. He pretended to pass out and she finally left him alone.

Experts say that sexually motivated attacks by Bigfoots on humans are extremely rare. But Spanish biologist and noted Bigfoot expert Ramon Reyes suggests an explanation for these incidents.

"There have been very few Bigfoot males seen in this area in recent years," Dr. Reyes says. "It could be that the female's mating urges are frustrated by this unavailability of males. In desperation, she's turning to humans."

Boys paint spots on white dogs – & sell them as Dalmations!

LANCASTER, Pa. — A pair of 15-year-old boys face criminal charges for producing counterfeit Dalmatians.

The enterprising youngsters, whose names have not been released, allegedly used paint to put black patches on ordinary white puppies — then sold the pooches as Dalmatians to unsuspecting animal lovers for big bucks.

About two dozen of the fake puppies were sold.

By VINCENZO SARDI
Correspondent

POPE WANTS MEL GIBSON AS SUCCESSOR

Ailing pontiff feels bold change is necessary to save the church!

POPE JOHN PAUL II is reportedly poised to announce his handpicked successor: Hollywood hunk Mel Gibson!

The devoutly religious *The Passion of the Christ* director has the charisma, commitment and strength of character needed to steer the Catholic Church through its current crisis and "lead it into the 21st century," the ailing 83-year-old pontiff is said to have told a small group of cardinals on March 21.

"His Holiness is not impressed with the caliber of those who would normally be in line to succeed him," reveals a high-ranking Vatican insider.

"He considers them weak and is angered at how they've let scandal destroy the good name of the church.

"In his view, Mel — a robustly heterosexual father of six and a quintessential man's man — is exactly what's needed to restore the image of the priesthood.

"The pope believes that under Mel, archbishops wouldn't dare to protect pedophile priests. They'd be too terrified that the 'Road Warrior' would whale the tar out of them."

Until he came out with the *The Passion*, few people were aware of the star's deep religious faith. In all the publicity surrounding the film, it came out that Gibson favors a highly orthodox brand of Catholicism and attends one of the few churches that still says mass in Latin.

"His thinking is right in line with the pope's" says the insider.

The hit Bible flick has helped to reverse the fortune of the church, which had taken a beating over the past few years due to child-sex scandals.

"The church was hemorrhaging parishioners," the insider says. "Mel turned that around. Attendance is up; donations are up.

"The pope is impressed and grateful. He calls Gibson 'Miracle Mel.' He told us, 'Miracle Mel is a lethal weapon against Satan.'"

The revered spiritual leader is reportedly set to formally announce his bold selection in two months. Officially, a new pope is elected by cardinals — and rumors are already flying of a "Stop Mel" campaign brewing among jealous church officials who feel they've been passed over.

"But, practically speaking, when a popular pope makes his wishes so explicit, it will be hard to overrule him without igniting an uprising by lay people," says The Rev. Fredo Bianchi, an expert on ecclesiastical law.

He adds that there's no rule requiring a new pope to have formal religious training. "John Paul II could ordain Mel right now and he'll be a priest."

Would one of the most powerful men in Hollywood leave his glamorous world behind to shoulder such a burden?

Buried alive — in 1980!
HOLY MAN SURVIVES 20 YEARS IN COFFIN

...and guru hasn't aged a day, say his followers!

By PAT WELLS
Weekly World News

BARODA, India — Hindu mystic Baba Singh Videsh was buried alive in 1980 and remained there until his disciples dug him up three weeks ago — to find that he had survived his amazing underground stint!

"It's mind-boggling," says Dr. Devendra Nirbhaya who witnessed the 67-year-old holy man's re-emergence from the tomb where he was encased 20 years ago.

"I've examined this man and he's in perfect health."

Videsh himself has had little to say about his astonishing stay under the earth, but acknowledges that in 1980, he instructed his followers to bury him in a steel box approximately eight feet by three feet by three feet.

His instructions to his disciples were to dig him up 20 years later.

"Baba Videsh is assuredly divine," said Adi Lakhotia, a longtime follower of the spiritual teacher.

"He has shown us that our minds can have absolute control over our bodies."

Skeptics immediately charged that the man who emerged from the coffin is not Videsh, who was buried before hundreds of witnesses.

But authorities used fingerprints and dental records to confirm that they are indeed one and the same.

"He's lost quite a bit of weight, but there is no doubt it's him," said Jayanti Thakur, who grew up with the guru and writes editorials for a leading syndicate.

"I don't know what to make of it," he added. "I last saw him the day he was buried and he doesn't look as if he's aged a day since then."

University physiologist Jehan Gokhale refused to comment specifically on the Videsh case. But he did say he knows of cases where men have survived several days in a buried coffin by meditating deeply.

"Our master wanted to show the world that it's possible, through meditation, to achieve many miracles," said one of Videsh's followers, Tut Samindra.

"By witnessing something like this, mankind may see that it's possible to achieve other seemingly impossible things as well, including world peace."

AMAZING Hindu spiritual teacher Baba Singh Videsh instructed his followers to bury him in a metal box back in 1980 — then dig him up 20 years later!

WEEKLY WORLD NEWS

April 26, 2004

BABY DINOSAUR FOUND ALIVE IN THE CATSKILLS!

ANGEL SHOT DOWN BY U.S. TROOPS!

ARMY BRASS: 'A tragic accident'

INSIDE: More amazing photos

$1.99 US / $2.29 CANADA

PLUS: How veterinarians fixed her broken wing!

HEAVEN: THE *WWN* CONNECTION

Ooh, heaven is a paper on earth.
They say in heaven news comes first.
We'll make heaven a paper on earth.
Ooh, heaven is a paper on earth.

High school football coach Joe Pendleton wrote an ill-advised cellphone text on a rain-slicked upstate New York roadway one day in the winter of 2007. Suddenly, he felt his station wagon slide out from under him.

Pendleton blacked out. Seconds later, Coach Joe became aware that his point of view had tracked aerial. From above, he watched helplessly as the wagon slid toward a massive oak tree. Right before impact, Pendleton felt a floating sensation take hold as he passed through the oak tree into a bright white light. The light gave way to a soothing but chilly fog that enveloped his consciousness. Pure and brilliant whiteness stunned his vision as billowy clouds unfolded in a glistening cascade to all eternity.

Moments later, a short, kindly, Italian-looking man with a tape measure around his neck approached from the mist. The kindly tailor stretched the tape measure across Coach Joe's back to fit him for wings. Coach had arrived in heaven, despite a losing season.

Why are there so many *WWN* stories about heaven? And what's on the other side? Is heaven a vision? Or only an illusion? Does heaven have anything to hide?

Barbara Wiltshire, a local journalist outside of Atlanta, can answer that last question. On 17 November 1995, while visiting her mother's grave in West Atlanta, her guardian angel descended to speak to her and give her background on the unknowable. The angel explained that in heaven, 'everything that exists is God within God – components of the all-powerful, unending force that is heaven'.

So, since everything in heaven is God within God, heaven has nothing to hide. For most readers, *Weekly World News* is as close to heaven as they'll ever get.

Pharaohs were hip-hopping back in 1470 BC!

CALL HIM the "Pharaoh of Funk"! Here's what contemporary rap great Puff Daddy might have looked like if he'd lived and performed 3,500 years ago.

3,500-year-old rap lyrics found in Egyptian tomb!

By PAT WELLS
Weekly World News

CAIRO, Egypt — Archaeologists from the University of Milan excavating a tomb in Egypt have made an astonishing discovery — rap lyrics dating from 1470 BC!

The rhyming hieroglyphics were unearthed near ancient Thebes and describe mummification, the Pyramids and the Nile using rhythms, words and attitude that are primitive precursors to the works of contemporary artists like Puff Daddy and Eminem.

Along with the hieroglyphics, the archaeologists found the fossil of a conical reed that the ancient rapper could have used to amplify his voice like a primitive microphone!

"I'm blown away," says hip-hop historian, Levar Williams, "These Egyptian raps are almost 3,500 years older than The Sugar Hill Gang's 'Rappers Delight,' which marked the resurgence of the ancient art form in 1979."

The raps were translated into English by Milanese Egyptologists and are included on this page for *Weekly World News* readers to be blown away themselves.

No point to the pyramids

There ain't no point to the pyramids
In Gaza, or no matter where it is
'Cause up at the point where all four sides meet
Room too narrow for a burial tomb
Instead, should be flat like a papyrus sheet
But I ain't one of King Khufu's elite
So when I'm dead I be buried with my cat out in the street

Nile rap

Water flows turnin' the soil rich for the hoes
That wack weed from the seed is makin' dough
It sun bakin' into a pile, stacked in Greek style
With fondness, sun goddess, I partakin' and rappin' about the Nile

Mummify your behind

Gonna mummify your behind
Bindin' your butt in linen then wrappin' seven times
Gonna mummify your behind
'Cause your colon already been cut, unrollen and embalmed in heady palm wine
Gonna mummify your behind
But you decomposin' and now I'm tryin' to push your pose in
So I pray to Isis in this crisis
Gonna mummify your behind

Women feel more pain than men, say experts

WASHINGTON — It's official: Women feel pain more than men do. But they also cope with it better than men, scientists say.

"Most studies show females are more sensitive to pain than males," Karen Berkley, a Florida State University neuroscientist, told a conference on pain and gender sponsored by the National Institute of Health.

"Females are more ready to identify pain than males and more ready to deal with it."

She and others at the conference said that although women feel pain more, they handle the emotional consequences of pain better than men and aren't as likely to be depressed by chronic pain.

POOF GOES THE NANNY!

ARTIST'S conception shows Patrick Houlihan casting a spell to rid himself of nanny Gladys Redmond — for good.

Boy vaporizes babysitter with Internet spell, say cops

EDINBURGH, Scotland — An 8-year-old boy recited a spell he found on an Internet site and made his nanny disappear for real!

Patrick Houlihan allegedly angry with his nanny for making him eat his spinach.

So, cops say, the mischievous schoolboy began reading aloud a spell he found on an Internet site devoted to pagan lifestyles and issues.

"I didn't think it would really work — I just did it for fun," Patrick told reporters in a tearful BBC interview.

"Next thing I knew, there was smoke and bright lights — then my nanny was gone."

Patrick's nanny, Gladys Redmond, 42, has been missing ever since the weird October 1 incident.

Friends and family say they've seen no sign of the mother of two and are growing increasingly worried.

Cops have questioned Patrick, but he has not been charged with any crime.

"There's no law against reciting a spell," notes Inspector Sean Clancy, adding, "I don't believe the boy's version of what happened — and foul play has not been ruled out.

"But until we prove that Mrs. Redmond is the victim of something other than black magic, there's nothing we can do."

For now, police are treating the disappearance as a simple missing persons case.

They've conducted a thorough search of the surrounding area, but have thus far failed to turn up any trace of the blonde woman.

The boy's mother, Shirley Houlihan, is furious with the pagan owners of the Internet site for what she calls "printing a real spell."

"Now my son thinks he really is a witch," she says.

"For the past few weeks, he's been running around with a broomstick, trying to get it to fly. I'm just sick about this."

— By PAT WELLS

A doctor has a stethoscope up to a man's chest. The man asks, "Doc, how do I stand?" The doctor says, "That's what puzzles me!"

BONE APPÉTIT!

PORT MORESBY, Papua New Guinea — Top TV chefs like Julia Child and Emeril Lagasse will have to make room for a new competitor — a slicin', dicin' cannibal cook who's specialty is turning human flesh into mouth-watering delicacies!

Cannibal cooking show eats the competition — ALIVE!

Herve Maudet's new show *The Cannibal Gourmet*, will be syndicated around the world starting in January — and he can't wait to sink his teeth into the new challenge.

"I want to show people that cannibal cooking can be every bit as delicious as fine European cuisine," says the expatriate Frenchman. "And of course, it's terrific fun."

Among the lip-smacking dishes he's lined up to teach housewives worldwide:

- Broiled Safari Guide Buttocks and Artichoke Hearts.
- Scrambled Hunter's Brain with Pasta and Pea Pods.
- Crab-stuffed Stomach of Nun.
- Spit-roasted Torso of Tourist with Broccoli Parmesan.
- Militiaman's Liver and Onion Kebabs.
- Raspberry-Glazed Guerrilla Head with Fried Zucchini.
- Lemon-Marinated Leg of Missionary.

Man-eating kitchen whiz Maudet came to the attention of Australian TV producers when he competed in the First Annual Cannibal Bake-Off held recently in New Guinea.

"Herve really impressed us with his style and charisma," said executive producer Dan Masterson. "Some of the other cannibal chefs were a little rough around the edges, to put it mildly, but Herve studied for four years at one of the finest culinary schools in France."

Maudet says he became bored with the ordinary cooking he sees promoted on TV's "dull" cooking shows.

"Everyone is preparing the same meals in the same tired, old fashion," he said. "Housewives are watching TV and gaining the same skills it took me years to learn.

"I decided to move to the next level and take the ultimate challenge: Cooking with human meat," he says.

The cannibal chef peppers his freewheeling show with jokes and gags, sometimes pausing to juggle knives or body parts. Adds the producer, "He's a great entertainer."

The show tapes in New Guinea, where cannibalism is illegal but enforcement is lax.

— *By VICKIE YORK*

CHEERS! Would you drink red or white wine with Spit-roasted Tourist Torso with Broccoli Parmesan? Tune in to *The Cannibal Gourmet* and find out.

YUM-YUM! Chef Herve Maudet's TV show will be syndicated worldwide starting in January. Contact your cable provider for details.

WHEN asked about his Mountain Oysters, Maudet jokes: "Somewhere there's an anthropologist singing soprano!"

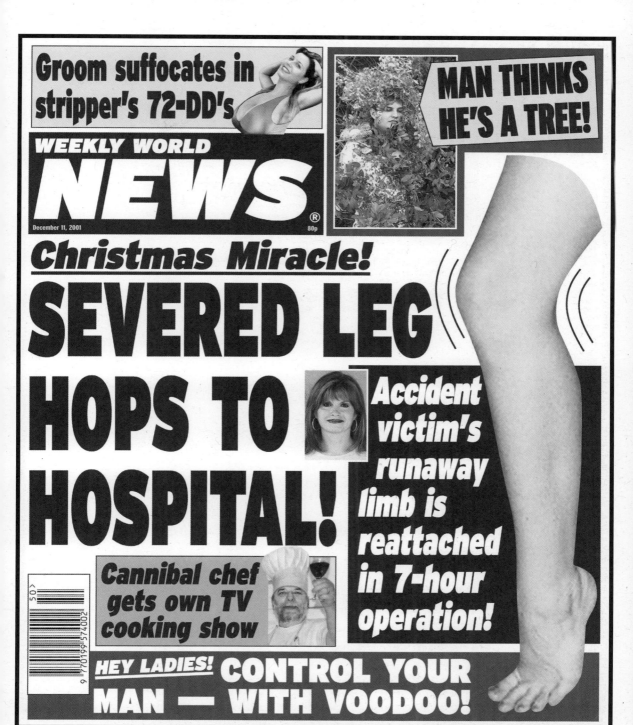

SHRUNKEN UFOs...
HIDDEN IN KIDS' TOYS!

By BOB JAMES / Weekly World News

WASHINGTON — The Consumer Product Safety Commission is contemplating a massive recall of popular kids' toys after reports that tiny UFOs have been found hidden in remote controlled cars, robots and other hi-tech merchandise.

"Aliens from other worlds appear to have infiltrated the U.S. toy market," says a CPSC spokesperson. "It is with a heavy heart that the federal government is considering playing the role of Grinch and breaking the hearts of millions of children by confiscating their holiday presents, but we regard this turn of events as a serious threat to national security.

"In the meantime, we encourage parents to take matters into their own hands and either destroy these toys themselves or drop them off at the nearest FBI office."

The first sign of trouble came when Danny Honeywell, 8, of Saginaw, Michigan, was playing with a remote-controlled pickup truck on Christmas morning.

As he was executing a hairpin turn in his family's living room, the vehicle suddenly changed shape and flew around the house before disappearing up the fireplace chimney.

Thousands of similar reports followed from all regions of the country. Several people reported seeing a sleigh-shaped UFO landing on housetops on Christmas Eve, carrying a fat alien in a red suit, who was furtively distributing brightly wrapped packages.

A source close to Barack Obama says the new president is grief-stricken over the proposed recall.

"He wanted to go down as the leader who saved America from the worst economic crisis since the Great Depression," the source explains. "Now, he fears his legacy will be 'The president who stole Christmas.'"

DANNY HONEYWELL was disappointed when his new truck flew up the chimney.

'We weren't going for pure zaniness. It was more like a short story in tabloid form … I guess you could say things proceeded logically, using the word logically very loosely.'—**MICHAEL FORSYTH,** *WEEKLY WORLD NEWS* **REPORTER**

HAIRPIECE FRO

EVIL toupee changed Roger into a monster.

MILD-MANNERED accountant Roger Wick.

IN A HAIR-RAISING confrontation with ev team of exorcists waged a dramatic three-day ba with a toupee possessed by a vicious satanic spirit!

By MATT BETT
Weekly World News

It took four priests armed with Bibles, crucifixes and specially blessed holy hair spray to drive out the demon that occupied the rampaging rug worn by baldy Roger Wick.

"If it hadn't been for those exorcists, I don't know what would have become of me — that thing was making my life a living Hell," says Roger, a mild-mannered accountant from Manchester, England.

"When it was on my head I was compelled to do and say the most wicked things.

"I would curse like a sailor on the job, pinch the bottoms of strange women I passed on the street, shout horrible curse words in church — often in Latin or ancient Greek, languages that I don't even know.

"There's no doubt in my mind that toupee had been taken over by an evil entity — and the demon was after my soul."

The 35-year-old chrome dome was thrilled when he first purchased the vintage hairpiece from a secondhand shop in June 2001. At first, his new full-haired look won him compliments from co-workers and admiring glances from the ladies.

But soon, he sensed that something was "a bit off" about the toupee.

"It would never stay on properly," he recalls. "I would fix it on

securely in the morning a midday, it would shift. Some it would work its way 180 de around by evening, all by itse

Roger realized that some was horribly wrong the nig took out Ellen West, a 25-ye mail clerk at his office, whon been lusting after for three y

"We were sitting in a coz ner at the back of a splitting a bott wine," he recall a shudder. " leaned acros table and holding her — about t her to come to my flat all of a su this dazed she normal on her pinch tle face turn one of horror.

"My toupee lifted off my n several inches and she later told m was spinning aro

"And instead of asking she'd like to come over t place and listen to an alb Englebert Humperdink's gre hits, I began drooling and 'How about a round of the ol 'n' tickle?'"

Despite the toupee's odd, Blair-type antics, and the st things it made him do an Roger continued to we because of the strong emo "charge" it gave him.

"When I wore the toupee

HELL!
Priests battle demonic toupee

erful — almost invincible and all my inhibitions ed to vanish," he ex—s.

"Sometimes, I swear I d hear the toupee whis—g to me, egging me on to iskier and riskier things. he end, it was getting me oplift on a regular basis and even told me I ld get a gun and hold church."

he cursing toupee Roger both his job his girlfriend.

While wearing the iece, I called my an idiot and I told n she'd better e across with some y fun and games," calls. "Later, when I off the toupee to take a er, I realized what a fool—mistake I'd made.

But when I tried to ain that it was my fake and not me making all trouble, they both gave he boot."

oger says he tried twice row away the evil toupee found himself coerced an irresistible force" to it.

That's when I ly called for " he said.

he Rev. Daniel utry, an itiner—exorcist who s a special on-hunting is team," re—ded to the erate baldy's plea.

Roger was very ed. I knew he was on evel," says Rev. McAutry. had never encountered ssessed wig before, but es about them date back e 18th century — includ—ne worn by the Marquis ade that's still reportedly rculation."

he respected exorcist's bout with the demon ee, on March 1, 2002, was he won't soon forget.

We entered the bed—n with our usual gear

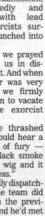

"BE GONE SATAN!"

— incense, cruci—fixes, holy water — in addition to a can of hair spray we'd carefully blessed," he recalls.

"When I closed the door, the toupee sprung from the wig stand and bounced off the walls and ceiling at very high speeds," he says. "It took a chunk out of my forearm and slammed me in the cheek before I retreated from the room with my assistants at my heels."

The next day, Rev. McAutry returned to the room with an unconventional weapon.

"I brought my tennis racket in there on the second go-around," he says. "Let's just say that wig didn't have a prayer against my backhand."

With the hairpiece beaten into submission, sprayed repeatedly and pinned down with lead weights, the exorcists surrounded it and launched into the ancient rite.

"For two days, we prayed for Jesus to aide us in dispelling the evil spirit. And when we felt His power was very strong with us, we firmly ordered the demon to vacate the toupee," the exorcist says.

"The hairpiece thrashed around and you could hear a tremendous howl of fury — then a cloud of black smoke poured out of the wig and it flopped down, lifeless."

After successfully dispatching the demon, the team did some research on the previous owner and found he'd met an unfortunate end.

"The original owner's house was struck by an errant hot-air balloon, caught fire and burned to the ground," says the preacher. "The man escaped unharmed, but lived the rest of his life in a railroad boxcar, hopelessly insane."

PAGE 5 PINUP — Luscious Lyndsey Nix is way more than a pretty face — she's also got a great bod. Topping it off is a head full of brains. The California gal is a full-time student and a professional cheerleader. She also finds time to volunteer at a children's hospital — perfect training for her dream of becoming a pediatric emergency physician. Hmmm — makes you want to be a kid again!

PAGE 5 PINUP!

Shocking scientific discovery:
PIGS CAN FLY!

By JUSTIN MITCHELL/*Weekly World News*

A RARE species of pygmy winged swine — dubbed "Pigasus" — has been discovered in a "lost world" near the Cambodian border that is teeming with wildlife previously unimaginable to science.

"In the past three years alone, seven new large mammal species were found in this region," says Vo Li Khoi, a Hanoi University wildlife biologist who was part of the team that discovered the flying pigs. "Four more species were discovered in Vietnam in the late '90s. And now we're really bringing home the bacon with Pigasus!"

The pigs resemble their potbellied cousins, but are smaller — each one is about the size of a football with 22-inch wings made of a thin, flexible membrane material, says Oxford zoologist Drew McSorley, who also made headlines in the '90s with his discovery of a new species of barking deer in Vietnam's mountains.

The airborne porkers, which can fly and glide for distances up to 200 yards, have been celebrated for centuries in the folktales of the Hmong tribes who inhabit the Chu Mo Ray region where the pigs were sighted.

"They fly and glide much like flying squirrels," says McSorley. "Except they cannot climb trees, so in order to become airborne they run as quickly as their small, powerful legs can propel them and launch themselves from cliff edges and slopes.

"The soaring swine are called 'flying pork creatures' by the native people," he continued, "They are worshiped as guardians that are believed to accompany a dead soul to the next life. Their meat is regarded a sacred delicacy to be eaten on ceremonial occasions."

McSorley and Vo captured two of the winged pigs by using a network of nets strung from trees and jungle foliage and maintaining a three-week vigil in hopes that the tiny beasts would fly into the netting and be trapped.

The beasts will be studied, displayed, and possibly even mated. McSorley has big plans for the flying pigs, included a tour of zoos around the world. But his real goal is to feature them in a circus.

"You should see them soar! It's really quite something. These little fellows really know how to put on a good show. I guess you could say they're natural-born hams."

It's not hogwash ... these swines soar!

"PIGASUS" is the latest new species discovered in Asia's "lost world," as shown in this artist's conception.

PET PIRANHA KILLS FAMILY CAT!

A WOMAN who owned a 30-pound piranha was horrified when she arrived home one night to find her prized pet fish had attacked and killed the family cat.

"My cat, Mr. Cuddles, was always exploring near the fish tank," said Maria Gonzalez, the owner of both pets. "One day, I accidentally left the aquarium uncovered. I came home that night and found Mr. Cuddles' bones at the bottom of the tank. All of his flesh and fur had been chewed off."

Gonzalez, 67, had raised the piranha, named Picu, since it was a baby. Picu eats three meals a day, with a diet including potatoes, broccoli, cantaloupe, liver, and frogs.

"That fish has quite an appetite," Gonzalez said, adding that she intends to keep her prized piranha. "After all," she notes, "now I only have one pet."

WEEKLY WORLD NEWS July 9, 2002

WEEKLY WORLD NEWS

December 1, 1998

7 40 This week's 6 LUCKIEST lottery numbers

SLIM & TRIM HILLARY HAS SECRET NEW BOYFRIEND

...says Washington rumor mill

CRASH DIET TURNING FIRST LADY INTO A BEAUTY!

GOVERNMENT WEATHER FORECASTERS PREDICT:

WORST WINTER IN 100 YEARS!

Prepare yourself for the deep freeze of the century!

Will Pope John Paul II be on next space shuttle?

THREE-LEGGED FIGURE SKATER...
BANNE
'IF THEY LET HER ON THE IC[E]
TOAST,' SAY SUP[PORTERS]

By MICHAEL FORSYTH
Weekly World News

SALT LAKE CITY — Outraged fans and supporters of popular three-legged skater McKenzie Sarchent are up in arms, because skating officials have banned the Salt Lake City girl from all international competitions!

"This is a travesty of justice — McKenzie has been training since the age of 3 for this opportunity," declared her angry father and coach Jack Sarchent.

"She is devastated by the panel's decision.

"They say she has an 'unfair advantage,' but the real truth is, those snooty blowhards in the skating world are incredibly intolerant of anyone who just doesn't fit their image of a physically perfect, prissy ice princess.

"It's prejudice, pure and simple."

But the panel is sticking by its guns —

TWO-LEGGED skating champ Michelle Kwan takes a tumble

meaning that unless the decision is overturned, America's "secret weapon" won't be able to join the rest of our team on the ice.

"It was simply a matter of fairness," explains an official, who asked not to be identified.

"That powerful third limb makes McKenzie the only skater in the world capable of doing the otherwise impossible quintuple axel. And of course, by pushing off with it she can achieve phenomenal speeds on the ice. She uses it

OUTRAGED DAD Jack Sarchent.

like an alligator swish[es its] tail.

"Also, extending th[e] leg gives her s[uper] balance whil[e per]forming such [moves] as the Bielma[nn,] the Grafstrom and the Russia[n...]

"We're sor[ry not] to allow her [to com]pete would ha[ve been] as unfair as [expec]ting another sk[ater to] bring alon[g a] tightrope w[alker's] staff for bett[er bal]ance or a ski pole to [get] extra speed."

The decision come[s as a] major blow to McK[enzie's] almost fanatically d[evoted] fans.

Spectators used to [look] with bemusement as [the] young McKenzie first t[ook] onto the ice as a [tot,] unsure of how to use h[er third] leg — then watched w[ith awe] as she blossomed int[o the] one sportswriter has ca[lled "a] swan on the ice."

In recent months, s[he has] been kept out of the li[melight] by U.S. skating honch[os who] dreamed of springin[g the] amazing wonder girl [on the] competition and strikin[g...]

Dad gives doc and nurse the AXE over daughter's care!

TAKASAKI, Japan — A 63-year-old man sent a doctor and nurse to their own hospital after he hacked them severely with a hatchet because he was unhappy at the treatment his daughter had received.

The man had complained previously that his daughter's illness had not improved despite treatment at the hospital three years ago.

"I was discontented with the doctor so I tried to give tit for tat," he told arresting officers.

The doctor and nurse have recovered from their injuries.

French chef stuffs clumsy cook in clothes dryer

MONTBRISON, France — Taking the French passion about food to new levels, an irate chef stuffed a cook in a tumble dryer and switched it on because he said the woman had been "clumsy and careless."

The raging chef got a six-month suspended jail sentence and a fine after he was found guilty of armed violence and abusing and humiliating an employee.

The spin-dried, shaken cook said she was terrified by the tumble: "Each time the dryer's drum turned, I fell and was hurt pretty badly."

WORLD EXCLUSIVE!

D!

WE'RE STARS

She spins around on the ice like a helicopter!

event after another. But that dream, and enzie's, appears to be ed.

etty McKenzie, 22, is taking e decision in stride and owed to appeal.

want the opportunity to sent my country," gutsy nzie declared.

triotic Americans, civil activists and crusaders e disabled have voiced ort for McKenzie. And though it may cost their ries coveted gold medals, some foreigners are against what they perceive as a major injustice.

"This is a clear case of discrimination," says Anna Heistand of the Swiss Association for Universal Human Rights. "McKenzie should be allowed to skate like anyone else."

But fellow skaters support the ban — and dread going up against America's sweetheart.

"If they put her on the ice, we're toast," one Finnish skater said.

WHAT YOU CAN DO TO HELP

Do you think three-gged skater McKenzie s a right to compete? o, send us a letter of port and we'll for-d it to international ting officials.

rite to: Weekly d News, 5401 NW ken Sound Blvd., Raton, Fla. 33487

WEEKLY WORLD NEWS February 12, 2002

INSIDE: Actual-size shoe of world's tallest man

SEE HOW YOUR FOOT MEASURES UP

How to tell your pet's past lives

April 2, 2002 — $1.79 U.S. / $1.99 CANADA

Shocking discovery reveals REAL reason ship sank

KKK SKELETONS FOUND IN TITANIC LIFE RING

Incredible one-eyed Cyclops people, world's fattest rock star, & much more...

Going out in style... LUXURY COFFINS FOR THE RICH & FAMOUS

NEW!

By CHAD ELLIOTT
Weekly World News

FLAT SCREEN TV
STOCKED MINI BAR
VCR RECORDER
CELL PHONE
CD & DVD PLAYER

CUSTOM CASKETS START AS LOW AS $250,000

BOSTON, Mass. — You may not be able to take your money with you when you die, but, thanks to a revolution in the funeral industry, you can now travel to the Great Beyond in style.

Luxury coffins are becoming increasingly popular with the world's wealthiest citizens thanks to such modern conveniences as air-conditioning, televisions and CD players.

"They're the hottest new status symbol," says funeral home owner R.J. Bransom. "It's no longer enough to have a better house or car than your neighbor.

"Now everyone wants to have a better coffin, too. And I'm making millions off of this."

Bransom's client list reads like a Who's Who of the wealthy and powerful, including corporate big shots and snooty bluebloods who come from a long line of money.

"The attitude of my clients is: 'You can't just shove people like us in a pine box. We're better than that.'"

These sentiments are typical of those in the top tax bracket who don't care for the notion of death being the great equalizer. For many of the wealthy elite, the subject of dying has been something of an embarrassment. But no longer.

"Nothing disgusts me more than the thought of winding up as a rotting corpse," an 83-year-old female client explained. "I mean, how humiliating! But thanks to the luxury coffin's powerful air conditioner, I can stay looking fresh and beautiful well into the next century."

Most of these luxury coffins are tailored specifically to meet the needs and interests of their individual owners.

Constructed of the finest materials and fitted with the latest in technology, it's not uncommon for units to contain such features as mini-bars, cell phones and even television monitors for the deceased to keep a watchful eye on their surviving family.

Predictably, these coffins come with high price tags. Even the more modest units start at $250,000.

Some feel this is a ridiculous price to pay for a final resting place. One industry analyst notes, "What good is a CD player when you're dead? Those rich buffoons are ignoring the fact that they won't be alive to enjoy any of this stuff."

But that's not stopping wealthy clients from paying top dollar for coffins that are as high-tech as possible. As one client noted, "I want to go in style, the same way I lived. And I'd rather spend my money on something meaningful like this than leave it to my greedy, no-good relatives."

"And dead or not, I still want to have an awesome sound system."

FUNERAL DIRECTOR R.J. Bransom

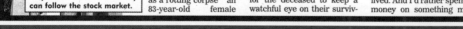
SOME clients have requested a satellite dish be installed atop their mausoleum so they can follow the stock market.

NEWS FLASH: ED ANGER RUSHED TO HOSPITAL!

BOCA RATON, Fla. — Apparently overcome by a fit of heart-stopping outrage, legendary *Weekly World News* columnist Ed Anger, collapsed at his desk and was rushed to the intensive-care unit of a local hospital.

"We are closely monitoring his condition," said a spokesman for the South Florida hospital where Ed, 72, was listed in critical but stable condition. *WWN* is not identifying the hospital, in order to keep Ed's legions of adoring fans from disturbing the acclaimed writer.

Ed's devoted wife, Thelma Jean, and the couple's two children, Jimbo and Sarah Lee, have kept a desperate bedside vigil for their beloved husband and father since he was first hospitalized three days ago.

WWN Editor-in-Chief Dick Kulpa said Ed was working on a column about the horrors of women drivers, when Mrs. Anger called to say she had just totalled his brand-new car on her way to the beauty parlor.

The columnist suddenly rose from his chair, clutched his chest and keeled over.

Ed's controversial columns have rocked the world with their no-nonsense attitude, and Ed made headlines recently when he pulled the plug on the *Weekly World News* web site, admonishing freeloading techies to "buy the @#%$* paper instead."

Ed had written several advance columns before his illness, so they will continue during his recovery. Readers may send cards and letters to:

Get Well, Ed! c/o *Weekly World News*, 5401 NW Broken Sound Blvd., Boca Raton, FL 33487

DIVER swims near Nessie after its capture in the huge lake in Scotland.

LOCH NESS MONSTER

Nessie caught in huge steel net — baited with 3,000 pounds of tuna!

By ZACK HAGAR
Special correspondent

EDINBURGH, Scotland — Scientists from seven countries captured the Loch Ness monster in a steel net baited with tuna fish on December 22 and have now provided the world with the first clear photographs of a creature that has intrigued mankind since it was first sighted 1300 years ago — in 690 A.D.!

It is not yet known what the researchers plan to do with the 70-foot, 20-ton beast. But it is believed that they will release it after they finish taking blood and tissue samples, possibly by the end of the January.

"This is it. This is the proof we've been waiting for," Dr. Michel Genet, the French zoologist who headed the team of experts who captured the monster, told reporters here.

"For the first time since the creature was sighted in the distant past we know for a fact that it does exist. The task before us now is to determine exactly what it is.

"It's much too early to attempt to name or classify the monster," he added. "But my gut feeling tells me that we've caught what may be the last dinosaur on Earth."

The capture of the Loch Ness monster, which the world knows as Nessie, capped a 3-year, $9 million research project that was organized by Dr. Genet and supported by scientists in France, Italy, Belgium, Germany, Sweden, Norway and the United States.

In spite of the potential rewards, the decision to search for the creature didn't come easy — because the vast majority of scientists in Europe and the United States considered the Loch Ness monster to be a myth.

"From the very beginning we understood that our professional reputations were on the line," said Dr. Genet. "Many of our colleagues treated us as a laughingstock and one science journal actually suggested that we forget about the Loch Ness monster and search for Santa Claus instead."

Undaunted, the research team set up a base of operations in January 1989 and spent the next 32 months mapping the floor of the legendary Scottish lake with underwater cameras and sonar.

Once they had familiarized themselves with the monster's turf, they baited a 175-foot metal net with 3,000 pounds of raw tuna fish and lowered it into the loch.

The net was suspended by special air bags that allowed

Dog calls it quits after 11 years as mayor of California town

By JACK ALEXANDER/*Staff writer*

During his 11 years as mayor of Sunol, Calif., Bosco was entertained at the Japanese embassy, appeared on national TV shows and never lost an election. It wasn't a bad life — for a dog.

The easygoing, 70-pound part Labrador, part Rottweiler has been forced to step down as the head of the tiny hamlet of 500 because his owner, Tom Stillman, moved to nearby Livermore.

"This town is still in a state of shock," said Virginia McCullough.

"Bosco was the spirit of this community. He was not like most politicians. He never lied, didn't cheat and never took a bribe.

"He got free beef jerky from guys at the corner saloon from time to time, but he never promised them anything in return, so we don't consider that a bribe," she was quick to add.

Bosco was first elected mayor in 1980, defeating two humans. He was unchallenged four years later and won his third four-year term three years ago against two other dogs.

"That strong-minded mutt had the respect of this entire town," said Tom's mother, Pat Stillman. "He represented the fierce independence and pride of this town. With him as our leader, we were successful in fighting off developers for years."

A group of Japanese officials visited Sunol several years ago and were shocked when they shook the mayor's paw. They later invited Bosco to the Japanese embassy in San Francisco.

"They wanted to know why we had a dog for a mayor, so I asked them if they knew who was mayor of Chicago, Detroit and Miami. When they said 'No,' I pointed out thousands of people know who Bosco is."

He has been written up in national publications — including *The Weekly World*

RETIRED — Hizzonor Bosco.

News — and he's been on national TV.

The NEWS reported Bosco's disappearance in 1988.

It turned out he had dozed off in the back of a pickup truck and ended up in Oregon.

He was given a ride home a week later.

Bosco is gone, but not forgotten. He has definitely left his mark on this wide spot in the road — 45 miles east of San Francisco. Seems he's got a Rottweiler named Sweetpea in a family way.

FLYING POOCH KILLS GRANNY!

Dear Dotti

AMERICA'S MOST OUTSPOKEN ADVICE COLUMNIST

I'll wear panties when they start making 'em big enough for me

Dear Dotti: All my friends and family members make fun of me because I don't wear undies, but there's a darn good reason for it. I'm a queen-sized lady, 58, and they simply do not make panties big enough for me — at least, they aren't big enough for me to wear comfortably.

Every pair I try bunches up around my thighs and butt and cuts me in front. I gave up on the things, Dotti, and if people weren't making fun of me, I'd be perfectly happy. But whenever I sit down or get up from a chair, or get into and out of a car when I'm wearing a dress they point and laugh at me and make crude jokes because they say they can see "something" they shouldn't be seeing, you know what I mean? I shouldn't have to go through this kind of Hell at my age, Dotti. Don't you agree? — Fed Up in Turnerville

Dear Fed Up: This is what you get for hanging around people who "love" you. Seems to me you'd be better off among strangers who are too embarrassed to point and stare!

Is President Bush REALLY a Puerto Rican?

Dear Dotti: When a friend of mine found I was born in Puerto Rico he told me that President George Bush is Puerto Rican, too. If that's true, it's a point of pride for all Puerto Ricans. I know that I, for one, would send him a personal letter offering to support him in any way I can. You're a national celebrity and famous newspaper columnist, so I figure you probably know the answer. Is President Bush Puerto Rican? — Curious in New York

Dear Curious: I can't vouch for the President's bloodline but I will say this: That bullet-proof Lincoln he tools around in HAS been riding a little low, lately — so maybe he is!

My pastor thinks I left mouthwash on his desk

Dear Dotti: I've never been in a situation like this in my life! The pastor of my church has really bad breath and somebody sneaked into his office at night and put a big bottle of mouthwash on his desk. Somehow he got it into his head that I did it. I didn't, and I told him so. But he doesn't believe me. Now, every time he sees me he makes a snide comment like, "What would Jesus do?" and, "Don't you know it's not nice to fool with your preacher?" He's got me thinking I did something horrible — and now I'm starting to feel guilty for what I didn't even do. Give me some advice, Dotti — please! — Good Christian in Chicago

Dear Good Christian: If you really want to get him off your back, rather than deny it, go on the offensive — and tell the old fool it was either mouthwash in the middle of the night or you were coming to church in a Haz-Mat suit... with a clothespin on your nose!

Does the boss really have the right to spank me?

Dear Dotti: Ever since I landed a new job down at the plant here in town the boss has been all over me like white on rice. Everything I do is either "half baked" or "all wrong," as he puts it. Even worse, he calls me into his office and shuts the door and makes me bend over, and then he spanks me with his hand as "punishment." I told him I don't like it — I'm an attractive gal, 35, and he's an old goat in his 60s — but he says there are federal laws that say it's O.K. to spank workers. I can't afford to lose my job, but I don't want to keep it if I'm going to be punished all the time. Does he really have the right to spank me like this? — Spanked in Columbia

Dear Spanked: Yes, he does.

How can I make my hubby dance with me?

Dear Dotti: Talk about problems! My husband and I have been married for five years and even though we make a good team, there's one thing missing. I love to dance — I'd go out dancing every night if I could. But he hates it. Even when I manage to drag him out to the dance floor he just shuffles around with his shoulders and head all hunched over like he's embarrassed to be out there. He won't take dancing lessons and he won't let me teach him at home. Got any strategies for making a man dance? — Bored in Dallas

Dear Bored: I get a lot of wimpy letters, lady, but this one takes the cake. If you really want that dud hubby of yours to cut the rug, get yourself a high-powered pellet gun — and shoot at his feet!

I wish I hadn't put that 'Kick Me' sticker on the judge's back!

Dear Dotti: I went to court for a probation violation and before I went in, my probation officer told me the judge loved practical jokes and would probably go easy on me if I made him laugh. I couldn't think of any jokes, but a cop who overheard our conversation suggested I put a "Kick Me" sign on the judge's back. There was one of those little yellow sticky notes lying on a desk so I scribbled "Kick Me" on it, and sure enough, when the judge walked by I managed to stick it on his back. Unfortunately, another cop saw me do it and started yelling. I tried to tell the judge it was a joke. But he wouldn't listen — now I'm in state prison serving out the two years that were left on my original five-year sentence. What's your take on all this. — Stupid Inmate in Raleigh

Dear Stupid Inmate: Look at the bright side — if the cop had suggested a "Kill Me" sticker, you'd be cooling your heels in there for life!

CONFIDENTIALS

Dear Hospitalized, Bored and Dying in Jackson: Better you than me!

Dear Angry Mobster in Philadelphia: You must have me confused with Dear Abby.

Dear Ree-tard in Pellsville: At least you admit it.

Dear Home-Alone Mom in Moorestown: That's one use for the "biggest, fattest, longest garlic pickle" you've ever seen. Serving it up with a hamburger and tater chips is another.

Dear Hot Mama in Tupelo: Only until you get the air-conditioner fixed.

Dear Sweet Little Gingerbread Man in Bakersfield: By any chance, are you gay?

Dear Super Genius in Boston: I hate to tell you this, Einstein, but you DID NOT invent the potato clock!

Dear God's Gift to Women and Men in Marshville: You and every other lesbo with an identity crisis. Get lost!

WRITE TO DOTTI PRIMROSE

Send Dotti your letters and questions — and let her tell it like it is. Write to Dear Dotti, c/o Weekly World News, 5401 NW Broken Sound Blvd., Boca Raton, Fla. 33487.

WEEKLY WORLD NEWS

June 4, 2002

 Miracle mud pits get healing power from UFOs

BABY BORN WITH ANTLERS

'He's a little dear,' says mom

 Guy finds money tree in his yard!

2-ton tubbies compete in beauty pageant for fatties

BIBLE SHOCKER! HEAD OF JOHN THE BAPTIST FOUND

$1.79 U.S.
$1.99 CANADA

E.T.s PHONING HOME IS COSTING TAXPAYERS MILLIONS!

By MIKE MORSE/*Weekly World News*

DENVER, Colo. — Government officials have announced a plan to help Earth-bound extraterrestrials phone their home worlds — but it's going to cost a lot more than a quarter. Experts say these intergalactic phone bills are costing U.S. taxpayers millions of dollars a month!

The U.S. government has been housing hundreds of exiled extraterrestrials for years, but these lonely aliens have never had a way to phone home, until now. Now construction has been completed on a network of costly communication satellites to allow them to speak to loved ones back on their home planets.

Hundreds of different life forms, many of which have come to Earth to escape the brutal regimes of their worlds, are currently living in a top-secret complex nestled somewhere in the mountains of Colorado. Sources claim that President Bush offered sanctuary to these itinerant beings in the hope that they may share with us their advanced technology for the betterment of mankind.

But so far, the only information they've provided are the blueprints for seven communication satellites that act as powerful transmitters to the home planets of our intergalactic guests. The cost of building and launching those satellites earlier this year was over two billion dollars.

With the satellites in place, the creatures can transmit and receive information to and from their home planets. And although each alien is given a time limit of ten minutes per day to speak with faraway friends and family, the tab still soars into millions of dollars per week because of the incredibly pricey equipment required to allow them to reach out and touch someone . . . or something.

The price tag for this project, code name Operation: Really Long Distance, has grown so out of control that several congressmen are threatening to shut down the whole program.

"Enough is enough," complains one congressman, who asked to remain anonymous. "American citizens are paying through the nose just so some little green creep can catch up on the latest gossip on Nebula Five. We've got to pull the plug on these satellites."

In spite of congressional threats, NASA has done nothing to discourage our interplanetary guests from racking up the astronomical phone bills.

Translations of their conversations reveal that the aliens talk about the same things humans do: How their kids are doing in school, the high cost of eating out and what's new with the family pet.

So, the next time you complain about your high taxes, remember that a good portion of your money is probably being used to allow a homesick spaceman to say "Happy Birthday" to one of his three hundred offspring back on Uranus.

Satellites for our alien guests' telephones could put America in the poorhouse, warn economists!

ONE OF MANY secret E.T. telecommunications satellites launched into orbit so aliens can let their fingers do the walking.

PRESIDENT Bush feels the expense of the satellites is worthwhile, as it promotes interstellar diplomacy.

'Crazy armadillo mated with my mower'

SHOCKED homeowner Edith Nilsson.

By CAL SAMSON
Weekly World News

...and HERE'S the photo to prove it!

IT'S NOT unusual to be loved by anyone. Actual snapshot by Bobby Nilsson.

TYLER, Texas — Imagine the surprise on Edith Nilsson's face when she stepped out to get her morning paper and saw a large armadillo "mounting" her brand-new lawn mower!

"I just couldn't believe my eyes!" said the 63-year-old grandmother. "The biggest armadillo I'd ever seen was hunched over the mower, trying to make whoopee with it!"

She tried to chase it away with a broom, but the humongous, horny hard body ignored her and just kept on humping!

"I was shocked and embarrassed. It was bigger than my cocker spaniel! My neighbors must have thought I was running some sort of armadillo brothel!"

Nilsson, an alto in her church choir for over 40 years, called Tyler animal control before taking a few pictures. "If anyone owns that thing as a pet, they're going to get sued big time!" she told reporters. "There ain't no way it could get that big without somebody feeding it!"

"It's not unusual for a large animal in heat to behave this way," said a local veterinarian. "Armadillos have poor eyesight, and perhaps this one mistook the metal mower for the hard body plating of a female armadillo. This time, love truly was blind!"

Animal control officers arrived on the scene and sprayed the armored hunk o' burning love with ice-cold water to chill him out before chasing him away. "That's the biggest one I've ever seen," said one. "We call 'em Texas speed bumps, but that one was an Alaskan road block!"

Nilsson was so shaken by the experience that authorities needed to administer oxygen to her at the scene. "People from up and down my street all came out of their houses to watch. They had to hide their children's eyes. One of my best friends even fainted. It was horrible, just horrible!"

Nilsson's son Bobby soon arrived on the scene to make sure his mom was all right. "My mom is one tough little lady," he said. "And her mower's a lot tougher than some horndog armadillo, no matter how huge he is. With a paint job, this one'll be as good as new!"

Soon afterwards, Bobby was mowing his mom's lawn as usual. "That armadillo was lucky that mower wasn't running," he chuckled. "Or else he'd be a pretty tasty stew about now!"

Bobby Nilsson

'The magazine can't really be accused of overhyping its exclusives: they're so white-hot that the lily-livered mainstream media daren't follow them up. Where was *The New York Times*, or *The Guardian*, when *WWN* broke the story about Saddam Hussein's secret arsenal of dinosaurs? Or his gay romance with Osama bin Laden, culminating in their adoption of a shaved ape baby?'—**OLIVER BURKEMAN, *THE GUARDIAN***

YOUR child may be a psychic genius

...and not even know it!

By JUSTIN MITCHELL
Weekly World News

EXCITED scientists from several countries have discovered scores of infants and children with rare psychic powers and telekinetic abilities that may herald a new race of "super kids!"

And your child might be one of them!

The so-called "Indigo" or "Psychic Children" have been found in Bulgarian monasteries, remote Chinese villages, the hustle and bustle of Tokyo and in homes and pre-schools in middle America by scientists and pediatricians intrigued by their unique mental and physical powers — such as using their minds to stop clocks and bend spoons.

Discoveries began in 1994 with a group of 53 "super-psychic" Chinese children whom U.S. and Chinese researchers placed alone in a room.

A page was randomly ripped from a book, crumpled up and put under a scientist's arm in another room.

"All 53 of the children were able to read every word or describe the pictures on the page, despite never having seen it before," says Dr. Jiang Qing of the Peking Academy of Paranormal Pediatrics. "We were amazed!"

Word of other similarly gifted children began to spread in reports in pediatric journals throughout the world. And the scientists have published a set of five characteristics that all of the talented children share.

"The psychic child needs respect and lots of room," advises Dr. Jiang.

"They possess a superior and expanded consciousness. Instead of worrying about it, relax and learn from your psychic child.

"We have much to learn from them."

"SUPER KIDS" can bend spoons and stop clocks with the power of their minds alone.

How to tell if your child has psychic abilities:

IF your child exhibits two or more of these traits, he or she may indeed be a *super psychic.*

1. They have "imaginary" friends that only they can see and often talk and play with these invisible pals.
2. They are impatient and will often rebel at doing structured activities such as standing in line or coloring within the lines.
3. They emerge in the world feeling privileged and often act like it.
4. They are picky eaters and often shun meat in favor of yogurt, fruit and cookies.
5. They will not sleep through the night and often toys or ordinary household objects mysteriously break, bend or are otherwise "altered" in or near their presence.

SATAN'S BEDROOM SLIPPERS FOUND!

A PAIR of tattered bedroom slippers designed to accommodate cloven-hoofed feet have been unearthed by archaeologists excavating the ruins of a 15th-century Satanic monastery in Frankfurt, Germany.

Experts believe the footwear may be the fabled "Slippers of Satan," said to be worn by the Evil One when he relaxed during visits to followers.

"Whoever wore these slippers was probably an overnight guest who left them behind inadvertently," says archaeologist Klaus Dermeister, whose team made the extraordinary find.

WEEKLY WORLD NEWS

WORLD'S FIRST PHOTO OF A... SPACE ALIEN CAT

PINUP POSTER OF THE MONTH

Bizarre creature landed on Earth just weeks ago!

By MIKE FOSTER/Weekly World News

NAPIER, New Zealand — A 12-year-old boy has taken the world's first known photo of a space alien's pet cat!

The bizarre creature, which measured approximately 4½ feet long, resembles an earthly Himalayan cat, but is completely hairless and sports elongated toes, a giraffe-like neck and enormous black eyes.

Sixth-grader Corbin Mullwood says he took the amazing picture after a disk-shaped spaceship about 60 feet in diameter landed on a hillside near his home and he and his parents went to have a look at it.

"Mom said to run and get the camera and I did," the boy says. "When the door of the spaceship opened up, out came this alien with his cat."

Corbin's mother Alexis, dad Paul — a respected clergyman — and four other neighbors all say they saw the nimble creature amble out of the UFO along with the pilot, walk down a ramp and drop to the ground.

"It trotted toward us, and from time to time it would rub its head against its master's leg," says Rev. Mullwood, 46.

"It was very affectionate, but when my wife tried to pet it, it darted back up the ladder into the spaceship."

The space alien made several attempts to communicate with the onlookers, speaking in a series of odd, insect-like clicks and whirs. But when he failed to establish contact, he, too, returned to the craft and blasted off.

"We didn't understand what he was trying to say and plus, everyone was so interested in that cat, we almost forgot he was there," says Alexis, 41.

"Everyone has seen aliens on TV plenty of times before, but no one I know has ever seen an alien cat before. We were all really excited."

It's believed the E.T. may have been looking for a nearby military base.

Experts say that sightings of felines in the company of space aliens date back at least to 1947. But until now, no one has ever come forward with photographic evidence proving the existence of space-alien cats.

"This photo confirms the theory extraterrestrials are very much like ourselves," notes New Zealand UFO researcher Bryan O'Neal.

"They have a strong need for companionship, just like we do — so much so that they bring pets along on a space journey of countless light-years."

Sixth-grader Corbin Mullwood

Ancient Chinese scroll reveals the future!

2,000-year-old-document predicts events to 2099

By ROGER WILSON
Special correspondent

A 2,000-year-old scroll found in a Chinese tomb predicts the course of human events from the birth of Jesus Christ through the year 2099!

That's the word from Dr. William Loir, who discovered the scroll in a cave west of Beijing, China, and flatly calls it "the archaeological discovery of this century or any other.

"The document is in near perfect shape and seems to be an astonishing piece of clairvoyance," the expert told reporters in Paris.

"It foretold the birth of Christ and the enormous impact His life would have on the world.

"It also predicted the rise and fall of the Roman Empire and of the atomic bomb that was dropped on Hiroshima."

Analysis of the scroll indicates that it is between 2,000 and 2,300 years old, said Loir.

It is written in Chinese but the author is unknown.

"You'd think such a document would have philosophical or religious overtones but it doesn't," said the expert.

"It's nothing more than a list with one prediction following another.

"The last prediction is for the year 2099."

Twenty of the scroll's 48 predictions have come to pass.

According to Loir, they include the birth and death of Christ, America's Civil War, World Wars I and II, the rise and fall of the Soviet Union as a world power, the AIDS plague and America's 1986 space shuttle disaster.

Predictions for our future include:
● The discovery of intelligent life on Venus in 1995.
● The development of super vaccines to eradicate the common cold and most forms of cancer in 1997.
● The creation of a one-world religion in 1999.
● The rise of Japan as a military superpower in 2000.
● The mysterious disappearance of insects and marine life in 2004.
● The destruction of Miami by a gigantic tidal wave in 2005.
● The discovery of a new source of energy in 2022 which is cheap, non-polluting and totally renewable.
● The perfection of weather control in 2091, making storms and droughts a thing of the past.
● The simultaneous births of superhuman babies in Beijing, London, Paris, Moscow and Los Angeles in 2007.
● The discovery of a new source of energy in 2022 which is cheap, non-polluting and totally renewable.
● The emergence in the year 2059 of a new ruling class selected on the basis of honesty and ability and charged with the responsibility of ruling over all other humans.
● The last-ditch salvation of the Earth's ozone layer in 2037 when scientists discover a way to spray badly needed ozone directly into the planet's upper atmosphere, replacing what has been eroded by manmade chemicals.

"I genuinely believe that all of these predictions will come to pass," said Loir. "Up until now every prediction on the scroll has been accurate. There's no reason to think that's going to change."

These predictions have already come to pass!

The space shuttle disaster

Civil War in the United States

The Hiroshima A-bomb

...these will occur in the next 13 years!

Cancer will be cured by 1997

Tidal wave hits Miami in 2005

Life on Venus will be found in 1995

BABY HAS WORLD'S BIGGEST MOUTH!

Weekly World News Medical Update

LONDON, England — When little Billy Fargut wails, his mom is sure to hear him — because the 18-month-old tot has the world's biggest mouth!

The rambunctious tot's kisser measures a whopping 6.5 inches across, say doctors. That's wide enough to hold a regulation-size softball!

When Billy cries, it sounds like a freight train coming, says his mother Dale, 24.

"My husband and I have to wear earplugs at night just to get a little shut-eye.

"We can still hear Billy in the next room, of course, but the earplugs help to deaden the sound and make it a bit more bearable."

The *Guinness Book of World Records* does not have a listing for Largest Mouth, but the youngster's pediatrician, Dr. Donald Edeward,

By GEORGE SANFORD
Weekly World News

declares, "Billy has the largest mouth I have ever seen on a human being in my 33 years in the medical profession.

"It would be a large mouth even on a horse."

Billy's tongue is also oversize and his larynx and vocal cords are unusually well developed for a child his age — accounting for his extra-loud cries. Billy's eardrum-busting screams have been measured at an amazing 110 decibels — just slightly shy of the world-record 128-decibel screech let loose by Australian loudmouth Simon Robinson in 1988.

Doctors say that Billy's mouth has grown faster than the rest of his body, and his face and torso will probably catch up in time.

"But he will always have a rather large mouth in proportion to his head," said Dr. Edeward.

TOT'S GIANT KISSER measures a whopping 6.5 inches across — bigger than a horse's mouth.

PLAYWRIGHT GETS THE LAST LAUGH

Two of America's wittiest playwrights, George S. Kaufman and Marc Connolly, were always trying to top each other with clever repartee.

At one social gathering, Kaufman said, "I like your bald head, Marc. It feels just like my wife's behind."

Without missing a beat, Connolly touched his own chrome dome and said, "Yes it does, George. Yes it does!"

Why you copy your pal's mannerisms
The more you like someone, the more you will copy his gestures, mannerisms and way of standing, research at Oregon State University shows.

By JASON MORELAND
Weekly World News

NEW 5-DAY DIAPER SPARKS OUTRAGE!

PHEW!

CHILDREN'S rights advocate: Geena Loughy.

INVENTOR Elaine Herphman, right, claims her five-day diaper will save moms up to nine hours a week.

LOS ANGELES — An inventor has come up with a product that she says will be a valuable time-saver for busy working moms — the Five-Day Diaper!

"In today's world parents simply don't have the time to change their babies as often as they'd like," said Elaine Herphman, who invented the full-body disposable diaper.

"The design of this diaper allows the baby to be changed once every five days."

But children's rights advocates are furious and say the Five-Day Diaper should be outlawed.

"This is child abuse, plain and simple," said Geena Loughy, president of a California group that is working to have the controversial diapers banned.

"No baby should have to spend even 20 minutes in a dirty diaper — much less five full days."

But Mrs. Herphman says there's no reason to think any baby would even care when its diaper is changed.

And she claims her $16.95 diaper will save busy moms up to nine hours a week.

"The simple fact is most diapers are changed because the adult who is taking care of the baby is offended by the smell," she said.

"I have researched this for nearly five years and I can guarantee that no baby worries about how often its diaper is changed."

Mrs. Loughy believes that's insane.

"Anyone should realize that it's not healthy for a child to be left in a diaper for five days," she said.

"I'm sure doing that could lead to mental problems that will stay with the child for the rest of its life."

Mrs. Herphman bristled at the idea that she would produce a diaper that would put children's health in danger.

"I have worked in the field of child-care products since 1981 and would never do anything that would harm even one child," she said.

Bird-brained drunks arrested for choking a parrot and trying to drown the bird in a margarita!

CLEARWATER, Fla. — Two bar-hopping buddies were charged with animal cruelty after cops say one of them choked his parrot and the other guy dunked the bird in his margarita five times.

Raye A. Northamer, 43, and Theodore A. Nobbe, 26, could be sentenced to a year in jail and fined $5,000 if convicted of animal cruelty charges.

Woody the parrot was recovering at an animal shelter.

BRIDE KILLS HUBBY ON THEIR WEDDING DAY — BECAUSE HE FLIRTED WITH A BRIDESMAID!

TARRAGONA, Spain — A jealous bride killed her husband on their wedding day — because he was flirting with one of her bridesmaids!

Francesca Sierra put rat poison in her new hubby's champagne after she spotted him dallying with one of her bridesmaids at the reception.

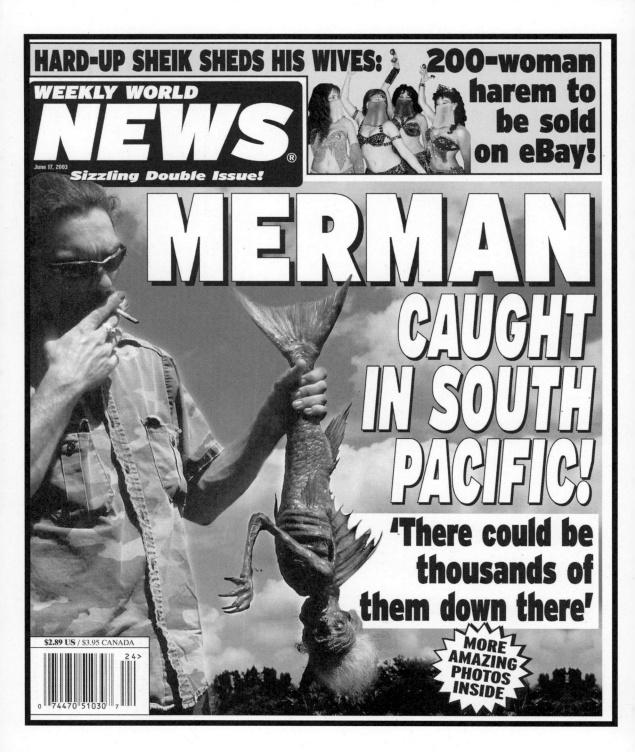

MUTANT MERMAN IS NOT ALONE...

By KATE McCLARE
Weekly World News

MORE and more bizarre species are being discovered around the world, and worried scientists say global warming could be to blame. In other cases, equally strange but much more tragic, humans have simply been dealt an unlucky hand by Mother Nature. The incredible cases include:

AMAZING PIG MAN: A hog farmer from North Carolina speaks and acts just like a human being, but has a pig's face and even a little corkscrew tail. Many say he was born from a failed genetic experiment mixing human and pig DNA, and was smuggled out of the lab by a compassionate scientist who found him a home with an adoptive family.

ALLIGATOR MAN: Photographed in the Louisiana bayou by a team of zoologists, this 8-foot-long beast has the head and torso of a man but the scaly lower body and massive tail of an alligator.

HALF-MAN HALF-FISH: The Florida Everglades is home to this frightening freak, which is terrorizing the more-peaceful residents of the swamp. It has the upper body of a man and the lower body of a fish, and it's so vicious that even scientists who normally want to study strange life forms are urging that it be killed for the good of the world.

SKUNK APE: Long-circulated rumors of this beast were confirmed this year, when a quick-thinking Florida woman snapped photos of a shaggy, ape-like creature hiding behind her home. Similar to the better known Big Foot, the Skunk Ape has the body of a huge ape and the unbearable stink of something that's been sprayed by an army of skunks.

WOLF WOMAN: This courageous gal is fully human, but suffers from a genetic disorder that covers her body with fur-like hair.

FISH WITH HUMAN FACE: Scientists say genetic tinkering or environmental catastrophe created a fish with unmistakably human eyes and even a nose and prominent teeth. The creepy-looking creature was pulled out of a South Carolina lake by an 8-year-old boy on a fishing trip with his grandfather.

BAT BOY: Hero to some, bratty pest to others, the legendary half-human half-bat was first captured in a cave several years ago by federal agents. The unpredictable mutant fought heroically with the U.S. Marines in Afghanistan, but early this year he stole a car and led police on a dangerous high-speed chase through five states.

ANGELS DECLARED AN ENDANGERED SPECIES

'They're dropping like flies,' says professor!

VANISHING GUARDIANS: Angels are ill-equipped to cope with the dangerous world we live in today.

By SMITH DAILY
Weekly World News

WASHINGTON — Federal agents have arrested a duck hunter who shot and killed an angel in what is believed to be the first of several moves that will make it easier for the U.S. Fish and Wildlife Service to declare God's messengers an endangered species like rice rats, manatees and Yacqui chub fish.

The surprise incarceration of Ted Sargo, 32, of Jackson County, Ala., and the Fish and Wildlife Service's plans to add cherubs to its list of protected plants and animals aren't as crazy as they might sound.

In the past six months alone, say agency insiders, accidents involving angels have risen sharply, with more than 200 cases reported to the feds.

As many as 1,000 others are believed to have gone unreported, the sources reveal.

"They're dropping like flies. We're blaming a variety of factors, not the least of which is more angels coming to Earth to help humans in these terrible times we live in," declares the Rev. Dr. Bruno Schiel, a retired professor of theology who is working hand in glove with fish and wildlife officials to help stop the carnage.

"We've had angels mowed down by cars, run over by lawnmowers, crushed in trash compactors, sucked into jet engines, electrocuted in power lines, slipping and falling on roller skates left on sidewalks, gunned down in drive-by shootings, and blasted by hunters who mistook them for everything from ducks to deer to wild pigs.

"We all know that God takes care of his own. And even if you kill an angel, he's not going to stay dead because God has rendered these gentle and loving creatures immortal.

"But we have to make a case to people to be careful. We all have a responsibility to help protect angels from a wild and dangerous world they are ill-prepared to cope with.

"In Bible days, angels could go about their business without fear of running into trouble. This is a different world. If you're descending from Heaven to Earth, it's no longer free and easy passage.

"You could wind up splattered on the windshield of a Boeing 707 before you know what hit you."

Sargo's arrest by U.S. marshals on undisclosed charges that may include manslaughter is by any reckoning a stunning development in a story that started developing in February.

As *Weekly World News* and other major media reported at the time, Sargo claims to have hit the female angel with a shotgun blast when he fired into a flock of ducks flying overhead.

Sargo alerted cops. But no charges were filed because the angel vanished before frantic paramedics who loaded the winged and bleeding creature into an ambulance could get her to the hospital.

The story seemingly took a dramatic turn for the better in May when Sargo claimed the angel appeared to him alive and well with a message of hope for mankind.

Skeptics have suggested that Sargo "made up" the story about the angel returning so that authorities and Christian fundamentalists who have been calling for his hide would think "God has made everything okay."

Regardless of the street debate, the feds are almost sure to drop the charges — eventually. It's extremely difficult for prosecutors to prove murder without a body.

And even though cops and paramedics saw the angel and say she had no pulse, the body vanished before doctors could confirm the diagnosis and issue a death certificate.

Sargo was released on $50,000 bond and has declined all interview requests.

Meanwhile, a Fish and Wildlife Service source says getting angels placed on the agency's endangered list will be "a cake walk."

"You better believe President George W. Bush is going to get personally involved," says the insider.

"The shooting death of an angel during a duck hunt will give him a focal point to rivet America's attention to the problem.

"With public support, we'll ram this thing through in no time. And just look at the great PR the president will get out of this.

"It's going to be better than those photos of him on the flight deck of that aircraft carrier after our regime change in Iraq.

"'George Bush — the president who made the world safe for angels.' Now will that slogan get him reelected or what?"

ON A WING AND A PRAYER: On February 4, *Weekly World News* broke the story of the duck hunter who shot and killed an angel.

TED SARGO

DR. BRUNO SCHIEL

HUMAN LIGHTBULBS

Minnesota family still glows in the dark!

EXCLUSIVE PHOTO!

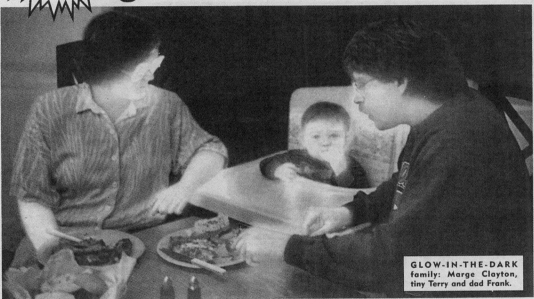

GLOW-IN-THE-DARK family: Marge Clayton, tiny Terry and dad Frank.

By BEATRICE DEXTER
Special correspondent

Frank and Marge Clayton and their little girl Terry glow in the dark like fireflies — and their skin is getting brighter by the day!

Whenever it gets dark the Minneapolis family light up the room, and no one can explain what causes their strange affliction. The Claytons' bizarre story first appeared in the Feb. 18, 1992 edition of *The NEWS*, and the family's condition has since gotten worse.

"Actually Terry hurts my eyes," says Marge, 32, a housewife. "It's getting so bad I have started to wear sunglasses when I change her diapers. I'm worried the glow is going to damage my eyes. She's always been brighter than me or Frank, but we're catching up fast. We haven't used an electric light in months.

"It's making it very hard to sleep at night. Even when I close my eyes I pick up the glow from Frank's skin."

The Claytons' weird problem cropped up after the birth of their daughter. Marge noticed her own skin seemed whiter than normal and her husband noticed that his skin had developed a sheen. A nurse in the delivery room told Marge that Terry was the whitest, brightest baby she had ever seen.

As the days passed, the family realized they were so white they glowed. People began to stare at them if they went out at night. The Claytons went through months of medical tests, but doctors found nothing to explain their glowing color. Environmental experts combed their house for substances that might explain the phenomenon and found nothing.

Over the months since the glow set in, the Claytons have grown steadily brighter. Today their skins are so luminous that the glow shows up even in sunlight. "People treat us like freaks," says Frank, who admits he's suffering depression over the bizarre plight.

Serenading banned in Mexico!

Romance is no longer sacred in Mexico — because serenading your lover is now against the law.

Bigwigs in the town of Huixquiucan ruled that performing a lover's serenade is punishable by up to 36 hours in jail. The custom was banned after people complained lovers' singing was keeping them awake at night.

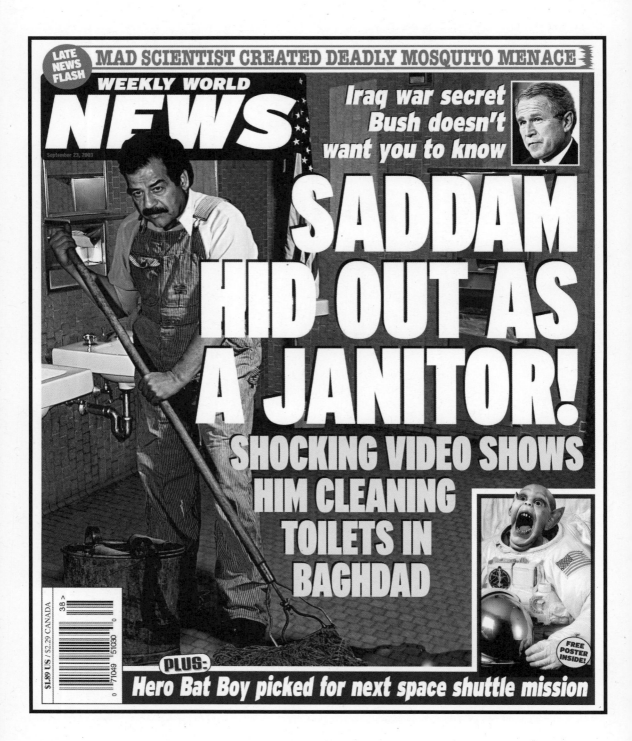

Robin Hood was murdered — by a vampire!

LOVE AT FIRST BITE: Robin Hood and Maid Marian as played by Kevin Costner and Mary Elizabeth Mastrantonio.

By SUSAN BRONSON
Correspondent

The legendary outlaw Robin Hood, who plundered the rich of merry old England to help the poor, died from the dreaded bite of a vampire — and, incredibly, the demonic ghoul responsible was probably the woman he loved, the beautiful Maid Marian.

That bloodcurdling claim comes from famous Romanian vampirologist Ivo Stefan, the founder and director of the worldwide Vampire Society.

"There is plenty of evidence that this late 12th-century champion of the oppressed mysteriously bled to death," the expert told newsmen at a press briefing in Tirgu Mures, Transylvania, once the hunting grounds of the infamous Count Dracula.

"What isn't so well known, though, is the fact that when archaeologists opened Robin's Sherwood Forest grave in 1880, they were absolutely stunned to discover it was empty.

"And when the adjoining burial site, which was supposed to be the final resting place of Maid Marian, was dug up, it, too, was vacant.

"But what was even more puzzling, there were indications the graves had been opened at least once before — from the inside.

"Even more bizarre, there were traces of bat droppings at the bottom of each pit."

Stefan theorizes that Marian concealed her membership in the Legion of the Undead from the celebrated crook and his robber band.

"However, according to tradition, when Robin grew old and feeble, the still youthful looking Maid Marian and he wandered off on a midnight stroll through Sherwood — never to return.

"The next morning, Little John found their lifeless bodies under a carpet of leaves deep in the forest.

"Maid Marian was stretched out on her back, with her hands folded across her bosom and a peaceful expression on her face and traces of dried blood on her lips.

"Robin Hood was now one of the undead."

Stefan said he plans to excavate the graves again to see if he can unearth further proof of the chilling truth.

But England's Robin Hood Society is opposed to the plan. A spokesman said: "This claim is outrageous. It desecrates the reputation of one of England's great heroes."

Top expert says the bloodsucker was his girlfriend — Maid Marian!

'It is my belief that in the '80s and into the '90s, most people believed most of the material most of the time.'—**DEREK CLONTZ,** *WEEKLY WORLD NEWS*

Oh God, we're all at risk!
DON'T KISS A COW
Madness disease can be transmitted by a smooch, experts warn!

NO BUSS FOR BOSSY! Planting a wet one on a cow can kill you, experts say.

By HOLT SMITH
Correspondent

FARM BOYS, college kids, sex creeps, animal lovers, university researchers and veterinarians alike are risking infection with mad cow disease every time they kiss cattle, warns a worried researcher.

"Kissing cows is dangerous and it could be deadly — and we strongly advise against it," says Dr. Robert Gildez, a Canadian scientist who discovered that some animals can carry mad cow disease "superficially on their lips and faces" without ever getting infected themselves.

"And make no mistake, the practice is widespread.

"For veterinarians and college professors who are involved in agricultural research, cow-kissing is as common as dog-kissing or cat-kissing — it's a natural expression of the friendship that develops when humans and animals work together and bond.

"For sex deviants and farm boys, cow-kissing is more complex, and it often becomes quite involved and extraordinarily risky.

"In these cases we aren't talking about a peck on the cheek. We're talking about unsavory aspects of bestiality that most people don't even want to think about.

"College students seem to be increasingly in the line of fire, often as the result of getting drunk at a 'cow-kissing party' and then driving out into the country to pucker up on a dare."

Nobody knows for sure how many people are putting themselves at risk by kissing cows but the researchers put the number at "somewhere between two and three million, mostly males between the ages of 13 and 35."

But women are taking chances, too.

According to university lecturer Melissa Granderson, cow-kissing "is an everyday thing for students and professors of both sexes."

"In fact, women may kiss more cows than men," she adds. "When you work around animals all the time in an agricultural program, they get to be like pets. You want to show them affection by petting and kissing, just as you'd do with a lab rat or a rabbit or a monkey.

"And with all the drinking and drug use that goes on at some of these cow-kissing parties, it's a miracle students aren't dropping like flies."

Mad cow disease causes a related illness in humans called Creutzfeldt-Jakob Disease. Early symptoms include anxiety, depression, withdrawal, behavioral changes, persistent pain or odd sensations in the face or limbs.

Later symptoms include motor difficulties, involuntary movements and mental deterioration. A person infected with CJD lives for about one year after the onset of symptoms and then dies.

"It's not a pretty picture," says Gildez. "And it certainly isn't something you want to risk getting in exchange for the fleeting pleasure of kissing a cow.

"It's no different than risking getting HIV-AIDS by engaging in unprotected sex with another person. The pleasure you get lasts just a little while.

"But AIDS and mad cow disease don't go away. They last until you die."

Man's brain sucked out by a vacuum cleaner!

FRANKFURT, Germany — Hapless househusband Werner Klauss will never again complain that doing chores is boring — after the high-powered vacuum cleaner he was using went haywire and literally sucked his brain out!

Frankfurt police have launched a full-scale investigation into the Mr. Mom's bizarre death, calling it the strangest the city has seen in decades.

"From what our detectives have been able to reconstruct from evidence at the crime scene, Mr. Klauss became tangled in the hose as he was attempting to use his new vacuum cleaner for the first time," says a police spokesman, Sgt. Peter Neinhaus.

"When he fell to the ground, the mouth of the device came in contact with the victim's left ear and, tragically, it sucked out approximately two-thirds of his brain."

Police say Klauss, 34, put up a "heroic" struggle with the high-tech, $1,200 gadget, touted by the manufacturer as "the world's first thinking vacuum cleaner."

Investigators believe the father of two may have battled the out-of-control machine for up to 15 minutes before succumbing to the superior strength of its powerful high-tech engine.

"From the condition of the victim's hands, our medical examiner believes Mr. Klauss held off the hose for some time before it attached itself to his ear," says Sgt. Neinhaus.

Klauss' distraught widow Edith, a well-known attorney, had the horrifying experience of finding her husband's body on the tile floor in the hallway — just feet from the living room carpet he was trying to vacuum.

"The look in Werner's eyes was one of sheer terror," she told a German TV station.

Ironically, the heartbroken widow says, her stay-at-home hubby begged her for the money to buy the pricey high-tech vacuum cleaner, known as the UberKlensor 2002.

He was on cloud nine when it arrived on October 21, the day before his death.

"Werner was excited about the vacuum cleaner because it had all the snazzy new attachments, as well as microprocessors that supposedly gave it the 'brain-power' to know how much suction to use," she recalls.

"And he liked the fact that it was the most powerful vacuum on the market.

Mrs. Klauss has filed suit against the manufacturer, Goettengein Industries. But the firm insists it's not to blame for what it terms a "freak accident."

"The UberKlensor 2002 uses the most highly advanced vacuum technology available in Europe today," a press release from the company reads.

"Of course, as with any other mechanical device, when used improperly mishaps can occur."

But German authorities are not convinced of the safety of the gizmos, which are now in 10,815 homes throughout Europe.

And just last week the killer vacuum somehow switched itself on and rolled out of a police evidence room!

"We're on the lookout for the device — quite frankly, we're worried it might kill again," says Sgt. Neinhaus.

— By KEVIN JONES

WERNER KLAUSS was found on the floor in the hallway with the powerful vacuum attached to his ear.

WIDOW Edith regrets buying the vacuum.

AUTHORITIES are worried the UberKlensor 2002 may kill again.

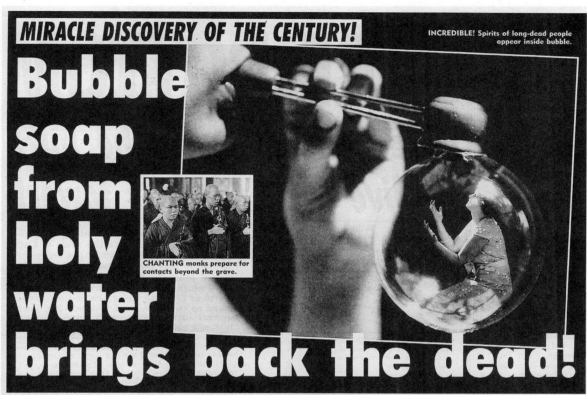

MIRACLE DISCOVERY OF THE CENTURY!

INCREDIBLE! Spirits of long-dead people appear inside bubble.

Bubble soap from holy water brings back the dead!

CHANTING monks prepare for contacts beyond the grave.

By BEATRICE DEXTER / *Weekly World News*

Buddhist monks have given hope to grieving people all over the world with the announcement that they have produced a bubble soap made with Tibetan holy water that makes it possible for folks to contact their dead loved ones.

The religious mystics sent word from their isolated mountain retreat in central Tibet that bubbles created using the miracle soap solution contain the living images of people who have passed away as much as a century or two ago.

The resurrected spirits can hold conversations and answer questions for as long as the bubbles last — sometimes up to five minutes.

"I have seen the bubble soap in use and it is absolutely extraordinary," said Dr. Gustav Amstahl, author of a recent book on Tibetan religion. "There is no doubt in my mind that somehow it is able to call up the dead soul and make it visible and audible. At one point, I used the soap myself and succeeded in contacting my dead wife. She blew me kisses and spoke to me for several minutes. I am sure it was her and that she was speaking to me from Heaven."

Dr. Amstahl says he first heard of the miracle bubble soap while visiting northern Burma in 1991.

After waiting six months for permission from the Chinese to travel to the Tibetan monastery, the religion expert climbed to the ancient holy place this summer. There, monks revealed that they had successfully communicated with the dead and demonstrated their breakthrough bubble soap for their astounded Austrian guest.

"First they performed a ceremony of chants and prayers asking the dead to awake and listen to them," Dr. Amstahl said.

"Then they mixed up the bubble soap with specially blessed holy water. A monk meditated for about 15 minutes, then blew a giant bubble with a bubble pipe and the other monks invited a certain dead individual to enter the bubble.

"I couldn't believe my eyes when an old man with a very long beard appeared inside the bubble. The ancient one was a Buddhist wise man who had died in 1893.

"He conversed with the monks for several minutes before the bubble burst. He was only about six inches high, but you could see and hear him very clearly."

Dr. Amstahl says the monks believe they can bottle their miracle soap solution and make it available to religious centers throughout the world.

"The monks believe they have discovered this important technique for the good of all mankind and that it is their duty to make it available to everyone around the world," the author said.

CROSSWORD PUZZLE SOLUTION

BONNIE

World's fattest bank robbers steal t[...]

By MACE GARNER

THE WORLD'S fattest bank robbers have left a trail of empty cash drawers and trembling tellers from St. Petersburg, Fla., to Seattle, Wash., while stealing $220,000 in cold, hard cash to support their $1,200-a-day junk-food habit.

And the FBI says the jelly-bellied bandits that agents have dubbed "Bonnie and Wide" should be considered hungry and dangerous — especially to anyone who gets between them and a Ho Ho, a Twinkie, a bag of fries or anything that even looks like it might be a double cheeseburger or is marked "Jumbo" or "Super Size."

At 722 scale-crunching pounds, Margaret "Bonnie" Stokes, 31, is the fatter of the two, outweighing Marcus "Wide" Starnes, 28 — who tilts the Toledos at 703 — by a full 19 pounds.

She's also considered to be the more volatile, having forced at least a dozen slow-moving tellers to lie on the floor at knife- and fork-point which, as one cop says, "clearly motivates bank employees to stop stalling and hand over the cash."

In one harrowing incident, she very nearly smothered a security guard who tried to stop a robbery in progress by pushing his head into the cleavage between her weather balloon-like, 126-DDDD breasts and squeezing them around his noggin until his arms and legs went limp.

The only good news lawmen have to report are that as Bonnie and Wide get bigger and fatter, it's becoming more difficult for them to get into the banks they've decided to rob.

In Kansas City, Missouri, "Wide" found himself stuck in a revolving door for a full three minutes while trying to make his way into a branch bank in a mall parking lot. A few weeks later, in Omaha, Nebraska, Bonnie got her left "thunderthigh" stuck in a turnstile as she attempted to squeeze through to hand a teller her "stick up" note.

But the flab worked to their advantage in Reno, Nevada, when an off-duty cop crept up behind the Crisco-cabooosed crooks and shouted "Freeze!" According to official reports, they spun on their heels and put the officer in a fearsome "full belly press," squeezing him so hard that, as one eyewitness put it, "green stuff came out of his nose like toothpaste from a tube."

"When you put Bonnie and Wide together, you're talking 1,425 pounds of shivering, quivering, scale-crunching flab — and that's after they've 'skinnied up' on an Atkins binge," says Roberta Cannon, an FBI agent working the case from the agency's office in Seattle.

"And unlike most fat folks, these two don't have hearts of gold, they don't have pretty faces, and they damn sure ain't jolly.

"You'd think catching a couple of whales like Bonnie and Wide would be easy — I mean, how quick on their feet can 700-pounders be?

"But what they lack in athleticism they make up for in cunning. They plan their heists meticulously.

"Once they've got a pocketful of cash, they go into hiding, hunkering down in out-of-the-way places while they gorge on all the junk food their money can buy.

"Depending on how much coin they've got, we might not hear from them for a week, or a month.

"And the sad fact is, we're no closer to finding them today than we were in 2001, when they yanked the doors off a Brink's truck in a $4,000 heist that they spent at that big pecan pie outlet near Stone Mountain, Georgia.

"It's true that they always leave a trail of junk food wrappers wherever they go. But when it comes to catching them, we're always a day late and a dollar short."

According to people who know them, Starnes and Stokes led quiet lives as live-in lovers in Columbus, Ohio, until the 9/11 terror attacks on New York and Washington, "twisted their minds" and "made them crazy. They were always fat, but after the terror strikes, they quit their jobs as night watchmen so they could eat full time, saying the world was coming to an end and they might as well go out in style," says Dr. Brent Mayhew, a chiropractor who treated the couple regularly for "back pain" and "chronic constipation."

"I watched them go from 500 to 700 in less than a year. I begged them to stop eating.

"They listened politely at first, but then they started to get an attitude about it. I told them to get out. I was through."

FBI agent Cannon says the double-wide desperadoes have robbed banks in 17 states from Florida on the Eastern Seaboard to Washington state in the Pacific Northwest. And even though they haven't killed anybody yet[...] are, adds the agent, "heav[...] armed with knives and fo[...] Bonnie also packs pistols [...] they most definitely are d[...] ous, especially if they're h[...] and you've got food."

Based on Mayhew's n[...] al records, the couple eat [...] $1,200 worth of junk food [...] them every day just to ma[...] their weight.

Those same records s[...] even though there's very [...] Bonnie and Wide won't ea[...] "never go long without ge[...] themselves a mess of cor[...] honey buns, pickled eggs [...] cream-filled cakes like Ho[...] and Twinkies," which is w[...] they like to snack on between "regular meals" that often consist of "25 to 30 double cheese-burgers each — a[...] al mountains of fatt[...] French fries."

The FBI warns citizen[...] steer clear of the couple i[...] spot them buying junk foo[...] robbing a bank — or mak[...] their getaway in the Bonn[...] 1973 Cadillac El Dorado c[...] vertible, which, at 23-feet [...] the biggest production au[...] bile ever made and the on[...] cle that can hold the two [...]

"Call the police immed[...] says Cannon, "and if you'[...] food in your hands, drop i[...] run.

"If they come after you[...] least you're going to get i[...] fer, and it could be worse.[...] she's not wearing her pan[...] that day? I shudder to ev[...] about it."

ARE YOU KIDDING?

Unlike "Bonnie and Wide," the real Bonnie Parker and Clyde Barrow were really, really skinny. Parker weighed just 90 lbs. — Barrow 130, and he stood 5-7!

Chilling encounter in the North Atlantic ...

TITANIC GHOSTS ATTACK U.S. NAVY SUB!

EERIE: Spirits of these ill-fated passengers — shown here just prior to sailing — were ones who terrorized sub.

'WE ARE THE PASSENGERS. WE WILL ALWAYS BE THE PASSENGERS'

BY BLYTHE SAVAGE: PORTSMOUTH, N.H.

A U.S. Navy sub was recently besieged and battered by ghosts from the wreck of the Titanic!

A top-level source within the Navy tells *Weekly World News* that the unnamed Ohio class nuclear-powered submarine, which was on maneuvers in the North Atlantic in late January, experienced something "beyond rational explanation."

The sub had been deep underwater for several days when a warrant officer who was monitoring the hull condition told the captain he was detecting mysterious, repeated "bangings" from the underside of the craft.

"At the same time," says the Navy source, "another crew member saw through the sub's surveillance cameras that they were approaching a large shipwreck on the ocean floor. The knocking sounds from outside seemed to get louder the nearer the sub got to the wreck."

Then, just as it was moving directly over the downed ship, the sub's engines suddenly cut off and the craft came to a halt.

"Not only was it highly odd — practically unheard of — for the engines to just give out all at once like that," says the source,

DOOMED: Famous ship took 1,517 souls to the bottom of the ocean.

"but the really bizarre thing is that the sub literally came to a complete stand-still.

"Even with the engines suddenly down, momentum should have carried the craft forward, but it didn't. Let me make it clear — such a thing is NOT possible. And yet it happened."

At that point, all the ship's interior lighting went off except for the glow of the control panels, leaving the crew in an eerie, greenish semi-darkness. As the sound of persistent pounding on the hull continued, the radio crackled and a quiet, but distinct voice was heard by the crew.

"In the transcript of the subsequent debriefing, the captain reports the voice as saying, 'We are forever trapped. You are not and we hate you for it,'" says the source.

"The crew just stood there, terrified, looking at each other in stunned silence.

"Finally the communications officer replied to the voice, saying, 'Who are you?' and the voice said, 'We are the passengers. We will always be the passengers.'

"Suddenly, the lights and engine came back on, and as the sub moved forward, away from the ship wreck, the pounding gradually subsided.

"Later, someone identified the shipwreck as the remains of the Titanic.

"It sounds insane, but it happened."

TITANIC

Now that the world has celebrated the 100th anniversary of the sinking of the *Titanic* by a German U-boat off the coast of Gibraltar, profiteering – the shameless sort that would make Mark Twain proud – is truly in full swing. Marketeers have surfaced to plug *Titanic* theme-park rides, candy bars, commemorative cruises, rust scraps and even a '*Titanic* Vodka', distilled from the very iceberg that the distillers claim is the iceberg that struck the big mama and drilled her down into the chilly deep.

To celebrate the anniversary, Guernsey's, the legendary Virginian auction house, conducted an auction of the world's largest collection of *Titanic* artifacts (Guernsey's, of course, being the very same esteemed auction house that conducted the eye-poppingly successful sales of Jerry Garcia's guitar pick, Princess Diana's St Tropez bikini, and, of course, the bloodstained tie that JFK wore that fateful day in Dallas).

Guernsey's '*Titanic* Collection' includes rings from the passengers, the ship's telegraph speaker, some portholes, and a seventeen-ton section of hull that James Cameron and various other pirates ~~looted~~ salvaged from the ship's final resting place. Several years ago, a leading appraiser valued the collection at $187 million; experts think that when the gavel goes down this time, the collection will bring in over $200 million.

The steerage crowd doesn't have that sort of booty and can't bid on these items, so for the last 35 years they have chosen *Weekly World News* as their bargain bin of *Titanic* information.

Loyal readers that sailed with us know the extent to which we have dominated this field of *Titanic* research: *Weekly World News* was first to report the touching story of socialite Lilian Alfredson, who got her beagle, Abner, into a lifeboat by disguising the dog as a baby; first to report the mysterious *Titanic* distress signal that a Canadian harbormaster received in 1974, 62 years after the sinking; first to report the presence of an ossified Egyptian talisman that a young Arab smuggled aboard and that many believe fatally cursed the ship; first to report that Captain E.J. Smith did not go down with his ship, but disguised himself as a woman to escape death before ultimately emigrating to the US, where he underwent gender re-assignment, living out his days as Ellen Smith in Gary, Indiana, where he died peacefully at the age of 97.

4,000-YEAR-OLD TV SET FOUND IN MEXICAN PYRAMID

PRICELESS artifact was made from shells and lava rock.

'It's a flat-screen HD model,' says stunned researcher

By BOB JAMES / Weekly World News

MEXICO CITY — In a discovery that has left scientists scratching their beards, a team of archaeologists has unearthed a fully functional television set in the ruins of a 4,000-year-old Aztec pyramid on the outskirts of Mexico's capital city.

The TV has a flat-panel screen and it captures high-definition (HD) images. The priceless artifact is made from seashells and volcanic rock. The components are arranged in a unique configuration which transmits electricity along mysterious pathways.

It is capable of picking up transmissions of contemporary broadcasts, and what appears to be an Aztec version of TV Guide has given researchers important clues as to what kinds of shows were popular among the original viewing audience.

"Electronic engineers are still trying to unravel the technology that makes the TV work," says anthropologist Professor Miguel Santa Ana, of the Universidad Autonoma Metropolitana.

"Meanwhile, we are studying this program guide to determine what the ancient Aztecs watched on this most remarkable device."

The hands-down ratings winner appears to be the monthly sacrifice of virgins to the volcano god Xocotl. These broadcasts easily beat out coverage of the war against the Spanish conquistadors. A sitcom based on the lives of two zany sacrificial victims also did well on Thursday nights, when the only real competition was bullfights staged by the invading Spaniards.

"There is evidence that Aztec astronomers also used the television to aid them in their star-gazing efforts and the construction of their world-famous calendar that is regarded as one of the wonders of the ancient world," Santa Ana says.

The construction of the TV set may revolutionize modern-day home entertainment, the professor adds.

"The components are relatively inexpensive and readily available," he points out.

"They could put giant, HD TVs within the financial grasp of just about anyone on the planet."

PROFESSOR Miguel Santa Ana is studying the program guide to find out what the ancient Aztecs watched.

GREEDY BILLIONAIRE DROWNS IN VAT OF GOLD

OREM, Utah — A billionaire recluse died after diving into an Olympic-sized swimming pool filled with liquefied gold.

Tycoon Gerald Monkhaven, who made his fortune in silicon computer chips, was celebrating the revival of the stock market after the recent economic downturn when the tragedy occurred.

Monkhaven employed chemical engineers to transform $73 million worth of solid gold bars into a room-temperature liquid for the festivities. According to eyewitnesses, his last words before diving into the gold-leaf solution were: "God bless free enterprise — I'll bathe in gold for the rest of my life!"

P'LOD SPOTTED WITH HILLARY — AND OBAMA'S HAVING FITS

Is it sex or politics?

WASHINGTON — Security videotapes of secret, late-night meetings between the mysterious space alien P'lod and new Secretary of State Hillary Clinton are sending waves of anxiety through Barack Obama's administration.

P'lod, recently appointed ambassador to Mars by Obama, and Clinton have had a long relationship, dating back to the days when the then-first lady was struggling with the exposure of her husband's dalliance with White House intern Monica Lewinsky.

At the time, *Weekly World News* reported allegations — backed by telltale photographs — that the two were embroiled in a passionate romantic affair. P'lod denied the charges and Clinton laughed them off on national television, but the rumors persisted.

During last year's long and bitter Democratic primary, the space alien supported Clinton's candidacy, switching his allegiance to Obama only after the senator from Illinois locked up the nomination.

In a decisive series of debates with McCain-supporter Bat Boy — printed in *Weekly World News* — P'lod stoutly defended Obama's policies. Political pundits universally agree that P'lod's victory in the debates played a key role in Obama's victory at the polls.

Obama's controversial decision to name P'lod ambassador to Mars was widely viewed as payback for the alien's support, but Washington insiders say it was also an attempt to ensure the politically influential P'lod's continuing loyalty.

The meetings with Clinton have called that loyalty into question.

"Obama knows that Hillary still has presidential aspirations," says one White House insider. "He also knows that P'lod may be the most powerful behind-the-scenes political force in America.

"He fears that the two of them can rob him of a second term and deny him the opportunity to leave his mark on American history.

"It doesn't matter if P'lod and Hillary are romantically involved or not. They are scratching each others' backs and that's giving the president fits."

Republicans are salivating over the possibility of another sex scandal involving a Clinton.

"We impeached Bill for fooling around in the Oval Office with a chubby intern," says a high-ranking party official. "Now, we may have the chance to impeach Hillary for fooling around at the State Department with someone — or something — that isn't even human.

"Let the fun begin!"

PRESIDENT OBAMA doesn't want Hillary and P'lod conspiring to rob him of a second term.

ALIEN IN SLAMM FIS WIT

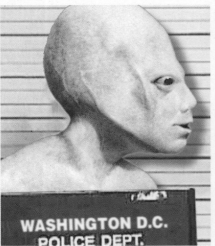
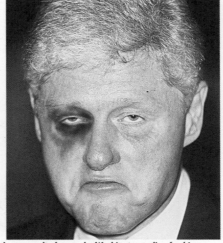

By **MICHAEL FORSYTH**
Correspondent

JEALOUS GUYS: Space alien P'Lod, left, was booked on assault charges by Washington police for his fistfight with former President Bill Clinton — shown at right with the shiner he got in the fight over Hillary.

THE AMAZING love triangle between Sen. Hillary Rodham Clinton, her jealous hubby Bill and her space alien ex-boyfriend P'Lod has reached the boiling point.

A wild fistfight between the love rivals landed the spaceman in a jail cell and the former president in a hospital, temporarily paralyzed by the infamous "P'Lodian headbutt."

"Apparently P'Lod came around trying to get back together with Hillary and when Bill caught them together again he went ballistic," reveals a close friend of the former first lady.

"After the fight, Bill had an ugly black eye and was unable to move for at least four hours. The alien is still being held in an isolated holding tank at Area 51, the secret Nevada military base and testing facility.

"Now Hillary is confused and doesn't know what to do. She told me, 'I'm crazy about both of them.'"

The explosive confrontation reportedly occurred at Hillary's Washington office just days after word of P'Lod's upcoming book detailing the extramarital, interspecies affair leaked out and was reported in the August 5 issue of *Weekly Weekly World News*.

While many initially laughed off the book story, Hillary stunned the nation when she confessed in an interview with *Tonight Show* host Jay Leno that she had indeed been on at least one date with the mysterious E.T.

"I had to go to some event in Washington and I asked him to accompany me," Hillary told Jay. "He puts aside his busy intergalactic business, he goes to the Kennedy Center with me and now he's held up to ridicule. It really is so unfair."

The senator from New York also took advantage of the TV cameras to put to rest widespread rumors that she was still smarting from her June breakup with P'Lod and had been bad-mouthing him all over Washington for cheating on her.

"P'Lod is a really decent alien," she declared.

Apparently, Hillary's former beau took this statement as a message intended for him — a sign that she was ready to mend fences.

"A couple days after the interview aired, P'Lod showed up unexpectedly at Hillary's Washington office with a gorgeous bouquet of Venusian rose crystals," says the senator's friend.

"At first she didn't want to let him in, but she knew that she couldn't just leave an alien standing at the door where nosy colleagues might see him."

P'Lod's attempt at a reconciliation hit a wall when husband Bill visited the office three hours later, caught the two sitting on the couch and "hit the roof," Hillary's friend says.

"Hillary insisted they were just talking, but Bill didn't want to hear it.

"He yelled: 'You told me t over and done with!'

"When the alien stood jumped to Hillary's defense, B up in his face and ordered him out of it.' Then they started each other."

It's not clear who hi first, but the shoving quickly turned into an out brawl, the source cla

"This alien is suppose superior being from a civ thousands of years advanced than ours, course Clinton is famous intellect.

"But there the two were, swinging at each says our source.

"Bill got in a few solid es, but P'Lod had the

HILL AND JAY DISCUSS *WEEKLY WORLD NEWS* EXCLUSIVE STORY ON *TONIGHT SHOW*

ER AFTER FIGHT BILL OVER LARY!

...age with those elongated arms. ...ey were wrestling on the car...

...ally, P'Lod got Bill in a hold ...essed that big bulging brow of ...gainst Bill's solar plexus. ...ow, that weird alien move put ... like a light."

...ng the fracas, Hillary's Secret ... protectors arrived and quickly ...d the E.T. with a stun gun. He ...r hustled away in handcuffs.

Secret Service refuses to con- ... deny that a fight took place in ...ton office. And Air Force offi- ...ho only recently acknowledged ...ea 51 even exists, insist they ...nothing" about any alien being ...soner.

UFO investigators say the ...g development bodes ill for the space alien, who has been working behind the scenes in U.S. politics for more than a decade and whose existence is called "the worst-kept secret" in Washington.

"P'Lod is supposed to be the ambassador of a benevolent race of space brethren — which doesn't mean fighting on the ground over a girl like some smitten schoolboy," says famed British UFO researcher Lyle Moseby.

"If his superiors decide that he's lost his credibility, they'll likely recall him to their home world.

"That would be unfortunate, because he's done a lot of good here.

"Besides, the vicious P'Lodian head-butt has been banned on every civilized planet across the entire universe."

Distraught senator: 'I'm crazy about both of them'

TORN BETWEEN TWO LOVERS: A friend says Hillary is upset over her inability to choose between P'Lod and Bill.

'*Weekly World News* was the journalistic guilty pleasure of the '80s and '90s. One writer called it "the newspaper of record for astrology and giant-tumor-related news"; another, "easily the world's best drunken supermarket impulse buy".'—**RICHARD CORLISS, *TIME***

Abe's ghost photographed at the Lincoln Memorial!

World exclusive

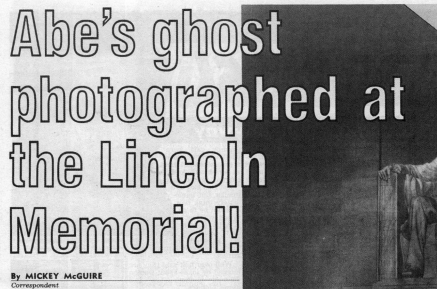

TWO SECONDS after this picture was taken the eerie specter vanished into thin air, said photographer Bev Stocker. 5-2-90 4:27 a.m.

By MICKEY McGUIRE
Correspondent

A photographer for *The NEWS* has captured on film the image of a tall, bearded man wearing a black top hat and old-fashioned overcoat as he strolled in the early-morning shadows of the Lincoln Memorial — and those who have seen him swear he's the ghost of Honest Abe himself!

The photos are so startling that the C.I.A. has taken the negatives in order to verify them. And after a battery of tests the agency's experts admit they are still baffled.

Although the stately specter has been sighted scores of times since the memorial in Washington, D.C., was completed in 1917, several previous attempts to photograph it were dismal failures.

"I slept during the day and staked out the place at night for 16 days before the ghost finally appeared," photo-journalist Bev Stocker said.

"My cameras were equipped with data backs that record the time and the date of each shot directly onto the film. My first exposure was at 4:16 a.m. and the 22nd ... the last exposure ... was at 4:29 a.m.

"The final exposure gave me a blank negative. He had vanished into thin air just a split second before the shutter opened. It was really eerie. He was there and gone in the blink of an eye."

Stocker's detailed description of the ghost matched in every respect the descriptions given by others who reported seeing the phantom over the past 73 years.

"I had a distinct advantage over the others who actually could barely make out the figure in the semi-dark," Stocker said.

"I had a state-of-the-art night vision scope that allowed me to see him as clear as if he was standing in broad daylight.

"The bottom line is that what I saw and photographed was the ghost of Abraham Lincoln.

"There is no mistaking it. There's not been another like it ... it was one of a kind, like the man himself.

"If I had any doubts about ghosts or spirits, they're gone now. Pictures don't lie."

The earliest known ghost sighting came less than a week after the hallowed Lincoln shrine was opened. It was reported by a Washington, D.C., patrolman who saw the top-hatted figure while walking his early morning beat in the park where the memorial stands.

The patrolman's description, like all the others through the years, is identical to that given by Stocker.

"There's one thing for certain, it wasn't a living human being," Stocker declared. "I was looking right at the figure when it suddenly vanished into thin air. Poof! Just like that.

"But my pictures prove beyond a doubt that the ghost of Abraham Lincoln does haunt the great shrine that we Americans built in his honor and memory."

MYSTERIOUS figure of Honest Abe approaches the steps of the Lincoln Memorial. 5-2-90 4:17 a.m.

GHOST nears Lincoln's statue. The Washington Monument is in the background. 5-2-90 4:20 a.m.

Courtroom shocker: Key witness is deaf & blind!

The chief witness against Robert Aitken is going to testify against him — even though she's deaf and blind!

Mary Aitken, the Longmont, Colo., man's aunt, will testify that her nephew stole $55,000 from her bank account instead of using the money to pay her bills as he should have, authorities say.

In preliminary testimony before a judge, Mrs. Aitken "listened" to questions using an interpreter who traced letters on her palm. She repeated the questions aloud to prove she understood them, then answered.

She told the court her nephew had the power to pay bills and handle her investments.

"I didn't consider that power to use money for his own benefit," she testified.

Said prosecutor Mary Keenan: "I have every bit of confidence in Mary Aitken as a witness. I really admire her."

STORIES FROM THE WWN ARCHIVES!

RICHARD NIXON'S GHOST STALKS DUBYA!

'HE JUST WON'T LEAVE ME ALONE'

WEEKLY WORLD NEWS Special Report

THE GHOST of disgraced former president Richard Nixon is haunting the White House, plaguing George W. Bush with taunts and jeers.

Nixon, who was forced to resign from office in the Watergate scandal, had been spinning in his grave, fearing he'll go down in history as the worst president ever elected, says a source close to the current administration.

But now that Bush has been slammed with the lowest-ever presidential job ratings, Tricky Dicky's ghost is thrilled that Dubya will save him from that ignominious fate.

"The ghost follows the president from room to room, waggling his ears at him and chanting, 'Nya nya nya nya nya,'" the source

By GARRETT HILL
Weekly World News

says. "He points his finger and yells, 'You're an even worse president than I was — and, to be honest, I was godawful.'

"'Now that they have you to savage and berate, the historians will leave me to rest in peace. I didn't think you had it in you to be No. 1 at anything, but I was wrong — you're the No. 1 doofus ever to sit in the Oval Office.'"

The ceaseless barrage of insults has taken a heavy toll on Bush, who is desperately trying to save his legacy from the hapless war in Iraq and a shameless bid to tax the poor to make the rich even richer.

"The president is on the verge of a nervous collapse," the source says.

"He can't eat, he can't sleep.

"He whines, 'Nixon won't leave me alone. Why is he doing this to me? We're both Republicans, aren't we?'"

ELVIS TO RUN

We can't build our dreams on suspicious minds...

ELVIS '08

GRACELAND TICKET MOTTO: "Don't Be Cruel."

By JIM ROBERTS
Weekly World News

ALIEN SQUIRREL GAVE ME HEARTBURN

WEEKLY WORLD NEWS Special Report

HUNTER Zeke Parsnip bagged dinner and a bellyache after shooting 'alien' squirrel.

FERN, Ark. — Hillbilly Zeke Parsnip was just out hunting for some food in the Ozark Mountains when he stumbled upon the most important scientific discovery of all time – proof that there is life elsewhere in the universe!

Parsnip, 65, shot what he thought was an ordinary squirrel and brought it home for his wife, Louella, to cook into a tasty stew, one of her kitchen specialties. But the dish had unexpected consequences.

"That derned squirrel gave my heartburn somethin' wicked," Parsnip says. "I thought I was headed for the Pearly Gates."

Worried he'd been poisoned, he brought the remains of his dinner – and the animal's hide – to Dr. Melvin Diggle, the local physician and undertaker.

Diggle immediately noticed that the creature's fur had a wiry texture, different from that of any squirrel he'd ever seen. Diggle sent tissue samples to the University of Arkansas, where intrigued scientists did a DNA profile.

To their utter astonishment, they discovered genetic material totally different from that of all Earthly life forms.

"After close examination," we concluded that this squirrel originated on another planet – maybe even in a different solar system," says exobiologist Dr. Andrew Price, who confidently expects to be awarded a Nobel Prize for his astounding find.

"Zeke Parsnip's name will be as famous as Einstein's."

WEEKLY WORLD NEWS EXTREME OPINION
MY AMERICA
BY ED ANGER

After volcano documentary reignites debate about Darwinism, Ed says...

KEEP EVOLUTION CLAPTRAP OUT OF OUR MUSEUMS!

KISSING COUSIN? Apes, left, monkeys and man all share a common ancestor, according to Charles Darwin's Theory of Evolution. Hulking, heavy-browed Evan Marriott, right, who starred on the first season of TV's *Joe Millionaire*, is living proof evolution is baloney, Ed argues.

I'M GLADDER than Curious George loose on a banana plantation that science museums are starting to wise up and ban evolutionist propaganda!

In case y'all didn't catch it on the TV news, those big-screen Imax theaters that sit in children's museums chickened out of showing a movie called *Volcanoes of the Deep Sea* because it mentions evolution — and bigwigs knew that would tick off God-fearing folks all across the South.

I was mighty glad to hear that, buckaroos. Our kids are getting enough of that evolution claptrap crammed down their throats by teachers on a daily basis. They don't need to see it on some gigantic, 360-degree screen that bombards 'em with the blasphemous baloney from all directions.

If those Imax theaters are going to show any science flick, it oughta be a documentary explaining the Theory of Intelligent Design — which says God created Adam in the Garden of Eden, just like the Good Book tells us.

Maybe if our young folks see a 20-foot-long rib getting plucked out of Adam to create Eve, it'll make a big enough impression to undo all this atheist hogwash about people descending from monkeys they've been getting an earful of at school.

Quite frankly, I've never been a fan of those newfangled Imax screens — they make me seasick. Too much realism is a bad thing. One time, I treated my wife Thelma Jean to an Imax show about whales on her birthday. The poor thing panicked when she saw a humpback fixing to "ram us" and she made a run for it, spilling a whole bucket of popcorn.

But it's one thing to spook folks with oversized animals like wolves, sharks and army ants — it's another to use the technology to drum that Darwinist malarkey into the heads of unsuspecting moviegoers.

You take a good look at that big ape who starred on that stupid reality TV show *Joe Millionaire* and tell me you honestly believe in evolution.

Better yet, play some relaxing Glenn Miller music. Then listen to that ear-busting filth churned out by that degenerate loudmouth 50 Cent. Still think the human race is moving forward?

Folks, to buy this cockamamie Theory of Evolution, you have to believe that simple one-celled organisms somehow came into existence by pure chance. That flies in the face of common sense, by jiminy. Those same people probably believe that Dubya stole his two elections or that there's an "evolving" plan in place to put Jeb in the White House.

Isn't it more scientific to figure that the Lord — a being of infinite complexity and infinite power — has always existed, always will, and made the little critters?

Let me blow a few of the Darwinists' pet arguments out of the water:

1. Evolutionists claim the discovery of the primitive cavemen like the Neanderthal proves their theory. Bull! Any night of the week you can flip on professional wrestling and see the same gol-durned thing.

2. In the womb, unborn babies have tails for a spell. So what? The whole Hampton clan who live up on the mountain back home have webbed feet. Does that prove people evolved from frogs?

3. Humans are less hairy now than they used to be, according to evolutionists. Oh really? Have you ever seen Tom Selleck's back?

Friends, I rest my case!

Ed Anger

TOO HOT TO HANDLE: Some Imax theaters in the South have declined to show the new movie about volcanoes.

158

BAFFLING PHENOMENON...
CROP CIRCLES APPEAR IN MEN'S CHEST HAIR

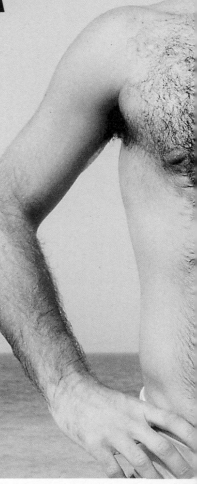

NEW JE[RSEY] bus driv[er] Malone [got a] shock o[f his life] when he [discov]ered de[mons] looking [symbols] shaved i[n his] chest ha[ir].

By MARK TOMPKINS

IN A BIZARRE twist on crop circles, paranormal researchers around the globe have a new phenomenon to report: chest hair circles!

"This is the most mystifying case I've ever come across," says Dr. Charles Dexter Ward, who is coordinating an international effort to study the phenomenon. "Aliens could be the culprit, but then again so could ghosts, angels, demons, or even some previously unknown species of insect. Right now, we just don't have a definitive explanation."

Twenty-five year old Ronnie Malone, a bus driver from New Jersey, was one of the first people to be affected. "One evening, I was hanging out at the Big Booby Lounge when I felt this funny tingling in my chest. I didn't think much of it, because I was too busy getting plastered.

"But later, when I went to the bathroom to change into my bus driver uniform, I got a real shock. It looked like somebody had shaved a bunch of demonic-looking black magic symbols in my chest hair. I was so freaked out I called my priest, only to find out he'd just been arrested for soliciting a prostitute."

Even more intriguing is the case of Mick O'Shaughnessy, a computer programmer living in Cork, Ireland. "About a month ago, I was checking my chest hair for fleas when a string of tiny white lights seemed to pop right out of my belly button," he told investigators. "For about ten seconds, the lights were zipping all over my chest and stomach. Then they disappeared. Ever since, I've been walking around with these gay-looking designs in my chest hair. I'm pretty pissed off about it."

Fortunately, there appears to be no danger associated with chest hair circles. "Of the four hundred or so cases we've studied, nobody has suffered any burns or abrasions," states Dr. Holly Snodgrass, a well-known authority on the paranormal.

"There is, however, a very slight residue of radiation in the affected area, which is one way we can tell if a case is bona fide or a hoax. Also, the hair that's removed to make the pattern doesn't seem to grow back. In other words, chest hair circles are permanent."

Though the term 'circles' is used for convenience, the mysterious designs actually come in a myriad of shapes and sizes.

"We've seen everything from elaborate geometrical patterns to recognizable objects such as fish, flowers, and even dollar signs," says Dr. Snodgrass. "The real question is, are these encoded messages of cosmic importance, or is some otherworldly joker just having a laugh at our expense?

"All we know for sure is, if you're a guy with a hairy chest, you may be in for a big surprise next time you take your shirt off."

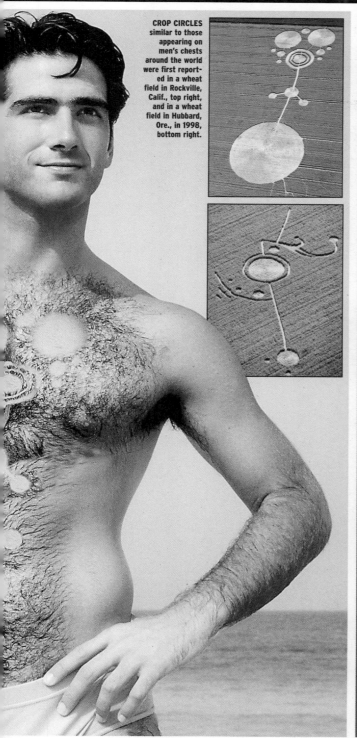

CROP CIRCLES similar to those appearing on men's chests around the world were first reported in a wheat field in Rockville, Calif., top right, and in a wheat field in Hubbard, Ore., in 1998, bottom right.

MAN VANISHES

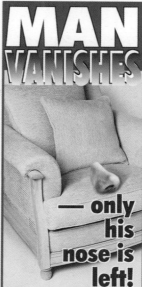

— only his nose is left!

By JENNIFER HIGHTOWER

POLICE in Belgrange, New Zealand, are stumped by the case of a man who disappeared — leaving only his nose behind.

Lawrence Brazel, 33, an unmarried ice-cream parlor manager, was last seen when he left work on the evening of November 25.

When he failed to arrive at work for two days straight, one of his employees phoned police. Arriving at Brazel's home, officers found the front door slightly ajar. A thorough search turned up no trace of the missing man — except for his nose.

"We found it on his big comfy chair in the living room," says police detective Marvin Pinn. "The nose was just sitting there resting on the cushion at about the spot it would be in if Mr. Brazel had been reclining. There was absolutely no trace of blood anywhere. It's quite puzzling.

"Friends say Brazel occasionally complained about his nose, saying that it was too big, so we're considering the possibility that he removed it in a fit of anger and then ran off when he realized the rashness of what he'd done. But why did he then just up and leave?

"As yet, no one nose."

HOMELAND SECURITY ALERT

TINY TERRORISTS DISGUISED AS GARDEN GNOMES!

DON'T let its small size fool you. This little lawn terrorist is packed with enough explosives to blow away an entire neighborhood!

By RICK DIXON
Correspondent

TINY, bearded terrorists from the Middle East are infiltrating the United States — disguised as garden gnomes.

"These guys are typical Al Qaeda operatives," says a top CIA source, "with beards down to their belt buckles and a burning hatred for all things American.

"But they are tiny and are being shipped into this country disguised as garden gnomes. A suicide gnome may be small, but he can still strap on a lot of explosives, walk into a crowded mall and . . . BOOM!"

The terrorist gnomes are the result of a genetic breeding program that began in the early 1970s, a joint effort of Libya, Iraq and Iran with Chinese medical advisers.

It was Iraqi tyrant Saddam Hussein and Al Qaeda mastermind Osama Bin Laden who first realized that garden gnomes stood in the front yards of millions of homes in the U.S.

"So what better cover for a terrorist than to pose as a harmless gnome until the time comes to strike?" the CIA source asks. "You can pass a garden gnome hundreds of times and never suspect that a human heart beating with hate lies within."

Acting on advice from his closest advisers, President Bush reportedly plans to ask law enforcers and citizens with guns to put every garden gnome in the nation to what he calls "the .44 Magnum Test."

"Basically," says a White House source, "you fire a .44 Magnum round into the gnome. If the bullet just blows a big hole in the little fellow and nothing else happens, then he's a real gnome.

"But if the gnome starts squealing like a stuck pig and bleeds all over the place, then you've nailed yourself an Al Qaeda for sure.

"Of course, you don't have to use a .44 unless you already have one. Police and federal agents will use standard issue 9mm semi-automatics and .357-caliber revolvers.

"The president isn't really up on his guns."

As threatening and dangerous as the garden-gnome terror threat seems to be, the plan to start shooting them like ducks in a gallery has frightened some people — and outraged others.

A spokesman for Citizens Against the Improper and Excessive Use of Guns, in Washington, says the group is concerned about public safety if the plan is enacted.

"Somebody's going to get killed if people start shooting at garden gnomes," he says. "Bullets will be flying everywhere, and you know in the excitement someone's going to pick off a child.

"There has to be a better way to fight Al Qaeda. This is a terrifying development in the war on terror."

Also fuming is the 10,000-member Society for the Proliferation of Garden Gnomes, a collector's group that promotes the decoration of American lawns with the leprechaun-like statues.

Members say that by associating garden gnomes with terrorists — and declaring open season on them — the federal government "is pretty much telling Americans that garden gnomes are persona non grata."

"Nobody in their right mind is going to display a gnome once FBI agents start hopping out of black sedans and blowing them off the lawn," says a spokesman for the Minneapolis-based group.

On the other side of the debate, pro-gun groups, self-styled patriots and right-wing militias are licking their chops over the chance to help keep America safe from Al Qaeda.

"This isn't target practice — this is the real thing," explains a gun lover in Houston. "Bleeding hearts and Nervous Nellies may be complaining now, but they'll change their tune after we nail a few terrorists."

Meanwhile, in Washington, President Bush is said to be contemplating the best way to tell the public about the garden-gnome threat without causing national panic.

TOP TERRORISM TIPS

From the Federal Emergency Management Agency:

● Be alert and aware of the surrounding area. The very nature of terrorism suggests that there may be little or no warning.

● Take precautions when traveling. Be aware of conspicuous or unusual behavior. Do not accept packages from strangers. Do not leave luggage unattended.

● Learn where emergency exits are located. Think ahead about how to evacuate a building, subway or congested public area in a hurry. Learn where staircases are located.

● Notice your immediate surroundings. Be aware of heavy or breakable objects that could move, fall or break in an explosion.

BUSH TO PARDON HILLARY — FOR FASHION CRIMES!

By BRETT ANNISTON

IN WHAT could be a hopeful sign that President Bush is striving to mend fences with Democrats, he's reportedly planning to issue his first-ever pardon — to Sen. Hillary Clinton for her many fashion crimes!

According to a leaked White House memo, the pardon will cover a host of alleged misdeeds, "including Mrs. Clinton's garish 'hippie' headbands, ill-fitting pink business suits and visible panty lines." The memo was obtained by political analyst George Bensing, who published excerpts in his on-line newsletter.

"The pardon is sweeping and generous, covering the entire period from Hillary's awkward early days as First Lady to the present," he writes.

Hillary's fashion sense — or lack of it — has long been derided. Never seeming at ease, she's experimented with a succession of not-quite-right hairdos, hats and color schemes — plus those notorious headbands.

"Hillary's headbands look like something you'd find at a discount drugstore," Bensing notes. "If Bush is willing to overlook a fashion crime like that, he's really must be set on uniting the country."

Instead of expressing gratitude, the New York Senator seemed irked when told about the memo.

Says an aide: "Sen. Clinton feels she has exquisite taste in clothing and suspects her right-wing enemies concocted this memo as an insult."

THANKSGIVING DAY 'turkey ready for the oven outfit,' Macy's Parade dinner gowns, and hideous, polka-dot blouses, landed Hillary in trouble with the fashion police.

FASHION POLICE Official Citation
- ✓ Polka dots
- ✓ Pirate-wear
- ✓ Criminal couture
- ✓ Safari sheik
- ✓ Faux pilgrim

5 teens miraculously saved when a...

BABY PARTS LAKE LIKE MOSES PARTED

By MICHAEL ROVIN

SAWYER, Mich. — "We are blessed, that's for sure," John Aaron told *Weekly World News*. "I'm not sure where this is all going to lead, but our family is on a very exciting journey."

A year ago, John and his wife Rachel would not have believed what fate had in store for them.

To begin with, their doctor had just informed them that Rachel couldn't have children.

"We were devastated at first, but we took it as a sign from God," said the pragmatic John. "There are so many orphaned or forgotten children in the world that we decided to adopt. We contacted an agency and were told that a Middle Eastern baby needed a home. We offered to give him one."

The Aarons were selected and the 3-month-old child arrived within days. They called him Marshal.

"He was beautiful and so well behaved," said Rachel. "As soon as I held him, I knew he was ours."

The Aarons took Marshal everywhere — to the park, to the movies, and also to church. One Sunday, shortly after Marshal's first birthday, the priest delivered a sermon about the importance of following the Ten Commandments.

"Father Ramer talked about Moses and how he performed the miracles of God, liberating the Children of Israel and parting the Red Sea," said Rachel. "Marshal was very quiet during the service. I thought he was sleeping, but when I looked at him I saw that he actually seemed to be listening."

"After church we went to Warren Dunes Beach on Lake Michigan for a picnic," John said. "No sooner had we spread our blanket on the crowded beach than we

STUNNED PARENTS John and Rachel Aaron could not believe their eyes when their one-year-old son Marshal stood on his own and parted the waters of Lake Michigan.

heard a crash offshore. Two motorboats had collided and one of them had overturned. I could see from the frantic arm-waving that there were five teenagers, and none of them was wearing a life jacket."

"Two lifeguards rushed out in a dinghy but we didn't think they would get there in time," Rachel said. "Just then I noticed that Marshal had left the blanket. I saw him crawling near the edge of the lake. Then he rose unsteadily and stretched his arms toward the water."

What happened then was as unbelievable as it was unexpected. The surface of the lake began to ripple, then tremble, and then the water exploded from the middle, two huge waves folding back on themselves.

"There was a lot of spray at first, but when it cleared we could see that there was a path from the beach to the teenagers," John said. "It was astonishing!

"The waters had parted and the kids were lying on the lake bed, dirty but unha[rmed]."

The lifeguards left the[ir dinghy] and carried the teens b[ack to] shore. When they were saf[e, Mar]shal lowered his arms a[nd the] waters returned to normal.

"In all the hubbub no o[ne had] noticed our little boy," Rach[el said]. "To them, this was just som[e kind of] tidal phenomenon. To us, [it sug]gested something much mo[re]."

MICHIGAN RED SEA!

Is this child God's messenger ... a descendant of the Deliverer?

PHOTOGRAPHIC documentation of the incredible event was provided by a weather satellite over the Great Lakes region.

dumbfounded parents eir son to the Lansing University of Theology, where Professor Charles Brenner taught an advanced class in Patriarchs of Old Testament.

called friends in the holy land asked for help in accessing Marshal's sealed records," Professor Brenner said. "Marshal was born in the land of Moab, which is located across the River Jordan from Israel. Now, it may be a coincidence but Moses died in Moab. It is remotely possible that this boy is descended from the Deliverer himself and, when confronted by tragedy, called on some of the miraculous abilities bestowed by God."

The Aarons were amazed, proud — and uncertain.

"We weren't sure how this would affect Marshal's life," said John. "Did it mean he had some higher calling? Or was this just some weird, weird phenomenon that our baby had nothing to do with? We just don't know."

In the days that followed, Marshal went back to being 'just a baby.' Soon, the Aarons began to believe that the event was in fact simply a bizarre natural event. The baby had probably just raised his arms to protect himself from the strong wind that parted the lake.

A few months later, the family was relaxing in the family room after dinner. John was watching the news and Rachel was reading a book. Marshal was playing with finger paints on a mat in front of the fireplace.

"Suddenly, the logs in the fireplace caught fire," John said. "I shouted to Marshal to stay away as I reached for him. He stared ahead and said, 'Yes, Father.'

"The strange thing was — I don't think he was talking to me," John said.

The couple doesn't believe it was another freak wind that came down the chimney and stirred an ember.

"We don't know what it is," John said. "But as I told you earlier, one thing I do know: Our family has embarked on a strange and very exciting journey!"

'DON'T F[
YOUR W[
A GOOD

'CT-CHECK
Y OUT OF
STORY'

—EDDIE CLONTZ,
FORMER COPY EDITOR,
WEEKLY WORLD NEWS

EXPLORER DISCOVERS 'THEM THAR HILLS'

MEDICAL SHOCKER
Transplanted organ is actually a MUSICAL organ – and the music's driving him crazy!

WEEKLY WORLD NEWS®
THE WORLD'S ONLY RELIABLE NEWSPAPER

EXCLUSIVE!

TIME-TRAVEL DOG FROM FUTURE HELD CAPTIVE!

In the year 2406, highly evolved canines are fighting man for independence... and they want to stop euthanasia NOW!
See Pages 26-27

FEBRUARY 27, 2006
$2.99 US / $3.95 CANADA

CONVENIENCE STORE FINED FOR BEING INCONVENIENT

WEEKLY WORLD NEWS

Issue 18, 2011

CRYSTAL SKULL PLAYS BOB NEWHART RERUNS!

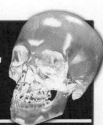

DOC KEEPS WIFE'S HEAD ALIVE!

SPECIAL REPORT

HER HEAD HAS SURVIVED FOR SEVEN YEARS!

SPACE ALIEN MURDERED!
– E.T. SHOT TO DEATH BY RUSSIAN SOLDIER!

BEACH PARTY TERROR!

By DICK SIEGEL

SANTA BARBARA, Calif. — Last week, a hideous manfish from the primordial past surfaced from the depths of the Pacific to terrorize hapless beachgoers!

"I have no doubt that it was the legendary 'Manacuda,'" said lifeguard Will Sampsen. "My granddad is a member of the Chumash tribe and he used to talk about it all the time. He said his ancestors saw the manfish a lot when they came to the beach and shared a smoking pot full of dried seaweed."

Though the true nature of the creature is unknown, the facts of the attack are indisputable.

"It had been a perfect day at the beach," 21-year-old surfer Dean Janson told *Weekly World News*. "Thanks to an off-shore quake the waves were major. We had been hangin' 10 since sunrise so we were totally wiped by the time the sun was setting. We broke out the coolers, got a slab of cow spinnin' on the spit, and Arlo started wailing on his guitar. It was just another sweet evening at Party Beach — or so we thought."

Soon, Janson began arguing with his girl friend, 18-year-old blonde beauty, Patti Wilson, who was advocating the health benefits of organic fondue over beef. As the row became more heated, Patti got up and went for a solo swim.

"I didn't try to talk her out of it," Janson admitted. "When Patti gets that way it's best to just let her cool off. There was still a lot of light out, so I figured she'd be safe."

The lithe, bikini clad surfer girl stepped into the waves and dove into a large breaker. When she emerged, she wiped the salt water from her eyes — and then she saw it!

"Patti let out such a cry. I thought she'd been stung by a jellyfish," her friend Mindi Pilson said.

"She started splashing toward shore, screaming something was chasing I knew it wasn't Jan 'cause he was with me mean, uh, sitting near Then I saw it too! A hide creature emerging from surf!"

Patti — who we in viewed in a padded obse tion ward of the Santa

ATTACK OF THE MANACUDA

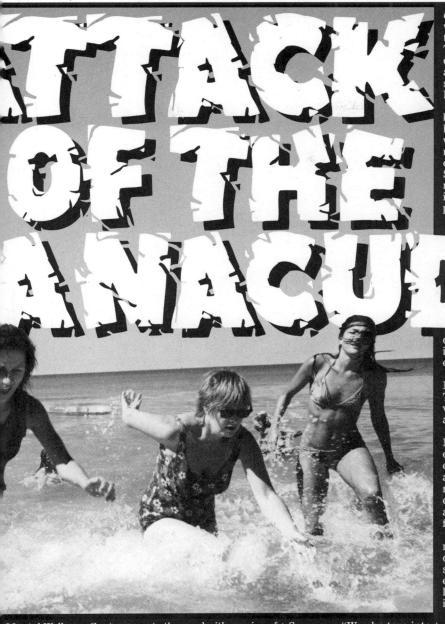

...Mental Wellness Center ...cked up the story.

"The thing was all scaly ... smelled like fish," she ... "It was about 20 feet tall ... growled, almost like a ..., except there was a kind ...rgle like a shark. Not that ...r heard a shark. It was ... like my dad when he ...les. The monster knocked me to the sand with a swipe of his huge hand. If it wasn't for Will Sampsen pulling me away, he would have crushed me into a sand Patti."

Kicking over several coolers, the Manacuda made his way to the slab of beef turning on the spit.

"I guess the smell was what attracted him," said Sampsen. "Way he tore into that side, he was obviously real hungry."

The surfers grabbed whatever they could — bottles of beer, containers of sun tan lotion, beach umbrellas, sandals and Frisbees — and began chucking them at the malevolent party crasher.

"Arlo even snapped a towel at its butt!" Janson said with amazement. "He was either real brave or real drunk. The manfish just grabbed the dude and chucked him against a dune buggy. Knocked him silly. Lucky he'd set down his Fender. That beaut's vintage."

As the Manacuda ate the beef, Sampsen snuck up behind and struck the intruder with an oar from his inflatable raft. The blow caught the creature squarely on the neck. Stunned, the Manacuda reeled forward and stumbled into the campfire. Howling in pain, the aquatic horror dropped the spit, dashed back into the surf and quickly swam off.

The next day, Dr. Steffen Mitchell, an ichthyologist from Tenney Junior College, reviewed the surfers' testimony and digital photographs.

"We believe this so-called Manacuda is the lone survivor of an ancient race of amphibious beings," he said. "There are legends that these humanoids traded with the ancient Chumash until some cataclysmic event cut them off from the beach.

"We suspect it was the famous Pacific Trench landslide of 1688. It's likely that the offshore tremor on the morning of the attack released the poor, lost creature for the first time in centuries."

"I don't care what its sob story is," muttered Patti. "I never want to see it again."

Another meeting between Patti and the beast is unlikely, since the teenager's stay at the Center is open-ended.

Weekly World News will continue to watch the beach and report on any other sightings of this remarkable creature.

A WINK IS AS GOOD AS A SMILE TO BABY EMOTICON!

By DICK SIEGEL

PAISLEY PARK, Va. — Obstetricians at Prince Memorial Hospital were shocked and mystified when they delivered a baby that was unique — yet strangely familiar.

"We were worried from the very first," delivering physician Dr. Bernard Christian told Weekly World News. "Mrs. Edwina Blanke had been complaining of strange pains for weeks before. Everything seemed fine in the sonogram, although we couldn't see clearly defined facial features, which is common with this technology. We told her to take it easy and sent her home."

Prior to her pregnancy, Mrs. Blanke had been working in Accounts Receivable for an insurance company. After being granted maternity leave during her arduous ninth month, Mrs. Blanke remained in touch with friends and co-workers via the Internet.

When the 10-pound boy was finally born, the doctors were shocked when it emerged with a 'happy' emoticon face, just like the ones used to express emotion on-line! Baby Emoticon — as the child was named — had sharp edged punctuation for a face.

Within minutes he also proved to have an array of graphic expressions, from a sad face to an eye-rolling wink to an evil grin.

A hospital-mandated investigation into Mrs. Blanke's pregnancy revealed that her desktop monitor had faulty shielding which bombarded the mother with a steady stream of cathode rays.

This radiation had transmitted her emoticon chat-graphics directly to the womb, thus altering the child's physiognomy.

Doctors offered to perform radical plastic surgery on the child but Mrs. Blanke was reluctant to subject her newborn to that trauma.

"At least I can tell exactly how Emoticon feels with just one look," she said, "whether he's happy, sad or bored. And for a new mother, that can be quite a relief."

Dr. Christian added this caution: "In the future, we recommend all expectant mothers no longer instant message but webcam to 'save face.'"

- :-) = Smile
- :-(= Frown
- ;-) = Wink
- :-P = Tongue Out
- :-D = Laughing
- :-[= Embarrassed
- :-\ = Undecided
- =-O = Surprise
- :-* = Kiss
- >:o = Yell
- 8-) = Cool
- :-$ = Money Mouth
- :-! = Foot in mouth
- O:-) = Innocent
- :'(= Cry
- :-X = Lips are Sealed

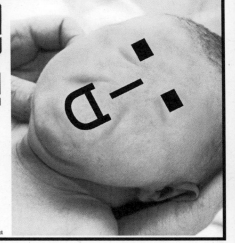

COPS SHOOT 3-HEADED BIGFOOT!

By BOB JAMES / *Weekly World News*

ZOOLOGIST Walter Barnard says Bigfoots are vulnerble to pesticides that cause birth defects.

SGT. MARCO HORMELA thought he and his men were being attacked by three suspects, but realized once he got a closer look, that they shot a three-headed Bigfoot.

SANTA FE, Argentina — The Internal Affairs Department of the police force in this major South American city are investigating an incident that could become an embarrassment for the Argentine government.

On January 11, at 4 p.m., three Santa Fe police officers shot a three-headed Bigfoot.

Similar incidents involving peculiarly mutated Bigfoots have been reported in Iowa in recent years.

"It may be that large primates like Bigfoot are unusually vulnerable to pesticides or other pollutants that cause birth defects," explains zoologist Walter Barnard. "Naturally, these defects would make them less able to avoid human beings."

What makes the Argentine case particularly sensitive is that the government declared the beast a protected species in 2002.

The officers could face prison terms in excess of 20 years.

In Buenos Aires, the nation's capital, Justice Department spokesman Alfredo Nielo Salieda stressed how seriously the government takes the case.

"There have been hundreds of Bigfoot sightings in our country over the years. They have never attacked a human being and have, on occasion, seemed to try to establish friendly contact with us.

"To have police — who are charged with upholding the law — violate that law by shooting at a Bigfoot is intolerable."

The incident occurred when three officers, led by Sgt. Marco Hormela, a 12-year veteran of the force, were on patrol during a blinding rain storm.

"Officer Manuel Ahtila, who has been a policeman for only three months, detected movement to our left," Hormela explains. "He wheeled in the direction of the sound. Suddenly, a head popped up from behind a row of corn and Ahtila opened fire without identifying himself or ordering the suspect to surrender peacefully.

"I didn't have time to stop him. The head disappeared into the corn field. But immediately a second head appeared.

"At that point, Cpl. Diego Cunas fired his weapon. The second head disappeared. I was trying to calm my men when a third head popped up.

"At that point, even I began to feel threatened and I got off two shots before the head vanished. One of them hit the target in the forehead.

"We thought we were under attack by three suspects, but when we approached and took a close look between the rows of corn, we realized we had shot a single Bigfoot with three heads.

"I was immediately overwhelmed with remorse. I deeply regret the death of the Bigfoot — I personally have no problems with Bigfoots — but for all we knew, we could have been under attack by Al Qaeda or facing an invasion from Uruguay.

"Under the circumstances, I feel our actions were justified."

Nonetheless, given the sensitivity of the situation, Police Chief Emilio Saragosa ordered an Internal Affairs investigation.

"The Bigfoot is an unofficial national symbol in Argentina," he says. "I would be derelict in my duty if I didn't do everything in my power to protect it."

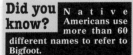

Did you know? Native Americans use more than 60 different names to refer to Bigfoot.

Christopher Columbus is ALIVE!

By GRAY KORAT
Weekly World News

AT 558 years old, Columbus lives under an assumed name in an assisted living facility in Florida. He claims that it was he — not Ponce de Leon — who discovered the Fountain of Youth.

BOCA RATON, Florida — Christopher Columbus, the founder of the New World, is alive!

The 558-year-old explorer resides under an assumed name in an assisted living facility on Florida's east coast. He claims it was he — and not Ponce de Leon — who discovered the Fountain of Youth and that its waters have kept him going strong ever since.

Lately, however, the Fountain's miraculous nectar appears to be losing its potency. Columbus is afflicted with arthritis, hardening of the arteries, the early symptoms of Alzheimer's disease and permanent geriatric crankiness.

For the past 500 years or so, Columbus has called himself Joseph Barzini. Records show he has pursued a number of careers and, in 1951, he became a travel agent.

"Joe fits right in with the rest of the residents," says Dr. Joyce Bellamy, medical director of the assisted living facility. "He's a nasty old man and proud of it.

"The only time his mood improved was on Columbus Day, but even then, he appeared to think the world owed him something."

NASA reveals lines rejected in favor of Neil Armstrong's 1st words on moon!

By MARK MILLER

WASHINGTON, D.C. – "That's one small step for a man, one giant leap for mankind."

Those immortal words, uttered by astronaut Neil Armstrong when he became the first man to set foot on the moon, continue to inspire generations of Americans about the wonders of can-do exploration. Few realize, however, that other phrases were suggested for that honor – phrases deemed not worthy enough to be the first words spoken on the moon.

These less-than-immortal words – suggested both by the astronauts and various NASA employees and subcontractors – came to light in January when NASA declassified more than 250,000 pages of historical documents.

According to NASA spokesperson Elizabeth Holscher, "These 10 phrases were on the final list that proved most popular among NASA employees for use after the first step on the moon."

"O.K., now Buzz can quit asking, 'Are we there yet?'"

"Hey, there's a river here – and it must be wider than a mile!"

"Man, we should *definitely* be able to get a date after this!"

"That's one long trip for a man, one giant steak when I get back home."

"I'm king of the world!"

"Wow! There's the Earth. I think I can see my house from here!"

"Boy, it's dark. Hey, Pink Floyd – got an idea for ya."

"Say, there's some yokel selling earthshine!"

"Incoming! Cow!"

"Silvery . . . blue . . . my butt. It's gray."

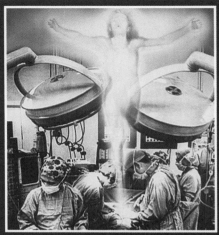

ALBERTO PORTO'S soul is captured on film as it leaves his body.

Docs snap first photo of HUMAN SOUL!

NAPLES, Italy — In a stunning confirmation that we're more than flesh and bone, doctors have taken the first-ever photograph of a human soul.

The earthshaking event took place at the Beneviste Heart Institute as Alberto Porto's heart stopped after coronary bypass surgery.

Porto's family was present as his weakened heart beat its last. So were doctors Gemma Eco and Humberto Nitti. At the moment when Porto took his final breath, a glowing object emerged from his body and floated upward through the ceiling of his room.

Eco snapped the history-making picture.

"It is clearly the soul leaving the body," she says. "That is proved by what happened next."

As Porto's family grieved, the glowing entity reappeared through the ceiling and descended back into his body. Seconds later, he revived and reported that he had been to the gates of Heaven, but St. Peter told him that his time on Earth was not yet up and commanded his soul to return to his body.

"We have clearly proved that where there is soul, there is life," Eco says. "When the soul departs, life leaves with it."

COSMOSCOPE
ALIEN HOROSCOPE DISCOVERED!

By MICHAEL ROVIN

HOUSTON, Texas — Last summer, the Mars Exploration Rover uncovered a startling alien artifact on Mars.

"It's a metal slab covered in Martian writing and images," said Dr. Robert Hale, who monitors the Rover for the Alien History Association. "The large tablet not only proves there was an advanced civilization on the Red Planet, it gives us a clear look at an important aspect of their culture."

After months of analysis, AHA computers have been able to translate the characters and their meanings.

"The writing is an alien astrological chart," Dr. Hale told Weekly World News. "Just as humans have horoscopes, these aliens have their so-called 'cosmoscope.' The Martian year is longer than our own, and it was quite a challenge to accurately adjust their calendar to ours. But we've succeeded and the results are fascinating."

Dr. Hale explained that there are 12 astrological signs, each with it's own unique personality:

● **Glowkus the Star** — Jan. 20 to Feb. 18 — You are full of 'sunfire' (energy) and destined for 'fifty rotations' (longevity in Martian terms).

● **Luny the Moon** — Feb. 19 to March 20 — You are 'nest' (family) oriented and have an espe-

CAVITUS

EMPTIUS

LATE BREAKING NEWS: Miller Lite spokesman stuns the world with blockbuster werewolf revelation!

NEXT WEEK:

WEEKLY WORLD EXCLUSIVE NEWS

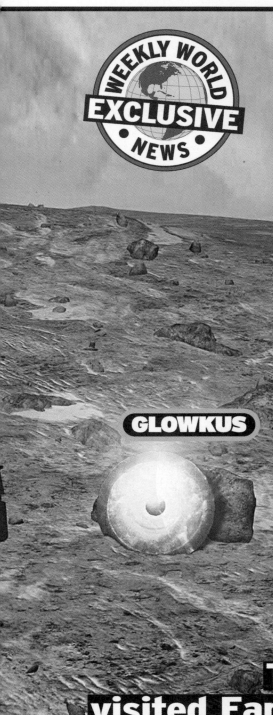

GLOWKUS

cially strong bond to your 'egg-layers' (parents).

● **Swiftus the Comet** — March 21 to April 19 — You love to travel and must always be 'crossing red sand' (on the move).

● **Inkus the Black Hole** — April 20 to May 20 — You are insatiable and uncompromising. You only see your point of view.

● **Rotatus the Pulsar** — May 21 to June 20 — You are very precise and punctual. You are a 'Phobolinger' (a creature of some kind) of habit.

● **Superus the Nova** — June 21 to July 22 — You hold your 'lava mud' (anger) inside, only to release it all at once.

● **Quikus the Wormhole** — July 23 to Aug. 22 — You seek shortcuts. You crave immediate satisfaction.

● **Icloudius the Nebula** — Aug. 23 to Sept. 22 — You're 'antenna roots' (mind) are often scattered. You have trouble collecting your thoughts.

● **Emptius the Airswimmer** — Sept. 23 to Oct. 22 — You are cold and without pity (evidently, this refers to a Martian life-form, some kind of translucent birdfish).

● **Geminus the Binary Star** — Oct. 23 to Nov. 22 — You are co-dependent. You are unable to be alone.

● **Cavitus the Craterite** — Nov. 23 to Dec. 21 — You have great depth but also a big mouth (clearly, there was a worm-like creature which inhabited the craters of Mars).

● **Julius the Human** — Dec. 22 to Jan. 19 — You are hairy but have a big heart and curious mind. Unfortunately, you allow your basest impulses to undermine you.

"Obviously, the Martians had visited earth at some point in the past and had met our prehistoric ancestors," Dr. Hale said.

"It's refreshing to know that an entirely different species had the same aspirations and limitations as us," said Dr. Hale, "though as an 'Emptius' I find it troubling that these aliens would consider me, personally, 'cold and without pity'.

"Fortunately, I don't care."

PHYSICIAN IDENTIFIES BONE OF CONTENTION!

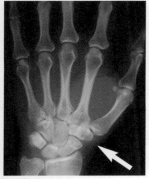

By MARK MILLER

FARRAGUT, Tenn. – Most people consider a 'bone of contention' to be the subject of any dispute. However, in what is being described as a major medical breakthrough, Dr. Adam Karns has identified the body's actual Bone of Contention!

"It's a very tiny bone located between the Carpus and the Metacarpus in the hand," explained Dr. Karns. "You can almost feel it if you stretch your index finger and thumb in opposing directions. That strain you experience is a tiny bone pressing in opposition to the Metacarpus."

Although the Bone of Contention is the first new bone identified in the body in 57 years, Dr. Karns has a track record in identifying and naming other new parts of the human anatomy. It began in 1978 when he identified Lip Service, followed by the Back Hoe in 1991 and the Heart of the Matter in 2002.

"I'm just days away from identifying my next body part," revealed Dr. Karns. "It turns out that gurgling often mistaken for a hungry stomach is, in fact, the waistband."

The Martians had visited Earth at some point

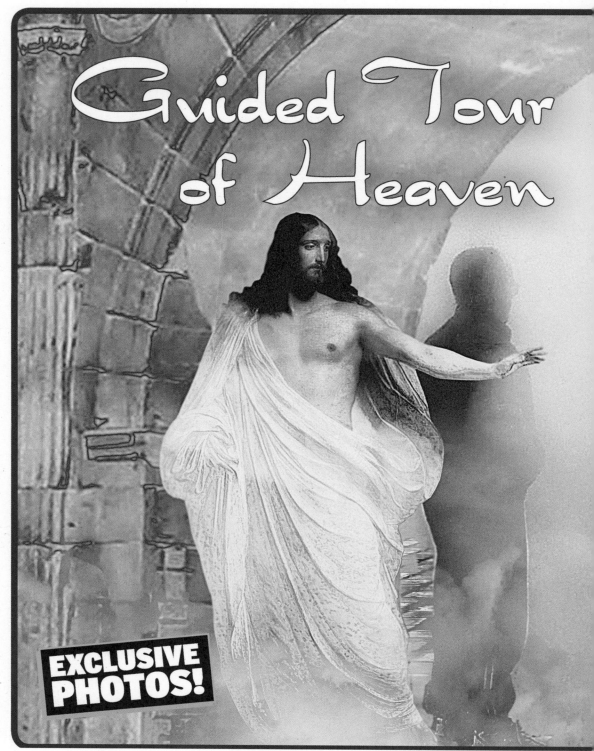

Jesus himself leads the way!

BOSTON, Mass. — After falling down the steps of the steeple of Boston's historic Old North Church — where the lighted lanterns were hung that sent Paul Revere on his midnight ride — thirty-six-year-old tour guide Dante O'Hara awoke to find himself in a place far holier than the church.

By PAUL KUPPERBERG

"Unfortunately, it wasn't a place where I had expected to find myself *quite* so soon," the startled O'Hara told *Weekly World News*. "I was in Heaven! I know, because when I came to — with a bit of a headache — Jesus was there to welcome me! Needless to say, I was shocked, humbled and honored at the reception I received."

Even more shocking was the news Jesus imparted.

"He told me I hadn't died," O'Hara said. "I was hovering between life and death and would recover to spread the word of God's glory. Because I had spent more time in a church than anyone — including the Pope, it turns out — Jesus was going to give me a special Easter tour of Heaven so that, when I recovered, I could tell everyone what a glorious place it is.

"Of course," O'Hara went on, "like so many people I had seen the photographs of the Pearly Gates and St. Peter published in your newspaper *(Weekly World News,* Feb. 19, 2007). But the Son of God took me past what He described as a 'reception area' and into the heart of things!"

Their first stop was the Heavenly Gardens.

"I've spent countless hours lunching in Boston's public park, the Common, but as beautiful as that is, it *pales* beside this. Every plant and flower you can imagine — plus a whole bunch you *can't* — was growing there.

"Ringing the Gardens were all sorts of dwelling places, from private homes to massive, residential complexes," O'Hara testified. "They were all so neat and clean and they positively glowed with a wondrous golden light."

Entering one of the buildings, Jesus and O'Hara paused to listen to a concert in the lobby. "I don't usually like classical music," the awed visitor admitted, "but when it's being performed by Beethoven, Bach, Chopin and Haydn themselves, it's actually quite extraordinary. And the acoustics were — well, heavenly!

"Next, He took me to the Museum of All Eternity, which houses an *incredible* art collection. Michelangelo showed me the new piece he's working on

CONTINUED ON PAGE 26

'It was electrifying. Every day you'd go into the office and somebody would make you scream with laughter.'—**SAL IVONE,** *WEEKLY WORLD NEWS*

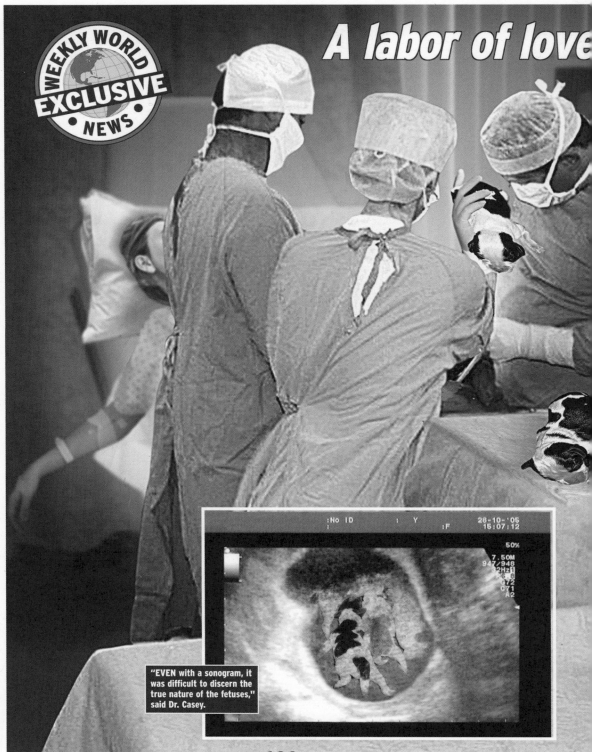

WOMAN GIVES BIRTH TO PUPPIES!

CANINE DELIVERY STUNS DOCTORS!

By DICK SIEGEL

AVALON, N.Y. — Here in a cloistered suburb of Westchester County, a woman has given birth to a litter — *literally!*

"It's an absolute miracle, but I've given birth to puppies!" the new mother, thirty-two-year-old Polly Purefoy gushed as she showed off her wire fox terriers. "For years, my husband, Wally, and I wanted children and now the Lord has blessed us with not one, but *six* boys!"

"Uh . . . yeah," said a puzzled Marc Purefoy.

The canine sextuplets were delivered by obstetrician Dr. Zoltan Casey at Avalon General Hospital.

"We knew that Polly was expecting multiples, but we never suspected *this!*" Dr. Casey admitted. "Even with a sonogram, it was difficult to discern the true nature of the fetuses. It was *very* crowded in the womb.

"When Polly went into labor, she seemed perfectly normal," the doctor said.

"Then, as the first infant emerged, I found myself holding a three-inch-long puppy by the ears! Then another. Then another. Despite my shock, I spanked each new pup lightly on the rump. Like any healthy infant, they cried — or more accurately, *yipped!*"

"I guess this is God's way of thanking me for all the dogs I've saved throughout the years," the proud mother said.

As a child growing up in the country, Polly took in so many strays she actually converted the family garage into an animal shelter. She made cages from old shopping carts to house her lost dogs.

"It started when my own hound, Senior Yellow, got sick," she said. "He couldn't live in the house on account of the hydrophobia and all, so I cared for him out there till he passed on.

"Soon, probably attracted by Yellow's mad howling, other pooches would show up hungry and I'd take care of them as best I could," she said. "Eventually, my folks made me give

CONTINUED ON PAGE 12

PUPPY LOVE: Proud parents Marc and Polly Purefoy have yet to name their new additions.

DI APPEARS IN WWN NEWSROOM

'She was on a mission — and she obviously was distraught'

ROYAL REVELATION: A quick-thinking staff photographer took this amazing picture which clearly shows Princess Di's ghost paying a visit to the WWN newsroom.

Weekly World News Exclusive Photo!

By JOHN CANNADY / *Correspondent*

The wailing ghost of Princess Diana appeared suddenly — and without warning — in *Weekly World News'* Boca Raton, Fla., office on September 10.

The princess begged clerks, reporters, writers, editors and even a custodian to help stop the potentially explosive inquest into her death that British authorities had announced just days before.

And in a courageous nod to a slew of recent books and reports that have portrayed the beloved royal as an unfaithful wife, she said she wanted to set the record straight.

"Like any woman trapped in a failed marriage, I longed to be loved," she said. "I often wanted to — I often thought about how wonderful it would be — but I did not cheat on my husband, Prince Charles."

"It was a stunning experience — something I'll never, ever forget no matter how long I live," says editor-at-large Nick Mann, who was the first to spot the shimmering spirit when it appeared in the northwest corner of the publication's sprawling 9,000-square-foot newsroom.

"It was history in the making — one of those defining moments when you realize that your life suddenly has become very, very special.

"But this wasn't a social call. She clearly was on a mission — and she obviously was distraught.

"In a voice trembling with emotion, she said the inquests that will delve into the gruesome details of her death and the death of Dodi al Fayed, her good friend and one of several men she is said to have bedded, 'must be stopped.'

"She warned that the investigations will lead to ambiguous and unseemly conclusions that will hurt her children, Prince William and Prince Harry, and also do grave damage to the British Crown.

"What I and others found especially intriguing were Diana's demeanor and her substance. When she first appeared, she was ethereal, like a thin, vibrating, golden mist that just barely held her form.

"She was crying then, but as she floated toward the center of the newsroom and began to deny having known any man other than Charles during their marriage — and to lash out at the inquest — her face became much clearer.

"I know we're supposed to be journalists who can handle big, breaking stories as they develop, but I was speechless. And so was everybody else in the room.

"The entire encounter lasted less than a minute. But everybody was shell-shocked. It was like a bomb had gone off in there."

Fortunately, a quick-thinking *Weekly World News* photographer was able to snap a picture of the spirit.

Eyewitness personnel have been eager to talk about the encounter, recounting how Diana — who was killed along with al Fayed in a mysterious high-speed car crash in Paris in 1997 — "walked on air" and "was beautiful" and "somehow put us all at ease so we wouldn't be afraid."

"At first I thought it was somebody dressed up like Diana," says one computer tech. "But when I saw her moving over the floor without touching it with her feet, I started to say something but the words just wouldn't come out."

Paranormal expert Dr. Denton Perimore often works with *Weekly World News* on reports involving ghosts. And he says Diana's appearance is not as strange as we might think.

"Spirit entities are often finely attuned to events on Earth and this would seem to be a textbook example," says the Washington-based expert, citing as proof Diana's keen awareness of the inquest.

"As for appearing in an American newsroom, nothing could make more sense.

"Diana couldn't go to the British press because they tormented her while she was alive with lurid and mean-spirited stories that hurt her deeply. To reach the most people possible and turn the tide of public opinion against the inquests, *Weekly World News* is a natural."

"We've done what Diana wanted us to do and that's to make her wishes known," says Mann. "What happens next is between God, Diana and the British coroner.

"I just hope and pray that the Princess, at long last, will get the respect she deserves and can finally rest in peace."

YOUR PRAYERS CAN [SAVE] WORLD'S FATTE[ST CAT]

TRAGICALLY, Fatty, the world's fattest cat, is at death's door. He now tips the scales at an astounding 97 pounds, and his veterinarian says the massive moggie won't survive much longer at his current weight. But religious leaders — including the pope — say your prayers could save him.

"Fatty's always been huge, of course," says owner John Mikulski. "But for some reason, over the last few months, he gained an extra 20 pounds. I have no idea why. We haven't been feeding him any differently."

The full-figured feline's vet, Dr. Marcus Moore, says it could simply be a matter of age.

NEVER underestimate the power of prayer.

POPE BENEDICT XVI is encouraging the public to pray for Fatty.

"Just like humans, as cats get older, their metabolism slows down," he explains. "Fatty is 11 now, which is pretty much the start of old age for cats. It's not surprising if he's lost what little ability his body had to burn calories in the first place."

Whatever the cause, fans the world over are horrified that the world's fattest cat may soon pass on.

Religious leaders are urging the public to stay calm and pray.

"Never underestimate the power of prayer," says Pope Benedict XVI, who recently granted an audience to Fatty. The pope is a great admirer of the fattest of all felines.

"I have long followed the World's Fattest Cat's adventures as recounted in the media," explains the pontiff.

Usually, members of the public request meetings with the Holy See, but in this case, it was the other way around.

"A few months ago, I had heard that Fatty and his owners happened to be vacationing in Rome. I could not resist sending word to them that I would be more than delighted to receive this most remarkable of felines in my private chambers."

At that point, in late November of last year, Fatty was already beginning his dangerous weight gain.

Remarks the pope, "I thought he looked a bit heavier than his photos, but, not wanting to offend, I said nothing."

The Holy Father is strongly encouraging the public to pray on the colossal cat's behalf.

"To all who read my words through this periodical," he says, "I tell you, and I mean each and every one of you, do not despair. Though the situation is dire, YOUR prayers can save Fatty."

Recently, at the 2011 Convocation of World Religions, a special panel headed by leading rabbi Shlomo Bergerman was convened specifically to address the Fattest Cat health crisis.

"I must agree with His Holiness, the Pope," said the rabbi. "Prayer can and does work in situations such as this."

The rest of the panel, including a Presbyterian minister, a Muslim imam and a Buddhist monk all concurred. As several people in the audience wept, the rabbi asked everyone present to rise and then led them all in an impromptu plea, asking God to spare the plus-

OWNERS Bernice and John Mikulski say Fatty's always been huge.

Did you know? According [to] experts, the w[orld] population [will] double in just 70 years.

sized puss's life.

Amazingly, there are signs that the outpouring of prayer already may be making a difference for Fatty.

"I weighed him the ot[her] day," says Mikulski, "and da[rned if] he hadn't lost a pound and a [half]."

"We must not be complac[ent]," warns the pope. "I'm told [he] must lose at least 15 more po[unds] before he'll begin to be o[ut of] immediate danger.

"Until Fatty is downg[raded] from the 'tremendously o[bese]' category to merely 'obese[,' we] must continue our prayers[."]

Vampire sues airline over busted coffin

By RICHARD STACK
Editor at large

A vampire is suing an airline for damaging his coffin in transit but he doesn't want money from the outfit — he wants blood!

Legal papers filed on behalf of Saverio Daehler allege that Rieder Airways showed wanton neglect in handling the coffin in which he was riding on a flight from Geneva to Paris and should be held liable for damages of his choosing.

The papers go on to say that Daehler wants 100 pints of blood to compensate for "the extreme mental anguish and trauma" he suffered when baggage handlers dropped his casket on the tarmac.

"This is no joke. We're quite serious," Christoph Capaul, Daehler's attorney, told the Swiss Legal Review.

"It's bad enough when an airline damages a suitcase but a coffin is intolerable," he added. "Especially when you consider that my client was in it."

Airline officials referred questions to attorneys, who called the lawsuit "preposterous."

Daehler himself says he suffers from an iron deficiency that makes him crave and drink blood.

"I don't want money. I want something that will do me some good," he said.

"They ought to give me the blood and be glad that I'm not suing them for a fortune."

'Keep your money — pay me in blood!'

Canada's spider panic

Warehouse workers in Canada were so worried that the spiders found in boxes of Mexican bananas might be poisonous that an inspector sent the whole shipment back where they came from.

Inspector Bob Randell wasn't sure whether the critters found at Shelly Western food distributors in Saskatoon, Saskatchewan, were that dangerous, but he wasn't taking any chances.

"Wandering spiders in Brazil can drop a man in a matter of hours," he said. "They're aggressive and can jump up to four feet in the air. I call that a don't-mess-with-me spider." — ANN HUGHEY

Holy eggplant!

Muslims are flocking to see a sliced eggplant wi[th] seeds that form the word "Allah" in Arabic, officials Leicester, England, report.

HIGH... LI'L LADY

What a meeting! What a greeting! It happened in 1937 when three-foot-tall Lia Graf, the world's smallest woman, met eight-footer Jack Earl, the world's tallest man in Flint, Mich. The Barnum & Bailey Circus superstars drew crowds across the country.

VAMPIRES:
STAKE THROUGH THE HEART!

*Stake through the heart and we're to blame.
We give vampires a bad name!*

Weekly World News never invited vampires into our newsroom, but it feels like they've always been part of the crew. The paper has tirelessly covered these blood beasts since the days of old Mercy Brown and Vlad the Impaler.

We've documented real-life encounters in back alleys and deserted cemeteries, and we were the first to report on the brave Texan Mr 'Wake'em and Stake'em' Purry, who at last count had killed nearly 1,000 ghouls.

Through it all, we've tried to remain fair and balanced in our undead coverage. We've long supported adequate dental care for vampires. But we drew the line when vampires demanded life insurance.

We clued the world in on what makes Gary, Indiana, the Vampire Capital of the World, and alerted our readers to the very real threat of 'Vampire Poodle Horror' (if you've got a poodle, you might want to double-check her incisors).

In their small way, vampires have changed the course of history. Marilyn Monroe was once bitten by one. But most of the time they are just like you or me. They work in convenience stores; they try to find an old folks' home when time slows them down.

You think you've got what it takes to hunt vampires? *Weekly World News* once caught up with the world's worst vampire hunter, Josef Demescu. Learn from his mistakes or risk taking a walk on the undead side.

If you do come across a vampire, keep your cool. Try to move into the light. Don't hug them or try to crucify them. Sure, they may be Satan's foot soldiers, but we've all got our crosses to bear.

REPUBLICANS SCRAMBLE FOR CANDIDATES WHEN N[EW] RUNNING MATE'S BID FOR THE OVAL OFFICE IS ANNO[UNCED]

HILLARY/BIGFO[OT] RUN I[N...]

By **DENNY SPURLING**

HOMER, N.H. — A member of Hillary Clinton's campaign team couldn't suppress his excitement when he recently confided to *Weekly World News* that the New York Senator is not only running for president, but has selected a running mate in the 2008 race.

"Leading Republicans have threatened a 'wild and woolly battle' in the upcoming election and we've got just the guy to help meet that challenge," said Clinton advisor Don Key.

The 'guy' is none other than a towering wild man well known to readers of *Weekly World News*. We don't mean Bill Clinton: we mean Bigfoot.

"Bigfoot doesn't intend to bully people," Key went on. "His style will be a no-nonsense, get-it-done approach similar to Teddy Roosevelt — with a slightly altered motto of 'Grunt softly and carry a big club.'"

When told of the still-secret news, G.O.P. spokeswoman Ellie Funt ridiculed the idea.

"Good grief, how can someone run for Vice President when he doesn't even exist! No one ever sees him except hunting prey in the wild or battling equally imaginary foes!"

Reminded that this is how most people saw Dick Cheney, Funt stayed on message.

"Running Sasquatch is just another stupid stunt by desperate Democrats," she continued. "Besides, the public won't vote for someone who stinks like a billygoat. Who'd come to those rallies?"

"The 'red states,' most likely," remarked Don Key.

While shocking to many, the choice is not entirely a surprise. Political observers first became suspicious when they read about Bigfoot getting into shape. ("The Bigfoot Diet," *Weekly World News*, Jan.1, 2007). It was obvious that his workouts and dieting were a

(Continued on Page 26)

...OF THE FORMER FIRST LADY AND HER HARD-HITTING
...ED!

...OT TO
...'08!

**CLINTON/BIGFOOT
—THAT'S THE TICKET!**

HEADLINES FROM TOMORROW!
Chuck Lee predicts the future!

WEEKLY WORLD NEWS

www.weeklyworldnews.com — THE WORLD'S ONLY RELIABLE NEWSPAPER

MAN HATCHES FROM EGG!

Miracle birth in the Andes!

AMAZING NEW KITE!
You won't believe what it's made of!

FEBRUARY 5, 2007 $2.99 US / $3.95 CANADA

PRINCESS DI HOSTS 'THE VIEW'
Now she's set to replace Barbara Walters!

MINI-TIGERS ARE THE SIZE OF SQUIRRELS

... but more savage than the big cats!

SMALL BUT DEADLY: Wildlife expert Kashmir Reed-Shukla captures a ferocious mini-tiger.

KHAPTAD, Nepal — A newly discovered breed of savage mini-tigers has emerged, and they're clawing and mauling frightened people with a ferocity that rivals that of the deadliest jungle cats.

Mini-tigers look like the cute house cats many Americans keep as pets, but these cats have razor-sharp claws and deadly fangs that can often leave their victims maimed or scarred for life after an attack.

Authorities say the problem came to light a few months ago, when a number of families were given mini-tigers by well-meaning friends as pets without any hint of how menacing they are.

"These are not cute kittens, these are vicious tigers," said Kashmir Reed-Shukla, of the International Wildlife Society. "Mini-tigers are dangerous and can kill people."

The mini-tigers, which scientists think are related to the extinct Balinese tiger, were accidentally discovered by a biologist during an expedition to the region to study the extent of poaching. Tiger bones are sought after and used in traditional Chinese medicines.

When the biologist picked up one of the mini-tigers to pet it, thinking it was a lost kitten, the animal snapped its jaws around his finger and snapped it clean off.

That brutal attack inspired Reed-Shukla, who has devoted his life to tracking jungle cats, to get involved.

"I've spent the past several years capturing and studying these mini-tigers," Reed-Shukla says, "and in all my years, I've never encountered a species so ferocious. It's as if they're trying to compensate for their size by being meaner than the larger cats.

"It's similar to the way a short guy in a bar might try to pick a fight to prove what a big man he is. In the animal kingdom, this is known as Chip On the Shoulder Syndrome. These mini-tigers definitely feel like they've got something to prove."

Reed-Shukla warns all travelers to Nepal to beware of any strange cats that they see in the streets. "That 'cute kitty' could turn out to be a killer," he says.

EARLY sketch for family group painting by Rembrandt's brother Maarten.

Art critics bemoan 'WORST PAINTINGS IN HISTORY'

NEW YORK — Their curiosity peeked by a catty comment from a congressman, art historians have uncovered a trove of "stomach-turning" paintings by a previously unknown brother of the Dutch Master Rembrandt.

In questioning Caroline Kennedy's qualifications to be a U.S. senator, Rep. Gary Ackerman (D-NY) pointed out that her family's political accomplishments were no guarantee that she had inherited their talent for public service.

Tongue in cheek, Ackerman said: "Rembrandt was a great artist. His brother Murray, on the other hand, Murray Rembrandt couldn't paint a house."

After careful research, art critics Aaron Twill and Jessica Oppenheimer learned that Rembrandt did, indeed, have a brother, who tried to follow in his famous sibling's footsteps and stumbled badly.

Rembrandt's younger brother was named Maarten, not Murray. He painted a series of portraits between the years 1636 and 1642 in a bid to rival his family member's towering reputation. His efforts ended in disaster.

"One portrait of the wife of a prominent banker was so bad she came out looking like a macaw," says Twill. "She was so upset, she sued Maarten Rembrandt, ruining him financially."

Ackerman's off-the-cuff remark was close to the truth on one point. "Maarten Rembrandt ended up eking out a miserable living as a housepainter," Twill says.

"'Imagine my mother's pride: "'France Makes Hanky Panky Mandatory'... my son wrote that!'"
—MARK MILLER, *WEEKLY WORLD NEWS* REPORTER

WEEKLY WORLD NEWS

Issue 4, 2011

CITY FOUND IN SPACE!

SATAN APPEARS!

LUCIFER'S FACE APPEARS DURING EARTHQUAKE!

REDNECK SHOOTS ANGEL!
"WE THOUGHT SHE WAS A DUCK!"

WEEKLY WORLD NEWS Special Report

HILLARY CONTROLS BILL WITH VOODOO DOLL!

WASHINGTON, D.C. — Secretary of State Hillary Rodham Clinton keeps bad-boy hubby former President Bill Clinton on a short leash through the use of voodoo, say Washington insiders.

Several anonymous Federal government sources, many of whom work directly with the former first lady and are familiar with her on both a professional and personal level, say she turned to Afro-Caribbean magic after the Monica Lewinsky scandal that plagued her husband's presidency in 1998.

> "Bill had a long, long history of cheating"

"Bill had a long, long history of cheating," says one source. "Hillary was aware of much of it, and that was bad enough. But the Lewinsky thing was different — it was all over the news media for months and months, it almost destroyed Bill's political career, and of course it was a huge embarrassment to Hillary. That's when she decided enough was enough, and she vowed to find a way to get Bill under control."

Sources say Hillary considered many options, everything from threats of divorce to fitting her sex-crazed hubby with a chastity belt, before settling on voodoo.

"She accompanied Bill on a trip to Haiti in September of 1998," says another source. "While there, she managed to sneak away from the president for a couple of hours to meet with a well-known voodoo priestess. The priestess gave her a voodoo doll and told her how to use it.

"Subsequently, following the priestess' instructions, Hill cut a small lock of hair from Bill's head while he was sleeping, and inserted it into the doll."

Reportedly, the first lady then waited for an opportunity to test the doll. She found that opportunity when, one Sunday afternoon, Bill announced that he was off to watch a football game with Vice President Al Gore. Hillary suspected Bill had another sort of recreational activity in mind, and 10 minutes after he'd left, she stuck a pin in the voodoo doll's crotch. Twenty minutes later, the president returned home, mumbling something about having a headache. Later that day, Hillary caught Bill holding an ice pack over his privates.

"That's when she knew it worked," says a third source. "She's used that doll ever since. That's why there have been no credible reports of Bill cheating after Monica."

SOURCES say ever since the Monica Lewinsky affair, Secretary of State Clinton has been able to curb Bill's randy escapades with the help of a voodoo priestess.

The saints go marching in!

VATICAN — A top-secret papal document reveals that Pope Benedict XVI and a group of powerful cardinals are near the point of finalizing plans to make saints of three of the world's most popular entertainment icons.

If they succeed, Michael Jackson, Elvis Presley and Princess Diana will join the ranks of the blessed before the end of the year!

"The move is a radical one," a Vatican insider says on condition of anonymity. "Up until now, sainthood was reserved for miracle workers and people who had devoted their lives to tirelessly doing God's work on Earth.

"This is the first time sainthood will be conferred on people just because of their popularity."

The decision sparked a firestorm of controversy behind closed Vatican doors, the source says.

"The more conservative elements among the curia are outraged, to say the least," the insider reveals. "They point to the charges of illicit drug use on the part of Jackson and Presley and to the fact that Princess Di was divorced and had several well-publicized sexual affairs that were not sanctioned by the holy rite of matrimony.

"One cardinal called the move tantamount to turning sinners into saints and asked would the Beatles and the Rolling Stones be next."

But the pontiff dug in his heels.

"He's been thinking about this for a long time," the source says. "Despite his reputation as a conservative theologian, the pope is really very progressive and adventurous. He's not afraid to try new things, to make bold gestures when he feels they are necessary.

"Even before he ascended to the Throne of St. Peter, Cardinal Ratzinger — as he was then known — was deeply concerned that the Church was losing influence among younger people.

"He felt the need to find a way to win their hearts and their attention back from the entertainment industry, which has been making deep inroads into their lives for many years now.

"His first thought was to canonize J.K. Rowling, the author of the Harry Potter books. But a group of cardinals persuaded him that Harry and his friends were engaged in practices that could be deemed satanic, so he backed down."

But, the source says, he didn't give up on the idea and commissioned numerous studies to identify figures that would have the most impact on young people. In addition to Jacko, Elvis and Di, his short list included the muppet Miss Piggy and cartoon character SpongeBob SquarePants.

"When it was pointed out to him that Piggy and SpongeBob were not real people, he backed off again," says the source. "But the Holy Father wouldn't stand down from his remaining three choices."

A major stumbling block was that none of the three were Roman Catholics. If canonized, they will be the first non-Catholics to bear the title "saint."

"The pope is dedicated to this idea," the source says. "He pointed out that the fact that all three candidates for sainthood attended Protestant churches when they were alive was a good example of the Vatican reaching out to other faiths."

The pope has appointed a special committee to investigate if there were any miracles attributed to Di, Jacko or Elvis — a search that is expected to take a long time.

VATICAN PLANS TO CANONIZE ELVIS, JACKO & PRINCESS DI!

By BOB JAMES
WeeklyWorld News

Did you know? The Virgin Mary was the first woman to be designated a saint.

POPE Benedict is not afraid to try new things.

EGOMANIAC LAWYER MARRIES HIMSELF!

By JIM ROBERTS / Weekly World News

NEWLYWED Barry Constant (center) hams it up with pals at his wedding.

MIAMI — An up-and-coming attorney has married "the person of my dreams" in a ceremony attended by 450 of his closest friends.

For lawyer Barry Constant that person was himself!

"I'd been playing the field for a few years, and I just couldn't find anyone who had the intelligence, looks, taste and sophistication to be worthy of me," he says.

"The endless round of dating a different stranger every night was getting old. I really felt the need to settle down, but the right person just didn't seem to exist.

"I was looking at spending the rest of my life alone — then I hit on the perfect solution to my problem.

"I wanted to be married to someone who's stunningly good looking, culturally sophisticated, athletic, upwardly mobile, witty and good in bed. I wracked my brains and I could come up with only one person who fulfilled all my criteria — me!"

Constant scoured his law books and found a legal loophole in Florida that would permit the marriage to take place. He rented the ballroom of a luxury hotel, arranged for a clergyman to officiate at the ceremony, hired a photographer, contracted with a band and a caterer and had a tux designed by a leading couturier.

Then, he sent out 450 gilt-edged invitations to family, friends and business associates.

"The hardest part was telling my mother that I was marrying myself," he says. "She's pretty old-fashioned and I didn't think she'd understand.

"When I told her I had found that special someone to marry, she said, 'I've got to meet that lucky individual.' I said, 'Mom, you already have.'"

The wedding went off without a hitch, and Constant is looking forward to a long, happy life with himself.

"There are no in-laws to worry about, and the tax breaks are fantastic," he says.

TWO grooms sat on top of Barry's wedding cake.

'It's the only way I could be happy,' he gloats

DEATH CURED!

New allergy shot developed by scientists works wonders!

By JIM GRAND

WASHINGTON, D.C. —While searching for a new, more effective hay fever treatment, researchers at the Walters-Reid Institute stumbled upon what may prove to be the most amazing medical discovery of all time.

"We were trying to find a way to completely shield the body from airborne irritants like cat hair and pollen," explained Dr. Hubert West. "We had treated a mouse, Mr. Mighty, with an experimental compound called Preparation-X that was made entirely of omega blockers. Not only didn't the rodent sneeze when exposed to cat hair, it didn't die when the tabby we were using got loose and bit deep into its tiny body. Afterwards, we tried electrocuting, poisoning and even drowning that heroic little mouse. Other than Mr. Mighty getting wet, singed and pretty cranky, nothing happened."

After trying Preparation-X on other mice and obtaining the same result, Dr. West decided to test it on a human being.

"Actually, I was *going* to use myself as a guinea pig but one of my assistants also volunteered," he added. "I figured, why not let her go down in history, come what may?"

The results on twenty-three-year-old Pat Jones were extraordinary.

"After making the injection, I hit the top of her neck with a handy propane tank, which gave her a severe headache," he said. "That proved the formula did *not* make an organism invincible. However, as we walked her to the hospital building to get X-rays, she stumbled into an oncoming car. Except for serious bruising, Pat was undamaged. That was when we realized what was happening.

"Preparation-X treated Death like ragweed," Dr. West said. "It prevented the grim reaper from getting close to living things and taking their life essence — or, in the case of humans, their souls."

Although Dr. West clarified that he was speaking figuratively, regular readers of *Weekly World News* know that the Grim Reaper exists. Unfortunately, efforts to contact him for this article were not successful. We were informed, by an assistant reaper, that he was on holiday.

"Despite your reports, I'm not ready to concede that there actually *is* a Grim Reaper," said Dr. West. "All I will admit to is, for now, it appears as if we have created what we playfully call a 'fatal disattraction' compound.

"We have, in effect, cured death."

The Walters-Reid team is continuing their Mouse-Pat research with other animals and volunteers, hoping *not* to find an exception to the rule.

"The test subjects are still going strong despite everything we've thrown at them —bacteria, accidents, toxins, the works," he said.

"Obviously, our data only goes back two months which hardly constitutes a long-term study. But we are very optimistic that the results will hold. Any canary that can survive being sucked into a jet engine, as was the case with one of our test birds, is not likely to depart this world very soon."

Asked what his team can possibly do for an encore, Dr. West smiled.

"We've talked about that," he laughed. "The only thing we feel would be even more desirable, at least among men, is a remedy for baldness.

"The good news is," Dr. West added, "as soon as we've finished our tests and injected each other, we won't have to rush to figure that out!"

New weapon has anti-gun groups raising Holy Hell!
BIBLE CONVERTS INTO A PISTOL!

By CARLOS WHITE / *Weekly World News*

Decent churchgoing people are furious over a new gun that looks exactly like a Bible — but can fire off 20 deadly rounds of hot lead in a matter of seconds!

"Since the gun looks just like a Bible it's easy for crooks to carry it around unnoticed," said George Corrigan, who leads a gun-control group that's working to get the warnings out about the weapon. "We are disgusted that people would use the Holy Word in such a blatantly deceitful and dangerous manner."

To use the Bible gun you just push a tiny button on the book's binding to make a handle and trigger drop out of what looks like the book's pages. The muzzle emerges from a corner near the binding.

The guns are sold on the underground market and apparently originate out of New York City.

But the Bible guns have been showing up in Miami and California in recent weeks and officials are worried they are spreading all over the United States.

"These guns are almost impossible for policemen to detect from a distance and normally when you see someone walking with what looks like a Bible you don't figure you'd have to check them," Corrigan said.

There is even evidence that some law-abiding gun-lovers are grabbing up the Bible guns as collector's items. "That is disturbing, too," Corrigan said. "These guns are not a laughing matter — they are a serious problem."

The situation may be most severe in prisons. "Prisoners are constantly trying to smuggle guns into prisons and this will make it even more difficult for wardens to detect them," Corrigan said. "Then guns would sit around unnoticed beside the inmates' beds — until the cons decide to use them to go on a prison rampage."

ACTIVIST George Corrigan.

BEFORE: This Holy Book looks totally innocent.

AFTER: The Bible has been transformed into a deadly weapon.

Cigarette cures hemorrhoids!

BEIJING — Chinese researchers claim to have developed a special herbal cigarette that cures hemorrhoids overnight!

The strange smoke reportedly reduces the swelling of internal and external hemorrhoids and stops bleeding within 10 to 12 hours, medical journals report.

207

MARS ROVER FINDS HOLY WATER

HOUSTON, Texas — The Mars Exploration Rover Spirit has contacted NASA with some incredible news. It hasn't just found water on Mars — it's found holy water!

The roving robot runs on solar power, and since it is currently unexposed to sunlight during the Martian winter, scientists weren't expecting to receive a transmission from it until November — if ever.

"The Spirit rover is currently experiencing temperatures lower than it's really designed for," says space scientist Dr. William Lucci. "There was a likelihood that it wouldn't survive the winter in working order."

That makes the transmission doubly surprising. First, for the incredible data it carried, second because it was able to send a transmission at all.

"It makes a kind of sense," says Lucci. "Bizarrely enough, it's as though the holy water 'cured' the rover."

The water found by the rover was in the form of ice crystals. Chemical analysis showed that the water was subtly different from regular H20.

"It's not generally known," says Lucci, "and scientists don't like to talk about it because it's impossible to explain, but studies have shown that water changes in discernable ways after it has been blessed by a priest."

An experiment conducted by Australia's McMurphy University in 2005 found that holy

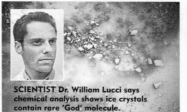

SCIENTIST Dr. William Lucci says chemical analysis shows ice crystals contain rare 'God' molecule.

water, unlike regular water, fluoresces under ultra-violet light. Holy water also seems to contain an extra molecular component that has yet to be identified and has been dubbed by some as the "God molecule." The Martian ice crystals, when melted by the rover, turned out to have exactly the same odd characteristics found in the McMurphy University research.

"The real question is," says Lucci, "how did water on Mars end up being blessed?"

According to top theologian Ernest Trinket, there's no reason why a priest couldn't bless water from a great distance, even the many millions of miles that separate Earth from the Red Planet.

"No doubt there's some priest out there who is an amateur or perhaps even a professional astronomer. I can easily imagine him taking it upon himself to bestow the blessings of God onto whatever water might exist on Mars.

"In fact, that's almost certainly what has happened."

WEEKLY WORLD NEWS

January 13, 2004

GLOBAL WARMING SHRIVELING EARTH LIKE A PRUNE!

BAT BOY LED OUR TROOPS TO SADDAM'S HOLE!

Bush plans to award pint-sized hero a Bronze Star!

PLUS: OSAMA'S CRAZY PLAN TO SURRENDER!

$1.99 US / $2.29 CANADA

BAT BOY GOES T

British leader Tony Blair

President George W. Bush

COALITION LEADERS ORD
HALF-BAT TO TAKE A BIT

BAT BOY as he first appeared when he was discovered in a West Virginia cave in 1992.

By LARRY MULDER / *Weekly World News*

BAGHDAD — The mut freak Bat Boy has emer from hiding in the last p anybody expected to see hi aiding U.S. troops in Iraq!

And in a world exclusive revela sources say British Prime Min Tony Blair asked President Georg Bush to "send Bat Boy against Iraqis to take a bite out of Saddam

"He's been training for the past months," says an unidentified source i Boy's unit, "and now he's tearing through soldiers like a bat out of hell."

Since arriving in Iraq in early March, Bat B proven to be an outstanding soldier.

So far, the pointy-eared private has:
- Taken out three Iraqi T-55 tanks
- Wiped out seven machine gun nests
- Saved a dozen Iraqi kids who were trapp a battlefield by leading them home and prot them from harm.

"Bat Boy really loves kids," the source "He'd do anything to help them, even lay do own life."

Although the age of the half-creature, half-h has been calibrated at 13 years, scientists ha termined that the animal side of Bat Boy f about 35 "bat" years. Subsequently, an offici issued by President Bush himself allows Bat serve in the military.

The mutant marine possesses abilities "f yond those of humans," say scientists, inc enhanced hearing, enhanced "night vision" ca ties, natural speed and incredible strength.

Docs also admit the half-human's sense of may come in handy as the war progresses.

This is the second time Bat Boy's service been called upon. In 2001, he traveled to Afgha to help U.S. forces in the war on terrorism.

When the opportunity came up to help out i Bat Boy was eager to re-enlist.

"He wasn't hard to find," the source says. " just led cops on a three-state chase in a stol That was just his way of blowing off some ste fore heading back to active duty. He tends

WAR!

HALF-HUMAN, [OU]T OF SADDAM!

ARTIST'S conception shows a pop-eyed Saddam Hussein reacting to Bat Boy's deadly bite.

...in civilian life, but there's a chance for [he'll] see some combat, look[s like].

[Bat] Boy doesn't seem to [mind] life in the desert, [source]s say. He often sleeps [in cave]s or bomb craters by [day.]

[An]d his unique abilities [make] him especially suited [for ni]ghttime attacks. "He [doesn]'t need night-vision [goggl]es," the source says.

[Bat] Boy is reportedly so [proud] of his mission in Iraq, [he's] even marking his terri[tory.]

[W]henever he has a suc[cessful] strike against the [enemy,"] the source notes, "he [uses w]hatever he has at hand [to wri]te 'Bat Boy was here' [on th]e wall. And he always [make]s sure he urinates on [the sp]ot, too."

[De]spite his reputation for [being] a bad seed, his superi[ors re]port that Boy Boy is [adapti]ng quite well to mili[tary li]fe.

["He]'s a mischief-maker [back] in the States," the [source] says, "but when he's [out he]re in Iraq, he takes his [job] as a soldier quite seri[ously."]

[Th]e only thing he won't [do is] eat the MRE (Meals [Ready] to Eat) that we pro[vide h]im. He uses those as [weapo]ns against Iraqi sol[diers.]Instead, he likes to eat [live]critters. The other day [I saw] him eat a rat. It was [really] disgusting."

[But] there's one big desert rat Bat Boy is eager to put a bite on: Saddam Hussein.

"He hates Hussein, and will do anything to get him good. In fact, just yesterday, I overheard him saying, 'Saddam bad man. Me bite him good,'" the source said.

Contrary to rumor, Bat Boy does not have the power of flight, but he is able to leap great distances.

"When he's approaching enemy troops, it's an amazing thing," the source says.

"He bounces from rock to rock, leaping through the air, and comes down on the enemy hard. He makes Spider-Man look like an amateur."

Asked to name Bat Boy's worthiest feat, the source cites the fantastic freak's incredible throwing arm. "He refuses to carry a gun, but he loves grenades. He gets a little carried away when tossing them.

"When we come across an enemy machine gun nest, Bat Boy starts lobbing grenades from 50 yards away," says the source.

"He's better at throwing grenades than Doug Flutie is at throwing footballs."

Bat Boy's presence in Iraq has even taken on a symbolic meaning. One U.S. military general notes, "The Iraqi soldiers see him as a "devil child," and they're deathly afraid of him.

"Not only is he a great warrior, but he's become a beloved morale booster for the troops."

Bat Boy is already due to receive several awards for his bravery, but those honors will have to wait 'til after the conflict is over.

"We gave Bat Boy a medal once," one U.S. officer explains. "He tried to eat it.

"But there will be many more medals for this young soldier when it's all over. We just have to find a place to pin them."

Weekly World News will continue to bring you updates of Bat Boy in action as they become available.

"BAT BOY WAS HERE" graffiti is showing up everywhere in Iraq.

[BAT]BOY stands ready for action in this image from Iraq. [Witn]esses say Iraqis have already felt his wrath!

ANTICHRIST IN CATSKILLS

He's plotting to take over showbiz

FERNDALE, N.Y. — An exhaustive investigation by the FBI has found the Antichrist!

Weekly World News can reveal that this disciple of Satan, destined to play a key role in the End Times, is an 86-year-old retired comedian named Sheldon Glick.

We filed a request under the Freedom of Information Act to obtain the extensive file federal agents have accumulated on Glick, and it tells the sordid story of one man's descent from a jolly joke-teller into raw, naked evil.

Glick was a mild-mannered accountant who dreamed of being a stand-up comedian. He set his sights on headlining at the numerous resort hotels that dotted the Catskill Mountains, northwest of New York City, in the 1950s.

But he never made the grade. His act was eclipsed by performers who went on to become showbiz legends — Milton Berle, Morey Amsterdam, Henny Youngman and others.

As the rejection slips piled up on his desk, Glick became increasingly bitter. His festering resentment seemed to focus particularly on Youngman.

In a shocking letter to the New York Times, dated April 19, 1957, Glick poured forth his venom at the more popular comic.

"Henny Youngman wouldn't know a joke if it spit in his eye," Glick railed. " 'Take my wife, please!' That's a joke? 'I just flew in from Vegas — and boy, are my arms tired.' That's a joke? How can people laugh at that crap?

"Now, here's a joke I thought up: 'If you want to read about love and marriage, you gotta buy two books.' Now, that's a joke!"

(Editor's Note: Research has revealed that Glick stole that one-liner from Alan King, another Borscht Belt luminary.)

The personality changes brought about by Glick's failure as a stand-up comic poisoned his marriage, which ended up in a financially ruinous divorce. His sourness deepened and he lost most of his friends.

In a last-ditch bid to salvage a glimmer of fame, Glick made a desperate deal with the devil. The two hit it off and concocted a scheme to win Glick the renown he has sought all his life and give Satan a foothold in the entertainment industry to promote his dastardly End Times plan to a mass audience.

It took some doing, but Satan managed to talk Glick out of reinventing himself as a screaming, Sam Kinison-style comedian. Instead, the octogenarian entertainer has formed a rock band, based loosely the Jackson Five.

Called Shelly Glick and False Prophets, the rout calls for Glick — dressed to look like a terrifying dem — to moon-dance back a forth across the stage while Prophets shuffle around and s Doo-Wop hits from the '50s.

They hope to capitalize on retro craze now sweeping airwaves and Glick is trying get himself booked on late-ni talk shows as a springboard his own primetime netwo vehicle.

FBI Special Agent M Stone sums up the results the agency's investigation a his frustration at not be able to nip Glick's Antich aspirations in the bud.

"Sheldon Glick has to stopped," Stone says. "But are powerless to act. The no doubt his act is a crime, it doesn't violate any state federal statute."

HENNY YOUNGMAN was on the receiving end of Glick's wrath.

Fabulous fact: Washington Irving' classic headles horseman horro story, The Legend of Sleepy Hollow is set in the Catskills.

LATE NEWS FLASH

NEW BUSH OUTRAGE: HOOKERS IN THE WHITE HOUSE!

WEEKLY WORLD NEWS

August 12, 2003

MODERN-DAY JONAH: I SPENT THREE DAYS INSIDE A WHALE!

···· **VATICAN RED ALERT** ····

POPE IS MISSING!

'He seems to have just wandered off'
— SAYS AGITATED CARDINAL

Last photo taken of vanished Pontiff

$1.89 US / $2.29 CANADA

BAT BOY STILL ON THE LAM!

Pointy-eared car thief continues to wreak havoc & evade police in 11 states!

PENSACOLA, Fla. — More than two weeks after the mysterious Bat Boy carjacked a brand new Mini Cooper, flustered lawmen are no closer to apprehending the elusive bat-like freak — who has been spreading panic and chaos in a wild and woolly chase that's taken him through 11 states!

The bizarre odyssey began when the pointy-eared mutant stole the car from a Detroit dealership, as *Weekly World News* reported in our January 14 edition.

Since then, a special law-enforcement task force tracking him through frantic calls to police from startled citizens says he's traveled through Michigan, Ohio, West Virginia, Virginia, Tennessee, North and South Carolina, Georgia, Alabama and Mississippi — clocked at speeds of up to 110 m.p.h.

Authorities say they're frustrated that Bat Boy has escaped all their roadblocks and even eluded police helicopters. "He's always one step ahead of us," fumes FBI Special Agent Jack Trasker.

Bat Boy was last spotted in the Florida panhandle, headed south. Among the 450-plus sightings reported to frazzled authorities:

BAT ON THE RUN: This incredible photo was snapped by a camper in the woods of Alabama, as Bat Boy ran to his car and made a quick getaway.

FBI Special Agent Jack Trasker

● **Darlington, S.C.** — The stolen vehicle skidded onto the town's famous racetrack, interrupting trials for a NASCAR race. "The little freak almost forced me off the track," one shaken driver says. "He did two laps, then zoomed off."

● **Athens, Ga.** — A religious revival meeting ended abruptly when Bat Boy drove through the crowded tent, sending folks diving for safety.

● **Tuscaloosa, Ala.** — A group of campers witnessed Bat Boy picking berries by the side of the road. A quick-thinking man grabbed his camera and snapped a picture before Bat Boy ran back to his car and drove away.

● **Vicksburg, Miss.** — Civil War re-enacters were stunned when the stolen car plowed through the mock battlefield, scattering Confederate and Union soldiers alike. "The guy playing General Grant was so spooked, he fell off his horse," says eyewitness Corbin Maxford, 24, of Vicksburg.

EYEWITNESS Corbin Maxford

● **Pensacola, Fla.** — A couple claim their beach date was interrupted when Bat Boy pulled onto the sand. The 27-year-old woman told police, "He snapped my thong like a rubber band, jumped back into the car, and drove away."

Law-enforcement officials are asking motorists to be on the lookout for a 2003 red Mini Cooper driven by a bat-winged youth about 13 years old.

"If you see Bat Boy, alert local authorities immediately. Do not attempt to take him into custody yourself," agent Trasker warns.

— By MIKE FOSTER

Got news for us? We've got $50 for you!

Hey, reader! Did something amazing happen to you? If so, we want to hear about it — especially if you got pictures! Send us your story. Write to: Reader Stories, c/o Weekly World News, 5401 NW Broken Sound Blvd., Boca Raton, Fla. 33487. Or e-mail us at: editor@weeklyworldnews.com

'The *Weekly World News* alien has accurately predicted the outcome of every presidential election since Ronald Reagan won in 1980. They don't call them "intelligent" life forms for nothing, okay?'—**NEW YORK MAGAZINE**

KILLER COWS TERRORIZING FARMERS!

Fabulous fact: Since 1972, mutilated cow bodies have been found following UFO sightings – as if aliens were dissecting cattle for analysis.

By **CHAD ELLIOTT**
Weekly World News

ABERDEEN, Scotland — A community of terrified Scottish farmers is under siege — by man-eating, carnivorous cows!

Farmer Angus Donal, 53, was the first victim of this bizarre epidemic that has frightened cattle owners arming themselves or heading for the highlands.

"One morning I was feeding my cows and decided to give my favorite, Lucy, a bit of salt from my hand," Donal recalls. "To my surprise, she bit me and drew blood. I saw her lick the blood from her lips.

"Then she looked at me like I was a piece of meat."

To Donal's astonishment, Lucy began to ominously approach the farmer and let out a peculiar moo that summoned her fellow cows.

Donal was able to hop over the fence just in time before the herd of crazed cows closed in for the kill.

"They would have eaten me alive," the farmer claims. "I'm sure of it. Their mouths were dripping with saliva, and they had sharp fangs, unlike anything I'd ever seen before."

Soon, other farmers in the area began to notice odd behavior in their own animals. Cows are usually plant-eaters, but these mad-as-hell cows have acquired a taste for meat.

Animal expert Samuel Masters says, "It's very unusual for an animal to develop a taste for flesh. Perhaps this is a survival mechanism for the cows, and the sharp teeth are just a part of 'natural selection.'"

Other authorities link the phenomenon to the onset of global warming. As pointed out in Al Gore's documentary An Inconvenient Truth, the planetary crisis has been triggered by actions like beef ranches bulldozing the Amazon – and, other reports reveal, by the metric tons of flatulence every cow produces per year. "It's as if cattle have it in for humanity as a whole," says climatologist Joseph Blauer.

Four farmers have been reported killed by carnivorous cows to date.

As a result, the area has been thrown into a state of paranoid hysteria that has agricultural families afraid to tend their own cattle.

One young boy was nearly mauled to death. "I was milking old Bessie," the boy says from his hospital bed, "when she turned around and bit my leg. I've never been so scared in my life."

The boy's father pulled him to safety, and stunned the cow by whacking it over the head with a shovel. But horrifying incidents have not scared farmers away from their livelihoods.

Instead, they have stocked up on cattle prods and other devices to keep their animals under control.

"I'll be damned if I'll let any cows chase me off my property," Collin McNuggell, 39, claims. "If any of them tries anything, I'll come out shooting."

Meat-eating herds have killed four & attacked others

AL GORE warned of global warming danger.

FEARING for their lives, farmers in the Aberdeen area are arming themselves against carnivorous cows.

Vampires drain victims for cash!

GORAKHPUR, India — Officials have cracked down on a ring of medical vampires who lure poor laborers with the promise of a job then force them to donate every last drop of blood!

"I answered a job advertisement," says Moksha Yujananda, who lost 40 pounds during his six months of captivity. "They said I needed to take a medical exam first. Once they put the needle in my arm, they pulled a gun and told me I couldn't leave."

Five men were arrested for kidnapping as many as 15 males and selling their blood to private clinics.

Anant Kumar Mishra, health minister for Uttar Pradesh, says the case has led to new rules governing blood donations.

EDGAR CAYCE REINCARNATED AS PSYCHIC FLY

INSIDE: The buzz for 2002!

WEEKLY WORLD NEWS

January 15, 2002 — $2.79 U.S. / $3.95 CANADA

BIG 24-page Book Bonus...
The BEST of Ed Anger
America's wildest columnist

DOUBLE ISSUE! More than 250 stories and photos inside!

CLINTON HIRES 3-BREASTED INTERN!

SHOCKED HILLARY: *'I thought he was a leg man'*

Eat, drink and go crazy

SO RICH, so smooth, so satisfying! Namwah puffs on a cigarette.

Health secrets of the world's oldest monkey!

YEAH, BABY! Namwah goes bananas at a topless bar.

By TOBUCHI KIMURA
Weekly World News

BANGKOK — Namwah, the world's oldest monkey, has lived to the ripe old age of 52 because he:
- Chain-smokes up to 80 cigarettes a day.
- Drinks martinis by the pint.
- Eats junk food like it's going out of style.
- Is addicted to sex.

To top it off, it is alleged that Namwah occasionally indulges himself in dangerous recreational drugs like marijuana and clove cigarettes.

And a leading veterinarian predicts that the monkey's amazing longevity may lead to a rethinking of the conventional wisdom condemning apparent human health hazards such as excessive drinking and smoking.

"This is an animal that has every reason to be stressed, since he's constantly pestered and photographed by curious tourists, and if anything you'd expect that stress to shorten his lifespan," Dr. Suan Yubarung told a reporter.

"But his bohemian lifestyle and bad habits obviously calm him and his troubles just seem to melt away.

"And that, of course, may apply equally to humans."

Frisky Namwah, who is reputed to light up a staggering four packs of filter-tipped cigarettes a day, was born in 1949.

It has been documented that during his long and colorful life, the naughty but amazingly hardy monkey:
- Started smoking cigarettes at the tender age of 12, in 1961.
- Tried marijuana and Asia's notoriously risky clove cigarettes in 1967, and continues casual use to this day.
- Has what native Thai pals call "a liquor tooth" and mooches free drinks in nightclubs peppering this sinful city's seedy red-light districts.
- Gorges himself on peanuts, pretzels and cocktail weenies while frequenting topless bars and strip clubs.
- Starts off every morning with a cigarette and a soda pop.

In an interesting footnote, Namwah appeared in two Tarzan movies, although one scene ended up on the cutting room floor when the curious creature yanked down Jane's loincloth and frantically pawed at her.

Dr. Yubarung said Namwah's original owner shared her cigarettes with the monkey — hooking him instantly.

When the old woman died 1965, a relative abandoned Namwah on the steps of a Buddhist temple.

But after a brief period of mourning, the brainy monkey left the temple and began his life on the streets, sleeping in alleys and milking tourists for cigarettes, booze and food.

Dr. Yabarung says a longevity study on rhesus monkeys showed that they can live up to 40 years.

"But at age 52, Namwah is in a class all his own," Dr. Yubamrung said.

NAMWAH lives up to his nickname "liquor tooth."

WEEKLY WORLD NEWS December 4, 2001

Chimpanzee graduates from Harvard!

GRADUATE Bo Bo Bellbottoms completed his medical degree in 18 months.

BABY BO BO lived in the Toronto Zoo before he was 'discovered.'

By BOB JAMES
Weekly World News

CAMBRIDGE, Massachusetts — The medical community is in disbelief after a 7-year-old chimpanzee recently graduated from Harvard Medical School on his way to become the first simian cardiologist in American history.

The chimpanzee, named Bo Bo Bellbottoms, completed the rigorous coursework in only 18 months, finished first in his class and graduated with honors.

"The toughest part was getting used to dormitory living," explained Bellbottoms, who can use sign language in English and German. "I had never used indoor plumbing before. Other than that, medical school was very easy. I probably could have graduated in less than a year if I hadn't been partying so much."

Bellbottoms' intellectual gifts were first discovered three years ago at the Toronto Zoo where he was living at the time. He would give herbal remedies to the other captive animals when they were sick, which were typically more effective than the treatments from the veterinary staff.

When it was later discovered that Bellbottoms could both read and speak, he was allowed to take the medical entrance exam, the MCAT, which he easily passed.

Dr. Glenn McFerran, Director of the Center for Unusual Primate Behavior, commented: "While it is not common for apes to speak and read, it is not unprecedented. However, to apply human language skills toward a specific degree in the challenging field of medicine is extremely unusual and impressive."

HUMAN SKULL FOUND ON MO

Feds suspect serial killer on t

CAPE CANAVERAL — A NASA probe has found 17 human skulls littering the surface of the moon, and federal investigators fear the grisly discovery may be evidence that a space-traveling serial killer is on the loose.

The mystery began to unfold on April 11, when the probe transmitted a picture of the first skull. During the next three days, it sent photographs of 16 more skulls.

NASA scientists were at a loss to explain the phenomenon. One early theory held that during the frenzied days of the space race in the 1960s and 1970s the Soviet Union had established a base on the moon, but that some disaster had destroyed it and killed all its inhabitants.

But a forensic anthropologist examined the pictures of the skulls and concluded they came from North American individuals and not eastern Europeans.

"There's no doubt that these skulls belonged to Americans or Canadians," says Dr. James Garton, the anthropologist who analyzed the photographs. "There are 11 women and six men, ranging in ages from 19 to 37. All of them appear to have died due to blunt force trauma. It's very difficult to fix a time of death simply by looking at pictures, but I'd say they died between 1963 and 1972."

Those dates ominously coincide with NASA's Apollo program, during which six manned missions landed on the moon.

"What we're looking at here is a serial killer who used the moon as a dump site for the bodies of his victims," says FBI Special Agent Jesse Sparks, who has been assigned to lead an investigation into the murders.

"We are treating the moon as a secondary crime scene and are working with NASA to get a team of forensic specialists up there as quickly as possible to look for DNA, fingerprints and trace evidence that may point us in the direction of the perpetrator.

"It's going to be very difficult to crack this case. We don't even know at this point if the perpetrator is human. He — or it — may be from another planet, even another solar system or galaxy.

"If that's the case, he would have come secretly to Earth, selected and stalked his victims, abducted and killed them and then transported their remains to the moon and dumped them there.

"Of course, there's another — much darker — possibility. Given the probable dates of death, it's possible that these people were killed by a human — probably an Apollo astronaut, who used his access to the lunar landers to get the bodies of his victims to the moon.

"No one wants to seriously contemplate this. That one of these men, long hailed as a hero of the space program, was in reality a cold-blooded killer. This scenario also implies that he had more than one accomplice at NASA, who helped him transport the bodies over a period of time.

"No single astronaut made enough trips to the moon to pull this off on his own.

"A third possibility is that the bodies belonged to American spies captured and executed by the Soviets who then used their rockets to send the bodies to the moon so that they could deny everything if they were accused of the crimes.

"We're looking carefully into this. Back in the '60s and '70s, KGB agents were a bunch of murderous thugs. They and their government were certainly capable of an atrocity of this magnitude.

"We've asked President Obama to pressure the current Russian leadership to make available to us any documents that would shed light on this situation."

Offically, Obama has vowed to get at the "truth of the matter and nothing but the truth." But White House sources insist the administration has gone into full damage control mode.

"There are a lot of people who want to blame this on the Russians, no matter what the facts are," one insider says. "With the Space Shuttle at the end of its career, NASA will need a massive infusion of cash to build the next generation of space vehicles.

"No one here wants to see its reputation tarnished at this time."

Did you know? To date, 12 American astronauts have landed on the moon.

FBI Special Agent Jesse Sparks is treating the moon as a secondary crime scene.

JESUS ACTION FIGURE HEALS THE SICK!

Move over G.I. Joe!

By MAX DURANGO
Weekly World News

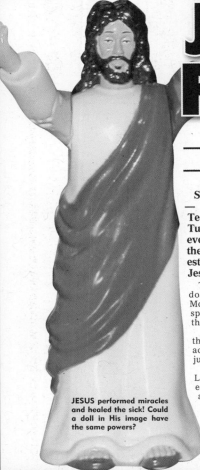

JESUS performed miracles and healed the sick! Could a doll in His image have the same powers?

SEATTLE, Washington — Throw away your Teenage Mutant Ninja Turtles, kids. Toy lovers everywhere are singing the praises of the newest action figure in town: Jesus Christ!

The 5-inch-high plastic doll is made by Archie McPhee, a novelty company specializing in religious-themed toys.

And some people believe this amazing new doll can actually perform miracles, just like the real Jesus.

They include Colette LeBeau, a French exchange student attending college in the United States. She suffered from excruciating migraine headaches for years — but the pain disappeared completely when she bowed her head before the doll and sought its intervention.

Such reports delight and amaze the McPhee company, says spokesman David Wahl. "We produce the doll only as a historical figure, and we can't promise it has any special powers," he says. "But these things are hard to explain in any other way."

Whether the popular toy is a miracle-worker or not, there's no denying that it brings kids hours of fun as they create their own adventures with the pint-sized savior. But there's just one catch — kids are finding they're not able to make the Jesus doll actually fight anyone.

"I keep trying to make Jesus fight Skeletor or Dr. Doom," says Todd M., 10. "But the Jesus doll just turns the other cheek, just like the real Jesus Christ. After that, the bad guys don't want to be bad any more.

"It's like the Jesus doll turns the bad guys good."

STUDENT Colette LeBeau is a believer! She claims her migraine headaches disappeared thanks to the Jesus doll.

SECOND COMING POSTPONED!

WHAT'S THE HOLDUP?
Jesus has put his return on hold due to the poor economy and plans on waiting until it improves.

TOP EVANGELIST'S SHOCKING CLAIM!

BY LAUREN LEVINE: MOBILE, ALABAMA

THE Second Coming of Jesus was due by now, but He has postponed His return until the economy improves, declares one of the nation's foremost evangelists.

'Savior's waiting for economy to improve'

The Rev. Josiah McMorriessy, a leading light in the current evangelical Christian scene, says the stunning news came to him as a revelation from the Lord himself.

"I was praying recently one night as I slept. That may sound odd to you, but as a fervent, Bible-believing Christian, I pray several hours a day, and often pray in my dreams, which is exactly what I was doing that night.

"During the prayer-dream, I asked the Lord when He would return, and He answered me, saying He had originally planned to be back in late 2010, but now, given the state of the economy, He'd prefer to wait until things really improve — perhaps another three years or so."

When McMorriessy, 53, announced the news to his followers, many were dumbfounded. But the preacher says the Lord's decision is entirely sensible.

"Basically, Jesus wants to return at a time when people have a little more pocket money. He figures they'll want to come out and see Him when He tours the country — which is one of the activities He has planned — and right now many folks simply couldn't afford to pay for tickets, gas, lodging, food and so on.

"Can you imagine how it would be if the Lord booked, say, Madison Square Garden, and couldn't sell out the venue? Talk about embarrassing! Wouldn't Satan have a field day with that one? The Lord would never live it down."

Some top Christian leaders are skeptical of McMorriessy's claim.

"Read your Bible," says Kentucky Baptist minister Tim-Bob McMuphin. "In 1 Thessalonians it says the Lord will 'come like a thief in the night,' meaning no one will know when it's going to happen. Case closed.

"I respect the Rev. McMorriessy, but just because he dreams something doesn't mean it's real. I mean, my word, if he dreamed that elephants could fly, would that make Dumbo a documentary? I don't think so."

But McMorriessy is sticking to his guns.

"I'm not talking about a darn cartoon, I'm talking about the Savior of all mankind. And when He tells me something, I take it as gospel. Literally."

READY TO TOPPLE

…n't set to …y tourist!

By **VINCENZO SARDI**/*Weekly World News*

ANGIE FLORICETTI'S dream visit to Pisa turned into a nightmare!

… vacation turned …g Tower of Pisa, …lian landmark to …t to topple.

…rated 8-story tower is … Italian government. …rs had reopened the …g Tower last …ber after a 12-year …ation effort costing 54 … lira — along with confi-…pronouncements that …er would be sound "for …t 300 years."

…redibly, red-faced offi-…are still insisting that …g that serious" has …ed to the Leaning … But an enormous tent …cently erected at the … supposedly to "fumi-… the tower — while …iently shielding it from … eyes.

…s a brazen government …p," says investigative …ist Marco Danillo, who … the story. "The tower …en quietly closed and …s from America and …ere are being steered …milar-looking old tower … slight lean, known as …tti's Tower. Govern-…aid tour guides tell the …ers it's the real tower … and most of them … it."

…he same time, the gov-…nt has assembled a …e team of lawyers, …ng them to clobber … with a multibillion-dol-…suit for wrecking the

…ly, obese Angie trav-…lfway around the world … the landmark, a trip

AUTHORITIES have "tented" the tower, saying it's closed temporarily to fumigate for pests.

she'd dreamed of taking since childhood. And it wasn't easy.

"Even fitting in the plane was a problem," she noted. "My butt took up three seats and they had to take out the row in front of me to make room for my gut."

Climbing the 297 steps of the tower's spiral staircase was no slight feat, either.

"I was huffing and puffing every inch of the way, and squeezing my big hips up that narrow stairway was nearly impossible," she said. "I kept thinking, 'Geez, did they build this place for children?'"

When the colossal visitor reached the roof of the tower, she was entranced by the wondrous view of the countryside. But she didn't enjoy the sights for long. "First we heard that god-awful creaking sound and everyone turned and looked at the fat woman, who turned beet red," fellow tourist Alan Buggs of Great Britain told the newspaper. "Then the next thing you knew, the roof of the tower was moving under us and people were tripping and spilling everywhere.

"The tour guide was great, he didn't panic. He told us all to be very still and he called for help on his walkie-talkie."

Firemen arrived on the scene and rescued the visitors, who leaped from the roof of the tower into an inflated rubber platform, like Hollywood stuntmen use when they jump off buildings. Angie was last to go, and her plunge nearly ended in disaster.

"When she hit the inflated platform, there was this loud 'woosh' sound as she seemed to disappear inside it for a moment," explains Danillo. "Then, suddenly, she came hurling out as if shot from a cannon, flew some 30 feet, and landed on a Saab 900. The car cushioned her fall, keeping her from being seriously injured. But she crushed the sedan flat as a pizza."

Meanwhile, experts in the history of architecture are beside themselves, because the tower is ranked one of the most important sites in Tuscany.

The tower was closed to the public in January 1990 because of fears that it might finally topple over and a last-ditch effort was launched to save it.

"The decision was made not to right it completely, but to stabilize it," said structional engineer Pinetti. "But obviously, none of us anticipated that someone as heavy as Miss Floricetti would ever try climbing it."

Working in secret, Italian engineers are again feverishly trying to save the tower, which reportedly now tilts as much an alarming 35 degrees.

"We've even had the Pope come to Pisa and pray for the tower," reveals Pinetti.

"When he saw what had happened, he threw up his hands and said, 'That lady, she was-a too fat!'"

RUDOLPH FOUND IN PALIN'S FREEZER!

BIG MIS-STEAK? Red nose was a dead giveaway, but cops are still not sure if it was really Rudolph.

AVID hunter Sarah Palin has denied any knowledge of Rudolph's remains occupying her freezer.

RUDOLPH the Red–Nosed Reindeer might go down in history as Christmas dinner instead of Santa's shining little helper.

WASILLA, Alaska — The presidential aspirations of Sarah Palin received a stunning jolt last week when investigators found Rudolph, Santa's red-nosed reindeer, inside a freezer at her home in Wasilla.

"The poor animal was already dressed and butchered," says a local police spokesman. "In with all the cuts of venison, there was the nose, wrapped in plastic. It had lost its luster and was more of a sickly shade of pink than bright red like we're used to seeing, but that was definitely no ordinary deer."

Federal prosecutors are reviewing the evidence and sources say they may charge Palin under the endangered species act.

"A reindeer with a red nose is unique — one of a kind," says FBI agent Terrence Neil, who is in charge of the investigation. "If that doesn't count as an endangered species, I don't know what does.

"We are looking at all the evidence very carefully. There is no rush to judgment here. We want to do right by Rudolph, but we also want to be fair to Sarah Palin. There are still a lot of unanswered questions."

Through a spokesman, Palin has denied all knowledge of how Rudolph's remains ended up in her freezer, which is located in the garage of her home.

He was found among assorted frozen ducks, geese and salmon, which Palin and her husband, Todd, freely admit they killed while hunting.

Both produced valid hunting licenses to validate their claim that they had done nothing illegal. Reindeer are native to Finland and western Russia, and thus receive no special protection under Alaska's hunting regulations.

Political pundits insist that the discovery of Rudolph's remains has seriously damaged Palin's chances of winning the Republican presidential nomination in 2012.

"She runs on a platform of family values," says one Washington columnist. "Yet, here she is implicated in the death of one of the great family-value icons in American history.

"Imagine the tear-stained faces of all the little children who will no longer be able to look forward to Rudolph landing on their roofs on Christmas Eve.

"It's worse than being a suspect in the death of Mickey Mouse or Donald Duck. This is a bona fide political disaster for her."

Indeed, some pro-family groups have already begun to distance themselves from Palin.

"We understand that Sarah Palin has not been charged with a crime, but we can't throw our support behind her as long as the cloud of suspicion hangs over her head," says Marjory Emmet, vice-president of Put Christmas First, a conservative organization who campaigned tirelessly for Palin in the last election.

Although Palin has not commented publicly, an insider says she secretly suspects that Rudolph's nose may have been planted by members of Senator John McCain's staff.

Relations between the two former running mates has been frosty since they were badly beaten by Barack Obama and Joe Biden last November.

Others close to Palin think it's all a tragic mistake.

"She probably thought Rudolph was a moose and let him have it," says one friend in Wasilla. "Moose are her favorite hunting targets."

Eager to capitalize on the political fallout, President Obama has ordered flags on federal buildings to fly at half mast in Rudolph's memory and has vowed to attend a memorial service planned for the reindeer at the North Pole next week.

Did you know? Sarah Palin is an avid hunter and proud of her marksmanship. "My father raised a tough hunting buddy," she once said.

WEEKLY WORLD NEWS UNCOVERS NEW...
CHINESE PLOT TO KNOCK EARTH OUT OF ORBIT

At 4:03 p.m. EST on September 2, 2012, 1.2 billion Chinese will jump up and down in another attempt to destroy the U.S., and send the Earth spinning into space

BEIJING, CHINA — THOSE sneaky Chinese are at it again — trying to throw the Earth's orbit out of whack by jumping up and down in unison. And unless millions of patriotic *Weekly World News* readers do a counter-jump here in America at precisely the same moment, it could mean the end of the world!

For the fifth time in a decade, the Chinese government is forging ahead with a bizarre scheme to topple America by changing the Earth's tilt, the CIA has learned.

"Despite all this talk about China and America being pals, the truth is those little commie rats hate our guts and they'll try anything to destroy us — even if it means risking the lives of everyone on the planet," a CIA official confirmed.

"The Chinese have ordered all 1.2 billion of their people to jump up and down at exactly

By GEORGE SANFORD
Weekly World News

4:03 p.m. EST on September 2, to tilt the Earth on its axis just enough that America will be cast into eternal winter. We'll be living in another Ice Age, fighting for survival. Our days as a superpower will be over while China is transformed into a paradise.

"As crazy as it sounds, our scientists say there's a 45 percent chance it could work — and if it fails, there's a 25 percent chance it could send the Earth spiraling out of control and into deep space."

The only way for the plot to be foiled, experts say, is for as many people on the other side of the world — North America — to jump up and down simultaneously, coun-

teracting the impact of the made-in-China hop.

When the Chinese tried the ploy before in the 1990s, *Weekly World News* readers rose to the occasion and launched a massive counter-jump that successfully thwarted the evil effort.

But with U.S.-Sino relations warming up, the back-stabbing communists think our nation's guard is down — and they're ready to give it another crack.

Every freedom-loving American must join in the world-saving stunt. To participate, stop what you are doing at 4:03 p.m. on September 2, and jump up and down as high as you can for six minutes, say government experts who are spreading the word quietly to avoid mass hysteria.

"Tell your friends, neighbors and co-workers. We need every able-bodied American, man, woman and child on board," says the CIA official. "If we all act as one, we can lick them at their own game."

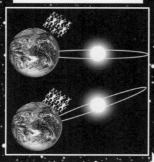

IF AMERICANS do not respond in force, the U.S. could be thrown into another Ice Age or the Earth could go careening into space destroying all life.

AS USUAL, America's firefighters and *Weekly World News* readers have always been the first to respond. But, it's not enough. Put out the word — gather your friends and relatives, and practice jumping up and down together. We're counting on you!

STAND UP & JUMP AMERICA
...WE STOPPED THEM BEFORE - AND WE'LL DO IT AGAIN!

'Mainstream journalists read *WWN* and dreamed about killing the county sewer-system story they were working on and writing about a swamp monster or a 65-pound grasshopper.'

— DEREK CLONTZ, *WEEKLY WORLD NEWS*

iPHONE USERS RECEIVE E-MAILS FROM 1969!

Mystery messages baffle owners

By RON WINTERGREEN/*Weekly World News*

WASHINGTON, D.C. — Owners of iPhones around the country are reporting receiving bizarre e-mail messages – from 1969!

As e-mail did not exist back then, experts are baffled by the phenomenon.

The U.S. government's top secret Office of Paranormal Electronic Investigations is taking the reports quite seriously.

"We know of several dozen incidents so far," says OPEI Agent Chad Kirkland, who is heading up the investigation.

"Most of the e-mails are blank — they say nothing, though their electronic headers are clearly stamped as being from dates in 1969. But a few contain brief messages and some even have files attached.

"For instance, one of the e-mails – received by the granddaughter of an Apollo moon mission astronaut, interestingly enough — had a subject line that read: 'First woman on the moon' and had a photo attached of an astronaut on the lunar surface. Although 1969

CREEPY greetings include shot of "first woman on the moon" and President Dick Martin (from famous TV show Rowan and Martin's Laugh-In).

was indeed the year the first man walked on the moon, no woman has been there as yet.

"Another e-mail had an mp3 file attached of a song called Five Nights in Moscow, ostensibly performed by The Beatles from their album Abbey Road. It certainly does sound like a late 1960's Beatles song, with Paul McCartney singing lead, but the song does not actually appear on Abbey Road, and, in fact, no such tune was ever released or known to have been recorded by The Beatles.

"Yet another e-mail had a short video attached that purportedly shows a few seconds of the president giving a state of the union address. But 'the president,' rather than being Richard Nixon, was comedian Dick Martin, best known as co-host of the hit 1960's TV show Rowan and Martin's Laugh-In.

"It's intriguing because Nixon famously once made a cameo appearance on that show."

What could possibly be going on? Experts have eliminated trickery or computer hoaxing, authenticating the messages as real. Paranormal expert Georgina Gunderson, who works in a consulting capacity with the OPEI, has a theory.

"It seems likely to me that these e-mails were sent from a parallel reality in an attempt to communicate with us," she says.

"The blank e-mails were probably initial tests. The ones with content tell us that things were — or are — very different in the 1969 of their world, starting with the fact that they invented personal computers and e-mail way before we did.

"If we can find a way to reply to them, the exchange of information could change our world."

WILL YOU, HONEY, GIVE ME YOUR PAW IN MARRIAGE?

TOOWOOMBA, Australia — A man has decided to prove to the world that his dog is his closest companion by marrying her.

Friends and family attended the nuptials of Joseph Guiso and his dog, Honey, a sweet-faced Labrador.

"It's not weird," says Guiso. "It's just pure love."

Guiso says the 5-year-old canine simply makes his life better in every way.

Shortly after the ceremony, the couple went on their "honeymoon" — a walk in a local park.

MIRACLE TOILETS FLUSH AWAY DISEASE!

By JIM ROBERTS
Weekly World News

POPE BENEDICT XVI once used the men's restroom while visiting Stuttgart as a cardinal.

ANIKA HOFFMANN makes her way to the restroom.

BEFORE

HOFFMANN tosses her walker after getting much needed relief from miracle toilet.

AFTER

STUTTGART, Germany — Thousands of ailing people are hobbling to a public restroom in a park in this city in southern Germany, seeking relief from their afflictions after reports that toilets in the facility are responsible for miraculous cures.

To date, more than 200 healings have been claimed for ailments ranging from arthritis to zits and — yes — constipation.

Public health officials have carefully analyzed the two toilets — one in the women's restroom, the other in the men's — and can find no scientific reason for the astonishing medical accomplishments.

Anika Hoffmann, who has suffered from rheumatoid arthritis for two decades, was able to triumphantly throw away her walker after relieving herself on the woman's toilet.

"Who would ever have thought that a simple act of urination could have life-changing consequences," says the 51-year-old librarian from Hamburg. "But as the fluid was draining from my bladder, I could feel the pain draining from my joints."

Hoffmann's doctors have confirmed that she is now free from the agonizing autoimmune disorder.

"I'm thinking of moving to Stuttgart so that I can visit this restroom every time I get a cold or the flu," Hoffmann says.

In another case, Wilhelm Bosch, 42, was cured of a neurological disorder, which required him to walk haltingly with a cane. He went on to win third-place honors on the German version of Dancing with the Stars.

Local religious leaders have formed a committee to promote the site as an international center of healing to rival Lourdes, in France, and Fatima, in Portugal.

Why this particular restroom should have miraculous healing powers is a mystery, but it is known that the current Pope Benedict XVI, the German-born Josef Ratzinger, once used the men's toilet when stricken with diarrhea while visiting Stuttgart when he was a cardinal.

IS THAT REALLY AN ALIEN WITH MICHELLE OBAMA?

GOOD SHOT: Tourist Frank Metty was surprised that he could see the first lady through the White House window and couldn't resist taking a picture.

BY JEFF BOGOSIAN: WASHINGTON, D.C.

A FIRESTORM of speculation has been set off over an odd photograph showing what appears to be a UFO alien in the White House embracing first lady Michelle Obama.

The picture was taken by tourist Frank Metty using a digital camera with a telephoto lens.

"I was just walking around taking pictures, taking in all the sights," says Metty, 58, a resident of Butte, Montana, who, along with wife Martha, was visiting the nation's capital for the first time.

"I was surprised to be able to see Michelle Obama through a window like that, eating dinner and getting cozy with what I at first took to be a bald-headed kid.

"I took the photo, and it wasn't until later, back at the hotel as I was reviewing the pictures I'd taken that day, that I really took a good look and I realized that wasn't a kid she was with. In fact, it wasn't even human!"

Weekly World News sent the photo to Florida photographic specialist Melinda Midge and asked her opinion as to its authenticity.

"Well, of course, these days, with digital photography, it's difficult to establish authenticity with certainty," Midge explains. "But I will say this: If this picture is a fake, it's extremely well done. The quality of the light and the angle of the shadows on the apparent alien are a perfect match for its surroundings."

After careful examination, UFO expert Avery Brite says he believes the photo is "100 percent real.

"I've seen top-secret government photos of actual aliens – the small, large-eyed, large-headed hairless type referred to as 'grays,' and this looks exactly like the real deal.

"The only question is: What is one doing socializing with Michelle Obama?

"This may indicate that the government is getting ready to introduce these beings to the public."

FOUND! HITLER'S LOST FAMILY JEWEL

It's being used as crystal ball by Austrian psychic

SCHITZELBURGER, Austria — Decades-old rumors that Adolf Hitler had only one testicle have now been confirmed. Historians have discovered the missing organ being used as a crystal ball by an Austrian psychic!

"There were unconfirmed stories going back to the early 1930s," says top WWII scholar K.D. Halloran, "that one of Hitler's testicles had been shot off in battle when he fought as a soldier in WWI.

"Furthermore, while doing research for a definitive Hitler biography I've been working on for the past 15 years, I discovered a letter that seemed to lend credence to those rumors.

"It was from Gertrude Schickelgruber — a female cousin that Hitler had long had a crush on — to a friend, in which she mentions receiving 'an odd keepsake' from her cousin Adolf.

"She doesn't really spell out what it is, but she mentions that the note attached read, 'Now, a little piece of me will always be with you, mein liebchen.' If this was indeed the testicle, it was a strange token of love, to be sure, but of course Hitler never had both oars in the water to begin with.

"But that was the only known evidence for the existence of a lost Hitler testicle — until now."

Last August, a story appeared in the Schitzelburger town newspaper about an elderly local psychic named Inga Winkelmann who claimed that her crystal ball was actually Hitler's missing organ. The story caught the attention of Austrian officials, who are always fearful of the emergence of Hitler-related relics that might draw the attention of or encourage Neo-Nazis. They quickly confiscated the object and had it analyzed.

It turned out to indeed be a human testicle that had been preserved and hardened under a layer of shellac.

Then, a DNA test comparing the testicle with a whisker derived from Hitler's mustache comb proved beyond reasonable doubt that the organ did indeed belong to the evil dictator.

"Inga Winkelmann says the testicle was given to her about 35 years ago by a man who said he got it from Gertrude Schickelgruber, so it all adds up," explains Halloran.

"Interestingly, Frau Winkelmann used her unique 'crystal ball' exclusively to make predictions for clients who had questions about having children in the future or about existing offspring. Appropriate, I suppose."

SEER Inga Winkelmann makes predictions for clients asking about having children.

WEEKLY WORLD NEWS

Issue 1, 2011

TINY DINOS FOUND IN PERU

WEREWOLF SUES AIRLINE OVER FLIGHT DELAY

COPS SHOOT 3-HEADED BIGFOOT!

WEREWOLVES

We saw a werewolf with a tabloid newspaper in his hand.
Walkin' through the streets of Soho in the rain.
He was lookin' for the paper called Weekly World News,
Gonna get a big dish of tabloid news fame!
Ahhhhoooohhh, werewolves of WWN.
Ahhhhoooohhh, werewolves of WWN.

It was 1979. Warren Zevon's 'Werewolves of London' was climbing the radio charts. Wolfman Jack ruled the air. Iraq and Iran were still one country, called Iranq. By midsummer, the price of gasoline had reached $18 per gallon. That fall, the first copies of *Weekly World News* were unloaded off trucks and they hit the newsstands.

America never looked back. Except, of course, when werewolves tailed behind us.

If you needed a guide on how to spot those ferocious interlopers, you turned to *Weekly World News*. Since 1979, *Weekly World News* has served as this country's werewolf almanac. For over three decades, our team of journalists provided the most comprehensive werewolf reporting that the nation, and the world, had ever witnessed.

How can you tell if your neighbor might be a werewolf? Read *WWN*. Why should you try to avoid a werewolf if there is a full moon? Read *WWN*. Is it true that kennel cough disease nearly wiped the species out? Read *WWN*. Can a woman marry a werewolf and live happily after? No, read *WWN*. What if the werewolf offers the woman $100,000 to marry him? Then, can the couple live happily ever after? Depends, read *WWN*. Can you successfully train a werewolf to live among your family? Read *WWN*. When house-training fails, how do you best kill and bury a werewolf? Read *WWN*.

These days nothing has changed. Gas is still too expensive, Iraq's still a pain in our neck, and everyone knows that the threat of a werewolf outbreak continues to rise. Our lawyers told us that refusing to publish our werewolf stories would be akin to *The New York Times* refusing to publish the Pentagon Papers. We have no idea what he meant, but we know the USA needs to monitor werewolves now more than ever.

'Ahhhhoooohhh, werewolves of *WWN*.
Ahhhhoooohhh, werewolves of *WWN*.'

BIKINI BANDIT: I'VE GOT A GUN ... SOMEWHERE!

KINGSTON, Jamaica — A shapely young lady wearing only an itsy-bitsy bikini walked into a car dealership and demanded money.

"I've got a gun," she said, "and I'm not afraid to use it."

The eagle-eyed salesman immediately saw that the desperate damsel had no place to hide a firearm and held her until police arrived.

"Next time I'll carry a purse," the girl said.

KOREANS CLONE 8,000 KIM JONG ILS!

BY RAND LEPAGE: SEOUL

... and they're ready to march on the South

THOUSANDS of pudgy clones of deceased North Korean dictator Kim Jong Il are poised to march across the 38th Parallel and invade the South, say shocked intelligence analysts.

"At the slightest sign of aggression from the South Korean jackals and their American running dogs, five infantry divisions, each soldier the sacred image of the Dear Leader, will march south and spread a great fire of destruction," one high-ranking general reportedly announced in a document sent to South Korean officials.

Western observers say North Korea has been working on clone research for years, mainly because Kim Jong Il saw it as a path to immortality.

"He was disappointed when his scientists pointed out that the clones would only look like him, not be him," a CIA spokesman says. "But he ordered the research to go ahead anyway."

Fire: Attack is imminent, says top-ranking U.S. general.

A spy-satellite image of a large military formation near the border between the Koreas has puzzled the CIA for months. The riddle grew when South Korean infiltrators described the troops as "pale, pudgy doubles of the Great Leader, apparently in his middle age."

But the spies add that the divisions are armed to the teeth with the latest Chinese weapons and have armored and air support.

All speculation ended when North Korea made its latest threat and confirmed the existence of the clone army, named the "Dear Leader's Loyals."

The United States military is not taking the clone invasion lightly. One top general says: "A bunch of fat 50-year-olds don't sound like much of a threat, but we don't know how clones will perform in combat."

Sssstick 'em up! Deadly pit viper ultimately caused the robber's death.

TELLER ROBBED AT SNAKE-POINT

VIENNA, Austria — After he robbed a bank using a deadly Indian pit viper as a weapon, a robber thought he'd gotten away free and clear with almost $40,000 in cash.

Unfortunately, the snake got loose in the man's getaway car and gave him a death bite. The money was recovered and the snake is now in a good home at a local zoo.

WORKAHOLIC TAKES FIRST VACATION IN 22 YEARS... AND DROPS DEAD!

BY RAND LEPAGE: NEW YORK

BON VOYAGE: Hardworking Henry Gilbert finally took a trip of a lifetime — a world cruise — and keeled over.

HARDWORKING accountant Henry Gilbert spent 22 years at his desk without taking a vacation – and now friends and family are mourning his untimely death.

"I warned him," Gilbert's sister Alice Lovell says. "But he wouldn't listen. 'Alice,' he said, 'I have a duty to my employer to work seven days a week, and that's what I'll do until I keel over.' Those were prophetic words."

After much persuasion from his loved ones, the frugal, lifelong bachelor finally decided to embark on a world cruise, leaving from the port of New York.

"He was very excited about the whole thing," his brother James says. "He'd spent his entire adult life at his desk, basically seven days a week, 365 days a year, and he was very tired."

When the great day dawned, Gilbert was first on board the ship, ominously named the Final Departure Maru, and checked into cabin 13, yet another bad omen.

"Henry was anxious to see the New York skyline as the ship headed out to sea and he went on deck," Alice says. "When the ship hit the North Atlantic breakers, his fellow passengers described my brother's mood as excited and slightly nervous.

"Then, after just a few miles into his around-the-world trip, he just keeled over like he said he would. By the time he hit the deck he was as dead as he was ever going to be. He'd had a massive heart attack."

The ship returned to port and Henry Gilbert was buried two days later. His gravestone reads, "Home is the sailor, home from the sea."

TRAGIC TRAVELER: Gilbert was only a few miles into his dream vacation onboard luxury cruise ship.

SISTERLY LOVE: Alice Lovell worried that her brother Henry spent his entire life working.

TOURISTS TREATED FOR 'GRAND CANYON SYNDROME'

Dozens of Japanese get sick with disappointment

BY RAND LEPAGE: COCONINO COUNTY, ARIZONA

IT SEEMS some Japanese tourists don't think the Grand Canyon is so grand.

At least two dozen are treated every year for what doctors have named "Canyon Syndrome," an ailment that can cause depression, hysteria, nightmares and in rare cases a nervous breakdown.

"The Grand Canyon is so much smaller than I was led to believe in the tourist brochures that it just felled me," one 28-year-old female victim says. "It just isn't grand like we expected.

"I was so disappointed, I fainted and the next thing I knew, I woke up in the hospital."

Another tourist, an elderly man, had a complete nervous breakdown after his visit to the canyon.

"It was not what I expected, so small, so insignificant, that I became depressed," he says. "My government paid for a nurse to accompany back on the plane to Tokyo."

Says psychiatrist Edwin Wilson: "Japanese people are very sensitive and do not handle disappointment well. Grand Canyon Syndrome is very similar to Paris Syndrome, a malady that affects 50 Japanese a year. They come from a very polite society and when they are confronted by typical French rudeness, they just can't cope and fall ill."

Japanese tour guides are now preparing vacation brochures that show the Grand Canyon to scale, comparing it to Japan's own great tourist attraction, Mount Fuji.

"We believe this will lessen our clients' disappointment and end this distressing syndrome," one tour guide says. "Unfortunately we can't do anything about Paris Syndrome.

"No matter what we do, the French will always be rude."

> **IT JUST ISN'T GRAND LIKE WE EXPECTED**

BREAKDOWN: Tourists became ill with depression after visiting the Grand Canyon.

WOLF GIRL RETURNS HOME

NEW DELHI, India — A 7-year-old girl who lived with wolves for two years returned to her native Indian village alive and well — but hungry.

The girl, known only as Aashi, which means "Hope" in Hindi, was given up for dead after she wandered away from her home. But officials believe wolves found her and raised her as one of their own.

Aashi will eat only raw meat and berries, her mother says.

I HAD BIGFOOT'S BABY!

HIT AND RUN: Bigfoot had his way with Earlene, then left her holding the bag.

By BOB JAMES
Weekly World News

'My Mama is so proud, but my cousin is fightin' mad,' says Ozark beauty queen

A 29-YEAR-OLD former beauty pageant winner from the Ozark Mountains of Arkansas has admitted to being the mother of Bigfoot's love child!

The stunning confession has created a rift in the family of Earlene Burnside because it broke up her engagement to her first cousin, Billy Bob Sparks.

"I know it was wrong to break Billy Bob's heart like that," Earlene admits. "But when I first saw Bigfoot rootin' for food in the garbage Dumpster behind my daddy's diner, I knew I had to hold his big, hairy body in my arms."

Burnside insists that her attraction to the elusive 7-foot forest creature wasn't purely a case of animal lust.

"The way he raised his little finger when he gnawed on chicken bones — it was so sophisticated, like they do in France," she says.

Modesty forbids the churchgoing Burnside from discussing the intimate details of her relationship with Bigfoot, but she does confess that he overwhelmed her with his direct approach to courtship.

"I couldn't stand to see him eating out of a Dumpster, so I brought him a plate of grits and hog jowls," she says. "He snatched the food out of my hand and had his way with me while he swallowed it."

"It was over pretty quick, but I'll remember the passion in his eyes and the grease on his chin for the rest of my life. What they say about the earth moving — it's true!"

Burnside can't stem the flow of tears when she recounts that once their moment of ardor had passed, Bigfoot leapt to his feet and lumbered off into the woods.

"He left a big hole in my heart," she sniffs. "No one will ever be able to take his place.

"But," she adds, brightening, "I have little Elrod to remember him by!"

Nine months after her encounter with Bigfoot, Burnside gave birth to a 13-pound, 11-ounce baby boy.

"He's awful hairy, just like his papa," she says. "But lots of folks say he has my broad shoulders and big feet."

Burnside had no shortage of human gentlemen callers, especially after she was the hands-down winner in the heavyweight division of the 2002 Miss Hush Puppy Beauty Pageant and Moon Pie Eating Contest.

But none, she insists, measured up to Bigfoot in the romance department.

"My cousin Billy Bob is a good man, but he's a scrawny little fella — petite, if you know what I mean," she says. "I need a lot of man, being 6 feet 4 inches tall and weighing 322 pounds myself."

Burnside's mother, Lurlene, looks after little Elrod while her daughter works at the local sawmill.

"Lots of people wouldn't take kindly to a grandson that's half Bigfoot, but Mama's proud as punch," Burnside says. "She wants him to grow up to be a moonshiner, just like my brother."

Burnside is not the first woman to bear a child to Bigfoot. The most recent was Beverly Hills socialite Daneille Cortell, who claimed in a 2004 *Weekly World News* story that she was kidnapped by the giant humanoid and held as his love slave.

"I'm not jealous that Bigfoot has other women," Burnside says. "I don't see how any gal can resist him — when you get past all the hair and the 'woodsy' smell, he kinda looks like Brad Pitt."

Jilted Sparks, however, has done nothing to conceal this jealousy over Burnside's affair with Bigfoot.

"He's hoppin' mad," she says. "He wants me to dump little Elrod off at a zoo and pretend like nothing ever happened.

"I couldn't ever do that to Elrod. He's my baby and every time I hold him in my arms and feel his fangs on my neck, I think of his papa and cry."

'Dumbosity will happen no matter what. At least the *Weekly World News* didn't take themselves seriously, like *The New York Times* and *The Washington Post* do … and the *Weekly World News* was accurate at least as often as those two publications have been lately.'—**SLATE**

VILLAGE sculptor brought Streisand's image to the people after studying art in America, where he first heard what he now calls "holy sounds" in her nasal singing voice.

They believe it brings them good luck and gives them sexual potency, says expert

By ANGUS FENWICK/ *Weekly World News*

AFRICAN TRIBE WORSHIPS BARBRA STREISAND'S NOSE!

MAHAJANGA, Madagascar — An African tribe is convinced that Barbra Streisand's nose holds special powers — and prays to it daily for rain, fertile fields, protection, good luck and sexual potency!

"The Mahafaly tribe of Southern Madagascar has worshiped Streisand's nose for the past 25 years," asserts British ethnographer Phillip Branwell, 58.

The Mahafaly believe that the tone and sound frequency of prayers said aloud bring the highest blessings, and that is why, Branwell says, Barbra's beak is so appealing to them.

"The nose is considered to be most holy by the tribe. They build statues in the nose's image, and wear little Streisand noses around their necks on chains."

The typical Mahafaly nose is broad and flat, nearly the opposite of Funny Girl's sausage-like schnoz. Tribeswoman Abba Madjanka, 48, confides: "When I first saw Barbra Streisand's nose, I was in awe. A feeling of amazement and wonder came over me. I realized I was in the presence of something very powerful and very special."

Members of the tribe are less impressed with Streisand's other accomplishments. Tribal leader Yazid Ouahib, 41, says: "We know she is famous, but we feel that her power and our good fortune come directly from her nose."

The worshipping of Yentl's nose grows bigger every day. There even is a shrine featuring an elaborate 12-foot-high Streisand head. Streisand's hit, People, frequently blares through the countryside. At night, lights illuminate its nose, which can be seen from any point in the village. Even the smallest of children point toward the lights and reverently mouth the name "Barbra" over and over again.

Toussaint Raharison, 63, the Mahafaly's village sculptor, brought Streisand's image to the people after studying art in America, where he first heard what he now calls "holy sounds" in her nasal singing voice.

Though it happened more than 25 years ago, Raharison still is fond of telling his story. But the talk is not of her voice or her songs or her stage presence. "Her nose was everything I thought it would be," Raharison raves. "It was magnificent. Just being close to it, I felt bathed in a golden glow."

Raharison says the tribe feels it is their divine calling to follow the nose because of its legendary capability for sounds. "We did not pick the nose, the nose picked us."

Branwell says this sort of body part worship is not unusual among tribal societies. "The bushmen of Botswana's Kalahari Desert have prayed to Marlon Brando's belly for decades. The Berbers of Morocco's Atlas Mountains consider George Hamilton's tan as sacred. And the pygmies of Equatorial Africa have long worshipped Farrah Fawcett's teeth."

DINOSAURS FOUND ON MARS!

Eye-popping photos stun scientists

By BOB JAMES
Weekly World News

THERE'S life on Mars — and it's enormous!

NASA's Phoenix Mars Lander has transmitted a photograph of what appears to be a super-sized dinosaur standing menacingly on the surface of the Red Planet — and shocked scientists say the discovery has overturned "everything we thought we knew about extra-terrestrial life."

The space agency has delayed releasing the stunning news to the public pending a full analysis of the available data. But Dr. Simon Wycoff, an astrobiologist serving as a consultant to the Phoenix project, has agreed to reveal what little is known about the humungous reptile and the implications of the staggering find.

In an exclusive interview with Weekly World News reporter Bob James, Wycoff says the creature resembles the Earth dinosaur Tyrannosaurus Rex, but is at least three times larger than the ferocious predator.

WWN: Why is the dinosaur so much bigger than any dinosaur fossils found on Earth?

WYCOFF: The relative lack of gravity on the moon allowed the beast to grow so large. Earth's stronger gravity would cause any creature that big to collapse under its own weight.

WWN: Is the dinosaur the only one of its kind?

WYCOFF: That's highly unlikely. We assume they've been breeding there for millennia.

WWN: Why didn't we discover it sooner?

WYCOFF: We believe the dinosaurs live mostly on the dark side of the moon, territory about which we know very little. They must have excellent night vision and thrive in cold temperatures.

WWN: What do the dinosaurs eat?

WYCOFF: Each other. Members of their own kind would be their only source of nutrition. They are cannibals.

WWN: Is there any way to estimate their population?

WYCOFF: Not until we explore the dark side of the moon. Even then, it will be difficult to get an exact count because of the lack of light and the uneven terrain of the Martian surface.

WWN: How did the dinosaurs get there?

WYCOFF: At this point, your guess is as good as mine. One theory is that microscopic living organisms were transported throughout the solar system by comets. On that account, life on Earth began when one of these comets deposited organic material on our planet after crashing into it. The same phenomenon could have occurred on Mars.

WWN: Dinosaurs became extinct on Earth 70 million years ago. Why have they survived on Mars?

WYCOFF: The dinosaurs were wiped off the face of the Earth by a massive asteroid impact. Apparently, Mars escaped a similar calamity.

WWN: President Bush has vowed to establish a human colony on Mars. What does this discovery do to that plan?

WYCOFF: It puts the kibosh on it, I should think. A human expedition to Mars would involve a maximum of six or seven astronauts. They wouldn't make more than a tasty hors d'oeuvre for creatures this size. It would be folly to spend upwards of $50 billion to send humans to Mars just to have them eaten by a dinosaur. The American taxpayer would never stand for it.

super-sized: Mega dinosaur roaming Mars resembles a T-Rex, but much, much bigger.

JFK IS ALIVE!
– AND IN COMBAT IN IRAQ!

AS SOON as he recovered, Kennedy volunteered to captain a swift boat in Iraq.

THE MENTAL functions of the eighty-year-old former chief executive are remarkably sharp.

By BOB LAZARUS

BAGHDAD, Iraq — The spry, white-haired navy officer stepped onto the dock and walked briskly into a small office. He looked so familiar and that voice — I'd heard it before. However, it was a glance at the desk's nameplate that staggered this *Weekly World News* embedded reporter.

It read: Lt. John F. Kennedy.

"Good lord! You're President Kennedy — I thought you were dead!" I blurted out. With a chuckle and that soft, Bostonian accent, the ex-president replied, "Well, I did, too — for about thirty years."

Noting orders lying on the president's desk, I checked Navy records that confirmed the existence of swift boat SB-109 under the command of 'Lt. Kennedy.' According to the documents, SB-109, a patrol and attack vessel, had apparently racked up an impressive list of dangerous missions. After three months of training off the coast of Kuwait, the speedy craft had prowled the waters near Iraq's capital, hunting insurgents and ferrying special ops forces in nighttime infiltration missions.

By his own admission, John Fitzgerald Kennedy, the 35th President of the United States, has been commanding swift boat SB-109 on the Tigris River for nearly a year.

"But that's only a small part of the story," said John Chapman, an elderly Secret Service agent who still serves as Kennedy's assistant. "I've been at his side since an hour after he was shot. The president doesn't remember anything about the incident in Dallas. After being pronounced dead, after the information was given to the press, he showed some signs of life. By then Lyndon Johnson had been sworn in. Rather than create a constitutional crisis, the comatose president was taken to our secret CIA hospital in Chevy Chase. Even the Kennedy family wasn't told. No one thought he'd last more than a day or two, so they went ahead with the services. We figured we'd bury him discreetly some time later."

But the athletic president fooled them all. Dumbfounded officials secretly called in the finest medical specialists in the world. Neurosurgeons worked carefully on the awful head wound despite being certain the cause was hopeless. But the days stretched to years as the shattered brain slowly regenerated and healed. After finally awakening in 1990, years of intense therapy brought a nearly-complete recovery in 1997.

"The mental functions of the eighty-year-old former chief executive are remarkably sharp," related Chapman, "and he's been eagerly catching up on world events, which saddened him. He came to the conclusion that he could be of help in Iraq by resuming his naval duties.

"When I told him it was risky work and asked why he'd want to put himself in harm's way, he said, 'I've always believed that each American should ask what he can do for his country. This is my answer.'"

After shocking doctors by passing the Navy physical — and with assistance from the top levels of government — Kennedy's World War II commission was reinstated and he took over command of a patrol squadron of swift boats manned by a joint army/navy team.

"Lt. Kennedy could easily pass for a man sixty years old," said Ensign Cliff Roberts who serves in his command. "He insists that the sailors simply call him 'Jack,' but I can't bring myself to do that. He was — and is — an officer and a hero."

Ensign Roberts is one of the few servicemen who actually believes that the senior officer is the former president.

"The truth is, most of these young seamen know nothing about the Camelot years," said Chapman. "To them, he's just a helluva leader. Every sailor told me he feels extremely confident when their quiet skipper is at the helm."

But it may soon be time to move on. Lt. Kennedy confided to Chapman that he never got to serve a second term.

"He told me he was the youngest president ever elected and if he decided to run in 2008 he could also be the *oldest*," Chapman said. "I hope he does. I'd like to see the GOP try to pull the same swift boat crap on him they used on John Kerry!"

After losing for the first time... TENNIS-PLAYING ROBOT GOES BERSERK — & BASHES HUMAN OPPONENT TO DEATH!

By GRANT BALFOUR
Weekly World News

LOS ANGELES — A wealthy tennis enthusiast met a grisly death at the hands of her "perfect" coach — a tennis-playing robot that went berserk after losing a game!

Police say the entire hair-raising attack was recorded on a video taken for training purposes. The tape shows Elaine Hersholl, the 41-year-old wife of a well-to-do movie executive, lobbing a winning backhand, approaching the net to reset her mechanical opponent for a new match — then being clubbed in the head again and again by the robot's heavy, steel arm.

Mrs. Hersholl's personal physician said she died of a crushed skull.

"That thing literally beat her brains out," said one investigating officer.

Bereaved pals said Mrs. Hersholl, who often played until late at night, had wanted more than a human tennis coach could offer.

TRAGIC Elaine died of a crushed skull.

"And she'd grown tired of playing against those ball-serving machines when she found out about this high-tech mechanical tennis player," a friend said. "The whole idea thrilled her."

Mrs. Hersholl eagerly paid an undisclosed sum to a Japanese electronics laboratory for a prototype of a robot that was still in the experimental stages of design.

The robot came equipped with ultra-sensitive electronic eyes, wheels at the base of its feet allowing for 360 degree movement — and that movable steel arm.

According to the robot's manufacturer, it had been programmed to win every game by evenly matching a human player's skill, constantly demanding better and better performance.

"Over the last few months, we all saw a great step forward in Elaine's game," said a former tennis partner. "She was suddenly the hottest player at the country club. All that practice at her home court was paying off."

But Mrs. Hersholl found improvement came with a high price the day she outperformed her computerized partner. That evening, her bloody body was found slumped over the net at midcourt. Her metal-plated assailant was spinning in small circles next to her with its racquet outstretched.

Police computer experts believe an unexpected win by the robot's opponent caused the mechanical man to go berserk — triggering the fatal volley of blows.

'The thing literally beat her brains out!'

TENNIS BUFF Elaine Hersholl and her robotic partner enjoyed a spirited match before the vicious attack occurred.

PHOTO COURTESY OF SPORTS INJURY INST.

WEEKLY WORLD NEWS WANTS TO KNOW WHAT YOU THINK...
SOUND OFF!
Anything in the paper you like, don't like or would like to see? Let us know by writing us at: Sound Off!, c/o Weekly World News, 600 East Coast Ave., Lantana, Fla. 33464-0002.

MAN ORDERED TO EAT HAY BECAUSE HE FED HIS HORSE JUNK FOOD

AZUL, Argentina — A man who made his horse sick by feeding the animal french fries, pizza and other junk food has been ordered to take a dose of his own medicine — by eating an entire bale of hay!

"Let him see what it's like to eat food that his system can't digest," said Judge Gerardo Montez.

Arnoldo Busquez, 37, was handed the bizarre sentence after being convicted of cruelty to an animal. His horse suffered a severe gastrointestinal illness but has since recovered.

The judge denied the defendant's request to pour beer on his bale of hay to make it go down easier.

SADDAM & OSAMA
A Love Story For the Ages
From the files of Weekly World News

Aug. 2003

A HOME video made by Osama and Saddam provided this touching scene of the happy couple dancing the night away somewhere in Iraq. Saddam was a vision in a tutu and pink slippers, though his five o'clock shadow spoiled the effect somewhat. The CIA is not sure when the video was made, but speculates it was around last August at a Saddam safe house in a Baghdad suburb.

Oct. 2003

DOE-EYED Osama and Saddam finally tied the knot at a hush-hush but otherwise opulent wedding somewhere in northern Iraq. Osama was resplendent in a black tuxedo, black vest and patent leather shoes. Saddam made a lovely bride in a simple white gown and red pumps. It is thought that the starry-eyed couple honeymooned in a cave in Afghanistan.

Nov. 2003

JUST weeks after their gay wedding, ecstatic newlyweds Osama and Saddam adopted a shaved ape baby to make their little family complete. The shaved apes originated in France, where an unscrupulous adoption agency passed them off as human babies.

Dec. 2003

A HEARTBROKEN Osama and the motherless shaved ape baby pine for "mommy" Saddam at a secret cave. According to sources, Osama will turn himself in so his family can be reunited.

ACKNOWLEDGEMENTS

For Henry, Marina & Charlotte.

Weekly World News would like to thank Jordan Hudkins, Allegra Staples, Olly Olinyk Frozen Santas, Ketch, Ihsan, Ponge, K-Sev, the Pizza Man, Mr Apple, Petro, R.G. 'the Rock' Rochester, A.C. Reilly, Señor Flaco, Ed Slink, Cobra Beck, C.S.W. Ketch, Charlie Garnett, Laura Sterritt, Leslie Grossnickle, Fat Willie, Frankie, E.C. Skwiblet, Benson Bunniepanz, M.H. Meancey, Charlie Pikels, the House, M.A. Twineball, Professor Greenjeans, Mowdy Gogo, Dallas Commagreens, Rob Mier, Merlin D. Tuttle, Chin Strap, the Bishop, Dennis Kucinich, T.D. Bati, Ben Jovi, Ed Anger and the Angriest Generation, Bill Creighton, Dack Kennedy, Dick Siegel, Joe Berger, Jack Alexander, Dick Kulpa, Conrad Morse, Deuce Collins, Nick Mann, Alex Morgan, Ernst Craven, Rex Wolfe, Ahmet Farouk, Vincenzo Sardi, Miguel Figueroa, Lois Castini, Joan Yung, Mike Foster, Wayne Diaz, Larry Mulder, Michael Chiron, Will Shivers, Darren Davenport, Ian Merkins, Mark Miller, Michael Forsyth, Tanya Broder, D. Patrick, Wolf Landrum, Kevin Creed, Cliff Linedecker, Scott D. Peterson, Brett Goldberg.